Aspiring Adults Adrift

Aspiring Adults Adrift

Tentative Transitions of College Graduates

Richard Arum and Josipa Roksa

The University of Chicago Press
Chicago and London

Richard Arum is professor in the Department of Sociology with a joint appointment in the Steinhardt School of Education at New York University. Josipa Roksa is associate professor of sociology and education and associate director of the Center for Advanced Study of Teaching and Learning in Higher Education at the University of Virginia. Together they are the authors of *Academically Adrift: Limited Learning on College Campuses.*

The University of Chicago Press, Chicago 60637
The University of Chicago Press, Ltd., London
© 2014 by The University of Chicago
All rights reserved. Published 2014.
Printed in the United States of America

23 22 21 20 19 18 17 16 15 14   1 2 3 4 5

ISBN-13: 978-0-226-19115-7   (cloth)
ISBN-13: 978-0-226-19728-9   (paper)
ISBN-13: 978-0-226-19714-2   (e-book)

DOI: 10.7208/chicago/9780226197142.001.0001

Library of Congress Cataloging-in-Publication Data
Arum, Richard, author.
    Aspiring adults adrift : tentative transitions of college graduates / Richard Arum and Josipa Roksa.
        pages ; cm
    Includes bibliographical references and index.
    ISBN 978-0-226-19115-7 (cloth : alk. paper)—ISBN 978-0-226-19728-9 (pbk. : alk. paper)—ISBN 978-0-226-19714-2 (e-book)   1. College graduates—United States—Social conditions. 2. College graduates—Employment—United States. 3. Education, Higher—Social aspects—United States. 4.Education, Higher—United States—Public opinion. 5. College graduates—United States—Attitudes.   I. Roksa, Josipa, author. II. Title.
    LC191.94.A78 2014
    331.11′445—dc23

                                                                                    2014012589

Contents

Acknowledgments   *vii*

1   College and Emerging Adults   *1*
2   Social and Academic Learning in College   *25*
3   Making It in the Labor Market   *53*
4   Parents, Partners, and Optimism about the Future   *83*
5   A Way Forward   *115*

Appendix A: Data, Methods, and Statistical Analyses   *137*
Appendix B: Survey Instrument and Interview Protocol   *171*
Notes   *207*
Bibliography   *229*
Index   *241*

Acknowledgments

The research that led to this book was organized by the Social Science Research Council (SSRC). The project began as part of SSRC's collaborative partnership with the Pathways to College Network—an alliance of national organizations that advances college opportunity for underserved students by raising public awareness, supporting innovative research, and promoting evidence-based policies and practices across the K–12 and higher education sectors. The initial phase of the project focused on students' experiences and development of general collegiate skills (critical thinking, complex reasoning, and writing) during the first two years of college, published in *Academically Adrift: Limited Learning on College Campuses*. Subsequent work followed this collegiate cohort through the end of the senior year and into life after college.

This research project was made possible by generous support from the Lumina Foundation for Education, the Carnegie Corporation of New York, and the Teagle Foundation, as well as by support for the initial stage of the project from the Ford Foundation. We are especially grateful to the following foundation officers, whose insights and support have been crucial to the project's development: Tina Gridiron, Dewayne Matthews, Jamie Merisotis, and Susan Johnson (Lumina Foundation); Barbara Gombach (Carnegie Corporation of New York); Donna Heiland, W. Robert

Conner, Annie Bezbatchenko, and Richard Morrill (Teagle Foundation); and Jorge Balan and Greg Anderson (Ford Foundation). We also are deeply grateful to the Council for Aid to Education for its technical collaboration with data collection while students were in college, as well as to Harris Interactive for its assistance with data collection after graduation. Our deepest gratitude goes to the students—and eventual graduates—who volunteered and agreed to participate in the various phases of this research project, as well as to the administrators and staff who coordinated the initial data collection efforts at their colleges and universities.

Early phases of this project benefited from the wise counsel of our advisory board, including Pedro Reyes, professor and executive vice chancellor for academic affairs at the University of Texas; Myra Burnett, vice provost for academic affairs and associate professor of psychology at Spelman College; William (Bill) Trent, professor of education, organization, and leadership at the University of Illinois; and Meredith Phillips, associate professor of public policy and sociology at the University of California, Los Angeles. We also received valuable feedback from colleagues across different universities where we presented the preliminary findings in 2013, including Stanford University's School of Education (January 6), the Joint Degree Program in Social Policy at Princeton University (September 30), the Sociology Colloquium at Yale University (December 6), and the Sociology Colloquium at the University of California, Berkeley (December 10). We are particularly grateful to Jonathan Zimmerman and students in the fall 2013 doctoral seminar "Educational Research in the United States: Problems and Possibilities," and to Joan Malczewski and students in the fall 2013 course "How Do Colleges Work?" at New York University. We also thank the anonymous reviewers at the University of Chicago Press for their close reading of the manuscript and constructive feedback.

At the Social Science Research Council, program coordinators Kim Pereira (2007–8), Jeannie Kim (2008–10), Esther Yoona Cho (2010–12), and Amanda Cook (2013–14) masterfully coordinated different aspects of the project. Additional assistance with data organization and coding was provided by Raynika Trent, while Rachel Wetts skillfully formatted the tables and figures for the book. Jeannie Kim and Esther Yoona Cho, who left the SSRC to pursue graduate studies at New York University and the University of California, Berkeley, continued to provide research assistance to the project and served as coauthors of chapters 3 and 4, respectively. Two additional NYU graduate students—Jason Thompson, coauthor of chapter 2, and Karly Sarita Ford, coauthor of chapter 4—contributed valuable insights to the book. Amanda Cook, who joined the project most recently, quickly became an indispensable part of the research team. She served as coauthor of chapter 3 and provided technical and editorial assistance for the book as a whole.

We owe a special thank-you to Elizabeth Branch Dyson, our editor at the University of Chicago Press. Her enthusiasm and belief in this project kept us writing, and her astute questions and thoughtful feedback sharpened our arguments. We are also grateful to the dedicated staff at the University of Chicago Press who assisted with the final revisions and the publication process. In particular, we would like to thank Nora Devlin for her technical assistance and Renaldo Migaldi for his careful and thoughtful editorial work. We are also grateful to Levi Stahl for his energetic engagement with this project.

Our deepest personal gratitude goes to those who have lived through every single page of this manuscript with us (multiple times!), and who patiently supported us. Thank you to Shenandoah for all the conversations, intellectual and personal, that fueled the long hours of writing, as well as for knowing when it was time to take a break. Gratitude to Joan for providing ongoing constructive engagement and steadfast support on the project. Inspiration and motivation for the project, was also provided by Sydney and Eero, who began college, Luke and Zora, who started high school, and Elias Jonathan, who joined our lives, since *Academically Adrift* was published.

While this research would not have been possible without the contributions from the individuals and institutions identified above, we, Richard Arum and Josipa Roksa, are fully responsible for all findings presented, claims made, and opinions expressed in this book. Our names are given in alphabetical order to represent our equal contributions to this volume.

1

College and Emerging Adults

"I can definitely do better," Nathan reported to us in an interview two years after finishing college: "I feel like I'm not using my degree at all."[1] On the surface, it was hard to disagree with him. Although he had majored in business administration, Nathan was living back at home with his parents, had significant college loans to repay, and—like many of his peers—felt lucky to have any job at all. He found his on Craigslist. Nathan was a delivery driver for a national retail chain. He picked up and dropped off items from the warehouse, shuttling materials to local branch outlets throughout the state. He had been working this job for the last six months and had annual earnings of less than $20,000. Nathan also reported to us that his employer had recently cut back his hours and that as a result he was spending five hours per week looking for other employment.

As far as college was concerned, however, Nathan apparently was considered an ideal student. He had graduated on time with a 3.9 GPA. Even so, when we asked Nathan about the experiences, events, or occasions at college when he had learned the most academically, he could initially think of nothing to report. After some prompting, he began to tell us about a final project for his business policy class that took "weeks and weeks and weeks of a lot of research." Nathan noted, "Each group was assigned a business and there [were] problems with the business and we had to come out with three different solutions and basically we had to look in every single aspect of this business and prove why our reasons would work." Nathan added that it was in "one of the toughest classes that I actually learned the most."

Nathan, similar to almost all of the graduates we interviewed, was socially engaged in college. "I went to a lot of events and parties and all that stuff," he reported. When we asked what he learned socially in college, he commented, "Not too much actually from college, I guess just hanging out with my friends." He readily admitted that he was what we have previously referred to as *academically adrift* while at college: "Like, when I first started, I really had no idea what I wanted to do. That is why I kind of took business—it was kind of a general thing that could help me with anything. I wish I would have put more thought in what I actually wanted to do with my life." He reported to us that he spent half his time studying at college with friends, and studied alone less than five hours per week. He also reported that he wished he had joined more clubs while in college.

As a college graduate, however, Nathan appeared to be no more engaged in voluntary associations than he had been at college. Aside from voting in the most recent national election, he did little that could be associated with civic awareness or participation. Although he spent his days crisscrossing the state's roadways, he seldom listened to the news. When we asked him how he kept up with current events, he reported, "Basically just the evening news. I read the Sunday newspaper and look at the string on the Internet that interests me." While his engagement with the news and public affairs was limited, apparently it was sufficient—coupled, perhaps, with his lived experiences—for him to conclude that the country was "kind of towards the bottom."

Given that he was struggling with college loan debts, living at home with his parents, and unable to find a job using his college-level education, one would think Nathan and his peers who were suffering similar fates since graduating college would be depressed, angry, or in general despair about the direction in which their lives were heading. However, this was far from the case. While Nathan reported that the country was "kind of towards the bottom," he quickly added that he thought "we're starting to improve." While he was frustrated by his post-college transition, he was hardly embittered. With respect to his college education, he noted that "I put a lot of money on this thing and I feel like I'm not getting much out of it at the moment, *but I think I will in the future*" (our emphasis).

In spite of current difficulties, Nathan and most of his peers believed that their lives would ultimately be better than those of their parents. "Just because I have had more opportunities," Nathan assured us. "That's the way the world is right now." College might not have delivered on all its promises, but one thing Nathan and his peers appeared to have acquired was a sense of social membership and entitlement. They were college graduates, and rewards would surely follow.

Other recent college graduates who were experiencing difficult transitions shared similar sentiments. For example, since graduating from a selective public university with a degree in public health, Sonya was back living at home with her mother. After struggling to find work, she had become a full-time babysitter. Two years after graduating, she was going back to school to become a nurse like her mother. Far from embittered, however, she was upbeat about how her life was going. "I'm very excited about the direction of my life," Sonya told us. "A year ago, I was depressed; I thought the world was going to end because I couldn't figure out what I was doing with my life." She went on to explain, "I guess it's just like my friends who graduated before me always say, that you go through that period of confusion and then you come out knowing, okay, 'This is what I want to do and this is where I'm going.'" Like Nathan, she told us she believed her life would be better than those of her parents.

And consider Alice, who was back living at home after graduating from an elite residential liberal arts college with a humanities degree. She worked as a grocery store cashier. But when asked about the direction of her life, she replied, "I feel generally confident in it." She continued with a statement that trailed off: "I wish I had a little more direction but . . . ." Or consider Lucy, who had been unemployed for months, was deferring payment on her college loans, and was back living at home with her mother. Lucy perhaps captured this sense of undaunted optimism best for the struggling members of her cohort: "I'm feeling OK about the way my life is going. It would be cool if I had a job. I don't know—I'm like, I tend to look on the bright side because I do what I can to change the things I dislike in my life, but I'm not going to hate things that I can't change, because they're going to stay, so I might as well accept them." She, too, expected her life to be better than her parents' lives had been, "in the emotional sense and more likely than not in the financial sense." While almost one-quarter of the college graduates we studied were living back at home with their families two years after finishing college, a stunning 95 percent reported that their lives would be the same or better than those of their parents.

While some graduates in our study experienced struggles in postgraduation transitions, others were flourishing. Consider, for example, Julie, who majored in biology at a highly selective college and found work as a research associate in environmental sciences at a flagship public research university. When asked about aspects of her college education that she was using in her job, she noted that "they run the gamut from specific information that I learned about ecology" to "theories, and ideas, and papers, and research methods." Julie in particular emphasized that at college she had "learned how to think critically about information, what is useful to me and what is not, how to be selective, and I also learned how to manage my time really well." She was living in a house with her boyfriend, whom she had met in college, and a second bedroom in the house was being rented out to bring in additional income. She kept up with the daily news by reading the *New York Times* online and listening to National Public Radio. She reported that she had voted most recently in a local election held a few months prior in the spring.

Or take the case of Michael, who was already married to a woman he reported having met in college, "the first semester I was there, during exam week." Michael and his wife, "now with the housing market as it is," were considering buying a house. Michael had majored in engineering and technology at a selective public research university. Two years after graduating from college, he had already earned a master's degree in engineering and had landed a job in his field of choice. He believed that his undergraduate education had taught him not only specific skills, but how to think. "I can take on any problem now," Michael noted. "Even if I don't know the answer, I know I can figure it out." Michael also credited college with promoting his active involvement with the American Society of Mechanical Engineers (ASME), an activity which connected him to employers and had led to a highly productive professional internship experience. Michael had voted in the most recent presidential election and occasionally kept up with current events by watching Fox News, because he was comfortable with "their more conservative approach."

We also have individuals such as Mindy, who found work as a fifth-grade math and reading teacher after attending a less selective public university and majoring in education. Mindy reported to us that she "spent probably all of my free time doing homework, and when I wasn't doing homework, I was either working or I was in like four or five clubs. All of them having to do with my major as well as a sorority." Mindy had recently broken up with her boyfriend and was living in a rental apartment with a friend. She could not remember the last time she voted, and she kept up with the news a few times a week by "looking on AOL news or like the local paper online."

C. Wright Mills, in *The Sociological Imagination*, argued that sociological research should work to illuminate how social and historical contexts shape individual life trajectories.[2] We will attempt to fulfill that disciplinary mandate by documenting how recent college graduates in our study attempted to make post-college transitions from the spring of 2009 through the summer of 2011, during a particularly difficult period for the US economy. Throughout this book we will take care to emphasize the high level of variability in graduates' employment outcomes, living arrangements, relationships, and levels of civic engagement, as well as to illuminate how this variation was associated with different components of undergraduate education. We will describe how colleges and universities were implicated in shaping the lives of these young adults. Given the character of our data, while we will not be able to identify the effects of college per se, we will be able to provide a rich description of how students' lives varied during and after college—as well as how these patterns corresponded with the majors those individuals chose, the institutions they attended, and the general collegiate skills with which they left college.

This book is based on research that tracks more than 1,600 students through their senior year at twenty-five diverse four-year colleges and universities, and then approximately one thousand college graduates from this sample for two years following their graduation in the spring of 2009.[3] The study does not include community colleges, a critically important part of US higher education, because of constraints on the original research design. Given that limitation, we focus our analysis and broader discussion in this book on four-year colleges and universities. We surveyed graduates each spring after college and conducted in-depth interviews with a subset of eighty graduates in the summer of 2011, not just to document their successes and hardships, but also to try to understand the extent to which their post-college outcomes were associated with collegiate experiences and academic performance. To what extent did it matter that students had performed well on an assessment of their general collegiate skills—that is, the Collegiate Learning Assessment (CLA), a measure of critical thinking, complex reasoning, and written communication—around the time they graduated? Was post-college success associated with college majors and the selectivity of institutions attended? And what about the social networks they had spent so much time cultivating and investing in while enrolled in college? Were these social networks helpful, detrimental, or inconsequential in terms of supporting post-college transitions?

Before documenting the different post-college trajectories of the graduates in our study and examining factors associated with variation in these outcomes, we find it useful to first sketch the broad features of the historical context that provides the backdrop for the variation we observed. As a cohort, the individuals in our study enrolled in four-year colleges and universities at a particular time in US history, one in which they faced high tuition, heavy debt loads, and relative institutional inattention to academic learning (as opposed to social engagement and personal development): a historic period when US colleges and universities as a whole, and many of the students enrolled in them, were academically adrift. Many of today's college students graduate, but then transition only partially into traditional adult roles. While the state considers them legal adults, social scientists have come to refer to them with a more open-ended term: "emerging adults."[4] The students in our study also graduated into a particularly difficult and unforgiving economic climate, where often they had little more than their own optimism and a diploma to sustain them in a quest to realize their expectations. In addition to discussing this larger historical and social context, we will provide readers with a brief outline of the ground covered in this volume.

Twenty-First Century Higher Education

The students in our study went through and were potentially shaped by four-year colleges and universities that existed in a particular historic moment—one in which the importance of rigorous academic study had been largely abandoned throughout many parts of contemporary higher education institutions. There are complex cultural, sociological, and historical explanations for the character of twenty-first century higher education that are worth touching upon to provide context for the empirical analysis that follows. While we have discussed some of this historical context in our prior work, we aim to extend those insights and focus more explicitly on the question of how higher education came to abandon academic rigor and promote social engagement for undergraduate students.

One widely shared explanation for the contemporary state of higher education, popularized by many institutional critics, depicts an organizational sector whose failings are a function of the creep of corporatization into academia's once-hallowed halls. This deepening corporatization is argued to have led to a decline in the role of faculty relative to school administrators, and a corresponding marginalization of academic pursuits and student learning. "Now, the Zeitgeist is the market," public policy scholar David Kirp has commented. "Still, embedded in the very idea of the university—not the storybook idea, but the university at its truest and best— are values that the market does not honor: the belief in a community of scholars and not a confederacy of self-seekers; in the idea of openness and not ownership; in the professor as a pursuer of truth and not an entrepreneur; in the student as an acolyte whose preferences are to be formed, not a consumer whose preferences are to be satisfied."[5]

Sheila Slaughter and Gary Rhoades refer to this as the emergence of "academic capitalism," where actors within higher education in recent decades have brought "the corporate sector inside the university." They argue that this corporatization manifests itself in multiple ways, including expanded ties with private-sector firms, growing attention to the economic utility of research endeavors, and increased market-based interactions with students, who have been redefined as consumers. The quality of instruction is compromised, according to Slaughter and Rhoades, because "expanded managerial capacity is also directed toward restructuring faculty work to lower instructional costs (although not costs generally)."[6]

Scholars looking for evidence of a corporate turn in higher education can easily find ample material to support this claim by turning to various provocations provided by contemporary higher education administrators. Consider, for example, Rick Matasar, former law school dean and current New York University vice president for university enterprise initiatives, who wrote in his "Commercialist Manifesto": "Commercialism is here, now, and it is not going away. . . . We are a business, deal with it."[7] Or perhaps consider the comments of the former president of George Washington University, Stephen Trachtenberg, who asserted that marketing colleges was similar to selling vodka—raising prices and improving packaging are generally sufficient to lure customers, as people mistakenly "equate price with the value of their education."[8]

Higher education, however, is a particular type of business. It is heavily subsidized by public provision and, with the exception of for-profit entities, untaxed. Higher education is also a business that has increasingly become characterized by the growth of administration and a marginalization of faculty. "Every year, hosts of administrators and staffers are added to college and university payrolls, even as schools claim to be battling budget crises," political scientist Benjamin Ginsberg notes in *The Fall of the Faculty: The Rise of the All-Administrative University and Why It Matters*. "As a result universities are filled with armies of functionaries—the vice presidents, associate vice presidents, provosts, associate provosts, vice provosts, assistant provosts, deans, deanlets, deanlings, each commanding staffers and assistants—who, more and more, direct the operation of every school."[9] Again, empirical support for these claims is not hard to find. Ginsberg presents an analysis from the National Center for Education Statistics showing relative changes in the number of full-time equivalent (FTE) students to higher-education personnel from 1975 to 2005. According to this analysis, student-faculty ratios have remained roughly constant—16:1 or 15:1—while student-administrative ratios have changed from 84:1 to 68:1 and student-professional staff ratios from 50:1 to 21:1.[10]

There is a good deal of truth in these popular critiques of higher education, but we believe that they often fail to adequately describe the transformation of colleges and universities in terms that are immediately relevant to our focus on students' collegiate experiences. For example, the increase in noninstructional staff and administration is not simply a case of bureaucratic bloat. Rather, the expansion is required by an organizational logic inherent to a particular higher-education model, which developed over the past century and has considerably strengthened in recent decades in the United States. One could imagine, after all, a corporate business that was focused on student learning—one that, for example, not only catered to satisfying students' nonacademic needs as consumers, but also carefully measured and reported student learning outcomes to demonstrate value to clients. As a whole, however, the higher-education sector has been at best ambivalent about such assessment efforts.[11]

It is not just that the relationship between faculty and administrators has changed as higher education increasingly has become managed along organizational principles found in corporations. More importantly, educators have increasingly ceded their authority to students, and administrators have shifted institutional emphasis from students' academic and moral development to their personal growth and well-being. Empowering and catering to students as consumers has only exacerbated these broader and deeper changes that have come to characterize US higher education.

Historian Christopher Loss has astutely highlighted the extent to which the current character of higher education developed from a convergence of several forces, including the development of a "personnel perspective" that, following World War I, was embraced and adopted by higher-education administrators; the legal and cultural undermining of school authority in the 1960s; and the willingness of the federal government to provide financial support to subsidize the enterprise without seeking administrative oversight or demonstrated student achievement. As higher-education institutions began to grow and become more diverse in the twentieth century, administrators moved away from their earlier commitments, often religiously informed, to ensure moral development and character formation for students. Instead, they turned to the field of organizational psychology and embraced models of personnel management. According to Loss, beginning in the 1920s, "personality and the belief in pliable selfhood eclipsed character as the 'chief purpose of college education.'"[12] Specifically, the institutional model of student services was developed and promoted organizationally by the American College Personnel Association (ACPA). According to proponents of the personnel perspective, colleges needed to be brought "into closer organizational touch with [their] students" to solve their problems of maladjustment and attrition.[13] College admission offices began to ask applicants for detailed information about their personal lives so that they could choose students who would fit the specific organization and, theoretically, so that they could provide individualized programs of counseling.[14] During this time period, colleges and universities also began to pay increasing attention to promoting extracurricular activities and university-affiliated housing. Beginning in the 1920s, students' involvement in extracurricular activities such as student clubs, athletics, and fraternities and sororities was argued to enhance their success.[15]

While the "personnel perspective" or the student service model was ostensibly promoted to address the high attrition rates colleges and universities were experiencing in the 1920s—when 35 percent of students who entered four-year institutions did not finish their first year and more than half of students did not graduate—the approach flourished, according to Loss, because it was aligned with institutional interests.[16] Specifically, administrators had a rationale for expanding their institutions' scale and scope, as well as their own role within those organizations. Although the student service model never worked as well as administrators hoped it would (college attrition rates have remained high to this day), "this fact did not weaken administrators' faith in the personnel perspective; it strengthened it."[17] The model's success reflected its fit with organizational interests, not its demonstrated efficiency in improving student outcomes per se.

If colleges began to adopt a personnel approach in the 1920s, it was not until the last fifty years, with the growth of student rights, changes in college financing, and broader cultural adoption of a therapeutic ethic, that the implications of this model for collegiate life were fully felt. Prior to the 1960s, US courts granted colleges and universities broad in loco parentis rights to regulate student behavior both on and off campus. Following a period of student rights contestation from 1969 to 1975, the ability of US schools, including colleges and universities, to regulate student behaviors was significantly diminished and constrained.[18] A landmark Supreme Court decision in 1975, *Goss v. Lopez*, guaranteed rudimentary due process rights to elementary and secondary students in public schools who faced even minor day-to-day school discipline. While *Goss v. Lopez* was about public high school students, lawyers quickly came to apply this precedent broadly and effectively to private schools and higher-education institutions, which were argued to have an implicit contract that afforded rights to students in these settings. As is often the case when organizations face uncertainty in their legal environments, schools began to develop internal structures that mimicked those found externally.[19] Colleges and universities detailed rights and procedures in student handbooks, administrative committees were established to handle disciplinary matters bureaucratically, the right to appeal administrative decisions through grievance procedures was articulated, and adversarial legal challenges became considerably more prevalent.

In 1974, colleges and universities were also faced with new federal regulations enacted into law through the Family Educational Rights and Privacy Act (FERPA), which prevented them from reporting student grades or disciplinary matters to employers, graduate schools, and parents without prior student consent. Students applying to graduate school had the right to view recommendation letters written by their professors. "Ours is the age of judges and legislators who routinely second-guess decisions with which they disagree," one education lawyer recently commented, "even if it means substituting their own views for the considered judgment of educational professionals."[20]

It was during this period that colleges and universities also began to require the use of course evaluations, in which students were further empowered to evaluate their instructors. Given these changes, it is not surprising that in recent decades researchers have found that cheating and plagiarizing have increased dramatically and the hours students spend studying have plummeted. One way to get a sense of the extent of these changes is to contrast the current situation with Howard Becker and colleagues' depiction of faculty-student academic relationships in the 1960s. In *Making the Grade*, they argued that faculty and administrator "subjection" of students was nearly complete: "They decide what students are to do, when they are to do it, something of how it is to be done, and what rewards or punishments will be given to those who do or do not meet the standards."[21] Today's students, by contrast, can rely on social networks to identify course sequences with few academic demands, tame professors whose standards are considered too demanding, and earn high marks by studying little more than an hour per day.[22]

Colleges and universities were reluctant to challenge student interests as they increasingly became financially dependent on satisfying the demands of students acting as consumers. "Students could not have won such hegemony if parents had not frequently abdicated their authority," sociologist David Riesman has noted, "often siding with their children against secondary school teachers over matters of student discipline, and at the postsecondary level unwilling to support institutional demands where these conflicted with student preferences."[23] Studying the revealed preferences of students, as demonstrated by their choice of which college to attend, economist Brian Jacob and his colleagues have shown that the majority of students manifest consumer preferences for institutional investments in college amenities, such as student activities, sports, and dormitories.[24] Of course it was not just permissive parenting, but increased public subsidies—including poorly understood guaranteed student loans—that facilitated this particular brand of student consumerism. Absent these forms of financing, it is possible that students would articulate a different set of consumer preferences more closely aligned with a conception of college as a long-term investment in one's future. As Riesman noted, "If they decided to attend, they might not feel that they were having a subsidized lunch whose nutritional quality need not be examined as carefully as if one were paying out of one's own eventual pocket."[25]

Increased higher-education institutional commitment to promoting a personnel perspective that celebrated self-exploration and social well-being was also well aligned with broader cultural trends occurring in society. Specifically, in recent decades a therapeutic ethic increasingly came to underlie modern conceptions of the self and society. Sociologist Christian Smith, for example, has argued that "the de facto dominant religion among contemporary US teenagers is what we might well call 'Moralistic Therapeutic Deism.'"[26] According to Smith: "Being moral in this faith means being the kind of person that other people will like, fulfilling one's personal potential, and not being socially disruptive or interpersonally obnoxious."[27] Sociologist Jennifer Silva has documented the broad diffusion of this therapeutic model in the lives of contemporary emerging adults. Silva argues that it has become ubiquitous in contemporary US culture, "propagated through school psychologists, family services, the service economy, self-help literature, online support groups, addiction recovery groups, medical trials, or even talk shows such as *Oprah*."[28]

Given these changes, colleges and universities became spaces where both students and the institutions they inhabited were increasingly focused on personal development and social engagement. As sociologist Steven Brint documented in his examination of undergraduate time use in the University of California system, while students spent thirteen hours a week studying, they spent more than three times that amount on recreation (twelve hours socializing with friends, eleven hours using computers for fun, six hours watching television, six hours exercising, five hours on hobbies, and three hours on other forms of entertainment).[29] Higher education institutions today are *academically adrift* but socially alive, active, and attentive. This emphasis on the social sphere at least partly reflects the role of schools in socializing students for adult roles in society.

Colleges and universities, like all schools, typically function to instill students with behaviors and attitudes aligned with the contemporary values of the society of which they are a part. "Educational transformations are always the result and symptom" of a set of larger social transformations that have produced "new ideas and needs," sociologist Émile Durkheim noted.[30] From this perspective, one would argue that if colleges, universities, and the students in their midst are increasingly focused on personal growth, individual well-being, and social engagement, it is likely the case that this new pedagogical orientation is seen by many as closely aligned with the personalities thought necessary for successful transitions to adulthood.

Following World War II, sociologist David Riesman, in *The Lonely Crowd*, described the emergence of young adults in the upper middle class of urban cosmopolitan areas who were increasingly "other-directed"—focused on getting along with others, rather than being grounded by their own deeply held "inner-directed" values and motivations. Sociability and sensitivity to social groups was understood increasingly as a requirement "for success and for marital and personal adaptation."[31] According to Riesman, schools that were focused on socializing students for middle-class adult roles would increasingly embrace approaches aligned with the development of these "other-directed" dispositions.

Riesman highlighted how extracurricular activities and group projects were increasingly promoted to socialize students for this new model of individual development. "Play, which in the earlier epoch is often an extracurricular and private hobby, shared at most with a small group, now becomes part of the school enterprise itself, serving a realistic purpose," Riesman observed.[32] In promoting group activities, the teacher redefines his or her role in a manner similar to that of an "industrial relationships department in a modern factory . . . increasingly concerned with *cooperation* between men and men and between men and management, as *technical skill* becomes less and less of a major concern"[33] (our emphasis). The teacher emphasizes that "what matters is not [students'] industry or learning as such, but their adjustment in their group, their cooperation, their (carefully stylized and limited) initiative and leadership."[34] According to Riesman, "The other-directed child is taught at school to take his place in a society where the concern of the group is less with what it produces than with its internal group relations, its morale."[35]

While Riesman's dichotomy of "inner-directed" and "other-directed" ideal types can easily be critiqued on both theoretical and empirical grounds—for example, we are highly skeptical of drawing such sharp distinctions between intrinsic and extrinsic motivation—his work successfully articulated an emerging feature of cultural and institutional life that is consistent with social science research and general observation. Media scholar Todd Gitlin wrote in a 2000 foreword to Riesman's book that contemporary students "born into a world of rock music and TV . . . [have] lived their entire lives as other-directed." Gitlin maintained that "by the 1980s, the 'exceptional sensitivity to the actions and wishes of others' . . . had long since been institutionalized into the norms of talk shows and 'sensitivity training.' "[36] More importantly for our purposes, the promotion of this other-directed orientation had been institutionalized into the structure of US higher education.

The "personnel perspective" that historian Christopher Loss shows came to dominate higher education's approach to student development was oriented to a general therapeutic ethos infused with cultural assumptions that social sensitivity, sociability, and interpersonal competencies were at the core of psychological adjustment and well-being. Higher-education institutions, largely through the promotion of social engagement, extracurricular activities, and group learning, focused on individual growth and self-realization, the development of personality and identity, tolerance for difference, and the ability to get along with others. Colleges and universities not only promoted these values, commitments, and activities on their campuses but also actively selected students on these factors when given the opportunity, as sociologist Mitchell Stevens has documented in his ethnography of selective college admissions:

> Admission to places like the College typically requires considerably more than academic accomplishment, and mothers and fathers with their eyes on top schools begin investing in the development of their children's extracurricular abilities many years before college begins. . . . At least part of their incentive for doing all of this is the hope that their incremental investments will sum to the "talented" athletes and musicians favored by admissions offices at the nation's most selective schools.[37]

Middle-class parenting that promotes "concerted cultivation" of youth through extracurricular activities is reinforced and legitimated by colleges that select on and emphasize these orientations for individual development.

After students enter college, institutions continue to support nonacademic pursuits, as is carefully documented in sociologists Elizabeth Armstrong and Laura Hamilton's recent in-depth qualitative study of a cohort of female students from college entry to exit at a flagship public research university. This research provides a detailed and illuminating window into the extent to which social, not academic, engagement dominates campus life for most students. Armstrong and Hamilton documented that while some students were focused on learning, mobility, and professional training, the largest pathway through college was a "party pathway" implicitly promoted and supported by the way in which the school was organized. "The party pathway is a main artery through the university, much like a well-paved eight-lane highway directing traffic into a major city," Armstrong and Hamilton noted. "On-ramps are numerous and well marked, and avoiding it completely requires intent, effort, and intricate knowledge of alternative routes."[38]

While college students' focus on social activities is not new, the extent to which those activities are now perceived as being closely aligned with adult development and the purpose of college arguably is.[39] The cultivation of character, grit, perseverance, social obligation, and duty are vanishing features of campus life at the beginning of the twenty-first century. Instead, college increasingly is focused on personal exploration and the development of young adults who are socially acclimated for middle-class societal roles. Many of the college students in our study have come to believe that "it's not what you know, it's who you know." The colleges where they enrolled did not fundamentally challenge that logic. Instead, they implicitly offered a friendly amendment: "It's not what you know, it's who you know *and who you are*" in terms of interpersonal competencies, psychological well-being, and capacity for social adjustment.

Emerging Adulthood and an Unforgiving Economic Environment

How these college graduates truly are and how their life course conditions and outcomes should be assessed is, however, subject to empirical investigation and general debate. One way to assess graduates' life outcomes is to ask whether colleges support their movement towards adulthood. In general, there is agreement from scholars and the larger public on the definition of what constitutes traditional markers of adult status. For example, sociologist Mary Waters and her colleagues have asserted, "In the United States, becoming an adult is achieved when a person takes on a set of socially valued roles associated with finishing schooling, leaving home, starting work, entering into serious relationships, and having children."[40] Transitions to adulthood do not require the accomplishment of all of these conditions, although it is generally assumed (given prevailing social norms) that the majority of them should be satisfied.

Social, economic, and cultural changes in society have led in recent decades to increasing numbers of individuals, including college graduates, not making traditional adult transitions either in their twenties or beyond. Indeed, researchers studying contemporary transitions to adulthood have noted that "much of the pertinent action occurs in the early thirties."[41] Social scientists have documented that "the transition from adolescence to adulthood has in recent years become more complicated, uncertain, and extended than ever before."[42] The likelihood of young adults living at home has increased significantly from the 1970s to today. In addition, the age of marriage has been delayed six years, from an average of age twenty in 1960 to older than twenty-six today.[43]

The reasons for these changes in life course development are complex. For example, some scholars have emphasized the importance of structural factors, such as changes in the economy. In a recent book, sociologist Katherine Newman has argued that "globalization has ensured that the economic conditions that underwrote the earlier, more traditional, road to adulthood no longer hold," and that "new entrants fall back into the family home because—unless they are willing to take a significant cut in their standard of living, the last resort these days—they have no other way to manage the life to which they are accustomed."[44] Other sociologists have emphasized cultural factors that underlie these changes. Christian Smith writes, "The adult world is teaching its youth all too well. But what it has to teach too often fails to convey what any good society needs to pass onto its children." Pointing to the rise of moral individualism, relativism, and consumerism, Smith asserts that "American culture itself seems to be depleted of some important cultural resources that it would pass onto youth if it had them."[45]

While a range of structural and cultural factors have been responsible for changes in the timing of adulthood in our society, one interesting institutional feature that has received less attention is the extent to which individuals, particularly from middle-class social backgrounds, have been spending more and more time in colleges and universities. The extent to which higher education is therefore implicated, not at the periphery but at the core of these changing patterns, is worth emphasizing. As a set of interdisciplinary scholars organized by the MacArthur Foundation and focused on transitions to adulthood succinctly noted, "The hope for and necessity, if not always the reality, of obtaining post-secondary education (or additional training through the military or an apprenticeship) has created the growing gap between the end of adolescence and achievement of adult statuses."[46]

What is accomplished and what fails to be accomplished at college is thus central to the transitions of many emerging adults. This is true for a number of reasons. As an increasing percentage of individuals are going to college and taking longer to complete undergraduate degrees, large numbers of individuals are living for longer periods of time in relatively unsupervised residential halls or independently, as opposed to living under the auspices of parental authority and commuting from home. National studies of college freshmen show a significant decline in the percentage of students living with parents or relatives, from 21.3 percent in 1973 to 14.3 percent in 2006.[47] With the exception of a handful of Scandinavian countries (Sweden, Norway, Denmark, and Finland), undergraduate students in European countries are much more likely to live at home with their parents and commute to college. For example, 75 percent of Italian college students, 55 percent of Spanish, 48 percent of French, and 22 percent of English and Welsh students live at home with parents during their college years.[48] In the United States, students are not only going to college but are increasingly *going away* to college, and are spending longer and longer periods of time there.

Consequently, large numbers of students—for increasing amounts of time—are deeply immersed in collegiate social life; they are embedded in peer climates that sociologists have characterized as "adolescent societies"—or perhaps, given the age of the students in these settings, what we might call "emerging adult societies."[49] As we have described above, the power of these young adult peer subcultures is enhanced by school authorities, as social engagement with peers is not discouraged but, rather, is institutionally advocated, endorsed, and subsidized. For many undergraduates, college is understood and experienced primarily in terms of social interaction with their peers. Sociologist Michael Rosenfeld observed that "by the 1970s, coeducational college dorms were common, curfews were a thing of the past, and the college campus had become an important site of social and sexual experimentation."[50] For many individuals from middle- and upper-class social origins, the college years begin a period of independence that allows for the exploration of a wide range of life-course pathways. This period of individual exploration and experimentation can last well beyond college as young adults attempt to "find themselves." Researchers studying transitions to adulthood have observed that "growing numbers of young people give themselves an early sabbatical to travel and experience life or engage in a community service project before deciding what they are going to do with their lives."[51]

While overall trends provide useful contours for understanding the transition to adulthood, as well as how colleges are implicated in this process, individual trajectories vary with respect to different components of undergraduate education—including development of general collegiate skills, college majors, and selectivity of the institutions attended—that are potentially associated with students' post-college trajectories. Individual lives also unfold and are profoundly shaped by social background and historic circumstances. In his classic work *Children of the Great Depression*, Glen Elder demonstrated that the cohort of people who had been children during the Great Depression experienced long-term consequences with respect to their subsequent adult careers, marital formation, health, and worldviews. Interestingly, Elder found that while working-class youth suffered long-term negative outcomes from the economic hardships in their lives, middle-class children who experienced economic deprivation but had familial resources as a buffer often assumed greater responsibility for taking care of others, and had largely positive adult outcomes. The consequences of delayed transition to adulthood in general, as well as the difficulties that recent college graduates experienced specifically as a result of the economic downturn, likely vary on the basis of social origins. As Frank Furstenberg and his colleagues have noted about emerging adulthood, "The ability of families to manage this long and complex period clearly varies greatly by the resources they possess or those they can access through formal or informal ties."[52] Whether delayed transitions to adulthood are a cause for concern is thus partially dependent on the extent to which emerging adults have resources that allow them to be adrift for a while, before they "find themselves" to lead more directed and purposeful lives.

The college students we followed in our study, who largely graduated in 2009, faced particularly difficult economic conditions associated with the 2007 recession. While they faced dismal economic circumstances that contributed to the labor market difficulties observed in our study, their conditions were perhaps not as dire as some social commentators have argued. Claims in the popular media, for example, featured unemployed and indebted college students joining Occupy Wall Street and suing their colleges for malpractice.[53] Increasingly, commentators were asking whether college was worth it, and often explicitly invoked our prior work to question the value of undergraduate education.[54] In spite of this sometimes shrill commentary, social scientific research on how college graduates fared during the recent economic downturn demonstrated that college-educated young adults continued to experience significant advantages in finding desirable employment, relative to those young adults without a degree. Sociologist David Grusky and colleagues write, "The deteriorating market situation of recent college graduates, while real and troubling, is nonetheless less extreme than that experienced by less-educated groups."[55]

Significance and Measurement of General Collegiate Skills

Our project is unique in that it includes an objective measure of student performance in critical thinking, complex reasoning, and writing as students move through college and then transition into the labor market as well as other aspects of adulthood following graduation. While we are unable to explore the extent to which other, subject-specific, competencies make independent contributions to improving graduate outcomes, our focus on a measure of general collegiate competencies is particularly relevant now, for multiple reasons.

First, there is increasing evidence that generic skills, such as analytical ability, have significant and growing consequences for labor market success. Recent research by sociologists Yujia Liu and David Grusky is particularly compelling in this regard. Analyzing data from several million respondents in Current Population Surveys (CPS) from 1979 through 2010, Liu and Grusky identify different skill requirements required for occupations by applying ratings developed by independent analysts at the Department of Labor as well as by representative individuals in those occupations who were surveyed about this issue. As the CPS data also include earnings reports, Liu and Grusky were able to track changes in the relative payoffs for different types of occupational skills over this time period. These returns can be thought of as the "revealed demand" for various skills, although changes in occupational earnings are also influenced by other institutional factors (such as the decline of unions).[56]

Liu and Grusky demonstrate increases over the past three decades both in the skill requirements of occupations—particularly for computer, creative, managerial, and nurturing skills—and in economic returns for analytic, computer, managerial, and nurturing skills. Some skills, such as creative competencies, which were rising in prevalence across occupations, had negative returns associated with them in general, and were actually experiencing rapidly deteriorating returns over the last three decades, indicating an oversupply of workers with skills suited for "dancers, journalists, poets, sculptors, creative writers, artists, and all manners of associated creative types."[57] On the other hand, increases in returns for analytical skills were particularly striking. According to Liu and Grusky, "Demand for analytic skills may be increasing because (1) they require intuitive problem solving skills that cannot easily be substituted with computer programming or software (unlike quantitative and verbal skills), and (2) the accelerating 'creative destruction' of modern capitalism places a growing premium on innovation, problem solving, and rapid response to changing market conditions."[58] A standard deviation increase in analytical skills was associated with 10.4 percent greater wages in 1980 and 17.5 percent greater wages in 2010. Analytical skills not only had the greatest increase in returns over this time period, but also had high returns overall. Liu and Grusky note, "The defining feature . . . of the last 30 years has been a precipitous increase in the wage payoff to jobs requiring synthesis, critical thinking, and deductive and inductive reasoning."[59]

Second, these generic competencies have broad applications; and multiple stakeholders, from colleges to employers, repeatedly assert that they represent core student learning outcomes. While students are expected to develop subject-specific skills and experience affective growth, the development of generic competencies in college has been argued to be increasingly important in the twenty-first-century knowledge economy.[60] Generic competencies—such as critical thinking, complex reading, and writing—are transferable across jobs, occupations, firms, and industry; given the broad character of these skills, they likely also have relevance for other aspects of individuals' lives, including citizenship. The potential broad relevance of these skills for individuals and society has led to extensive support for developing these competencies in college. Commitment to these competencies is found in institutional mission statements and faculty surveys, as well as in employer surveys of desirable skills sought in job candidates.[61]

Third, there is growing concern that the US higher education system is failing to adequately develop generic collegiate skills in its graduates. For example, recent surveys of employers have highlighted dissatisfaction with the preparation of college graduates, noting that only approximately a quarter of college graduates entering the labor market have excellent skills in critical thinking and problem solving, and only 16 percent have excellent written communication.[62] "Woefully unprepared" is how one employer described college graduates in a 2012 survey conducted by the *Chronicle of Higher Education* and American Public Media's radio show *Marketplace*. According to this survey, employers tended to "ding bachelor's-degree holders for lacking basic workplace proficiencies, like adaptability, communication skills, and the ability to solve complex problems."[63]

More troubling still are the recent results of the Programme for the International Assessment of Adult Competencies, a study of adult skills in twenty-three developed countries conducted by the Organisation for Economic Cooperation and Development (OECD). The study measures individuals' ability to understand and use information from written tests; to use, apply, interpret, and communicate mathematical information and ideas; and to use technology to solve problems and accomplish complex tasks. The OECD disaggregated the results by education level, so that it is possible to compare US college graduates to individuals in other countries with similar levels of education. The results for US college graduates on these assessments were not impressive: on most measures they scored below the average of college graduates in other countries.[64] In addition, the results were discouraging when considering change for the population as a whole over recent decades. The OECD states that in spite of increasing percentages of adults in the US having gone to college, "there are few signs of improvement. Today, adults in the U.S. have similar or weaker literacy skills to their counterparts in the mid-90s, and the average basic skills of young adults are not very different from older adults."[65]

In addition to new cross-national research on adult competencies, an important development in efforts to measure general collegiate skills in the United States was also undertaken by the Council for Aid to Education (CAE). The CAE brought together leading assessment experts to design an instrument, the Collegiate Learning Assessment (CLA), that required students to perform a task akin to what they might be asked to complete by an employer following college graduation. Students were given a prompt that required them to analyze and think critically about a set of documents, synthesize information across these documents, and then write a logical response that used evidence from the documents to support the arguments being made. Although all instruments that attempt to measure student competencies are by definition limited and imperfect, the CLA was adopted as a reasonable proxy for students' general collegiate skills by a large number of organizations and higher-education institutions. For example, the OECD used a modified version of the CLA for its cross-national institutional Assessment of Higher Education Learning Outcome (AHELO) project, and the Association of Public and Land-Grant Universities (APLU) and the American Association of State Colleges and Universities (AASCU) promoted use of the instrument through the Voluntary System of Accountability project. Other measures which rely on multiple choice questions, such as the Collegiate Assessment of Academic Proficiency (CAAP) and the Proficiency Profile (formerly known as the Measurement of Academic Progress and Proficiency or MAPP), yield similar findings at the institutional or aggregate level.[66]

Additional Motivations and an Outline of the Book

In exploring graduates' life-course transitions after college, and particularly the extent to which different components of undergraduate education facilitate successful transitions, this book seeks to extend our prior research. In *Academically Adrift: Limited Learning on College Campuses*, we joined an existing longitudinal study of several dozen colleges and universities that was being fielded by the CAE and documented the limited learning and lack of academic rigor that large numbers of students experienced during their first two years of college. Specifically, during the fall of their sophomore year, 50 percent of students had no single class which required more than twenty pages of writing over the course of the semester, 32 percent had no class that required more than forty pages of reading per week, and 36 percent studied alone five or fewer hours per week—less than an hour per day. Given this limited educational "treatment," student gains on the CLA were modest. The average student only improved by 0.18 standard deviations, after two years of college—meaning that if, after two years of college, he or she were to take the assessment with a new cohort of freshmen, he or she would move up only from the 50th percentile to the 57th. If the assessment was scored on a scale from 0 to 100, 45 percent of the students would not have demonstrated an improvement of even one point on this measure at the end of their sophomore year. These findings were not likely an artifact of the assessment instrument or the sample in our study, as researchers using data from the Wabash National Study (WNS), which used a different measure of general collegiate skills and followed several thousand students in a different set of schools, found similar results in a replication study.[67]

In *Academically Adrift* we also explored the variation in student outcomes to understand better the factors that were associated with student learning. As with learning outcomes in elementary and secondary schools, we found variation in test score gains to be greater within colleges than across colleges. Which schools individuals attended made a difference, explaining 24 percent of the variation in student learning gains, but student outcomes varied much more across than within colleges. For example, students majoring in traditional arts and science fields had higher gains on the CLA than students in other fields, corresponding in part with the greater likelihood of experiencing courses with greater reading, writing, and homework demands. Providing an organizational perspective on these findings, we argued that the incentive structures that administrators, faculty, and students in higher education encountered were poorly aligned with the production of positive learning outcomes. Our earlier work, however, implicitly assumed and emphasized the academic functions of colleges and universities. We did so in part because our bias as educators was to assume that academic activities were at the core of these institutions' logic.

In this book we move beyond the conceptualization and findings in our earlier work. Rather than again demonstrating lack of academic rigor and its consequences for student learning outcomes throughout the entire four years of college, we illuminate other aspects of collegiate experience that students themselves value, and also examine the relationship between collegiate experience and transitions to adulthood after college. In the pages that follow, we document variation in the extent to which 2009 college graduates in our study progressed towards successful transitions to adulthood within two years after graduation. Specifically, following prior scholarship on emerging adults, we examine these college graduates' ability to secure employment, and the quality of the jobs they attained. In addition, we examine whether they moved on to graduate school, whether they returned home to live with family, and the extent of their romantic relationships and civic engagement. If graduates moved successfully into the labor market or postgraduate education, what factors were associated with these trajectories? While we will be unable to resolve the larger cultural debate, given its normative character, about the relative costs and benefits to individuals—and society—of the extended period of emerging adulthood, we pay particular attention to how the college graduates in our study understand and speak about their experiences. If they have taken on large debt to socialize rather than study in college, and later as emerging adults they are underemployed, living at home with their parents, but reporting to us high levels of satisfaction and well-being, is there really any problem requiring social reform or institutional remedy? We will return to this normative question in the concluding chapter of this book.

In the current study, we indeed observed many graduates who were unemployed, underemployed, heavily indebted, and economically struggling;

but we also found many who had made successful adult transitions and were flourishing economically and personally. Although the lack of academic rigor and positive learning outcomes that we identified in our research is disconcerting in its own right, one cannot conclude a priori that negative economic consequences are associated with variation in undergraduate experience and academic performance. As social scientists, we find it imperative to document and learn from the real and observable differences that graduates experienced both during and after college. Parents, policy makers, practitioners, and students themselves would benefit from knowing more about how college experiences and academic performance track with graduates' ability to make successful transitions into adulthood.

We begin chapter 2 by listening to graduates' reflections on their college experiences, including what they learned or regret not learning; how they describe their academic and social engagement as undergraduates; and how, two years after graduation, they appraise the value of their college experiences. We also identify the extent to which students developed general collegiate skills, such as critical thinking, complex reasoning, and writing, as measured by the CLA. In addition to reporting average learning gains, we explore variation within and across institutions, highlighting how different individual and institutional factors contribute to variation in learning gains. We end the chapter by exploring whether graduates continue their education after college, and whether CLA performance is related to their pursuit of graduate degrees.

Chapter 3 presents a portrait of how graduates are doing economically approximately two years out of college during a historically difficult economic period. In particular, we explore how senior CLA scores and other college experiences are related to early labor market outcomes, including individuals' ability to avoid unemployment and marginal employment (in terms of part-time status and low skill requirements) as well as job loss. In addition, we explore the extent to which college graduates are finding jobs that are satisfying to them, and we identify the features of their college education that they report to have been useful in the labor market. While many aspects of college are potentially related to subsequent labor market success, we pay particular attention to senior CLA performance—as it is a unique feature of our data—as well as to the selectivity of college attended and the student's choice of major.

Labor market outcomes, of course, are only one important part of a graduate's hoped-for transition to adulthood. In chapter 4 we take the other parts of that transition seriously and focus on a range of outcomes, from being financially dependent on parents to finding romantic partners and being civically engaged. Specifically, we explore the extent to which different aspects of undergraduate education and labor market experience are related to graduates' financial dependence on their families, in terms of both living at home and receiving money from parents. We also examine whether graduates have romantic partners two years after college, and the extent to which graduates find partners who are similarly highly educated or have attended institutions of similar selectivity. Finally, we highlight the predictors of graduates' civic and political awareness, and conclude with their own assessments of their lives in relation to those of their parents.

In the concluding chapter of the book, we shift from analysis and reporting of empirical results to a broader discussion of what we believe these findings suggest for higher education. We focus on how our findings illustrate the extent to which colleges today are spending inadequate attention on academic rigor and the promotion of critical thinking, complex reasoning, and writing skills. We argue that appreciating the relationships between variation in college experiences, student learning, and graduate outcomes can reveal ways to improve undergraduate education. We also highlight the role of improved assessment for expanding educational opportunities for all. What one does in college matters, as does how much one learns. Systematically addressing the problems we have identified will, however, require institutional commitment to both measuring and improving learning outcomes.

2

Social and Academic Learning in College

College provides an environment conducive to exploration—to learning about oneself and others, and to considering different options and beginning to chart a path toward the future.[1] It also provides a context for a range of new experiences. For many students attending residential four-year institutions, this is their first time away from home without direct parental oversight. Some students are better prepared and able to manage this newfound freedom than others. Given the segregation of neighborhoods and of primary and secondary schools, college can also present increased opportunities for engaging with students from different walks of life, whether in dorms, classes, student organizations, or informal gatherings. College can thus provide a unique opportunity for personal development, which has become an increasing emphasis of higher education over the course of the twentieth and twenty-first centuries.[2]

This aspect of college life is often given inadequate attention in scholarly and policy debates, which have overwhelmingly focused on credentials—whether students complete their degrees—and, more recently, on whether they get jobs afterwards. When social life is attended to, especially in the popular discourse, it is often of the disconcerting kind, whether it be Greek life or the party scene

Jason Thompson coauthored this chapter.

surrounding college sports.[3] While college life provides opportunities for excessive drinking, inappropriate initiation practices, and revelry that can capture media scrutiny, understanding its patterns and consequences requires that attention be paid to a broader set of more subtle everyday processes. As Émile Durkheim asserted more than a century ago, the goal of education is the "socialization of the human being."[4]

Six decades ago, David Riesman provided a thought-provoking proposition of what this socialization might entail in modern times.[5] He argued that with the source of conformity moving away from tradition and towards one's peers, the crucial skill becomes the ability to pick up signals from others, to gauge the flow of the times, and to mesh with that flow. "Other-directed" individuals have to be socially attuned; they have to have appropriate social sensibility to respond to myriad possible situations smoothly. In this context, schools "[underplay] the skills of intellect and [overplay] the skills of gregariousness and amiability."[6] Thus, while the general curriculum may teach students how to be better thinkers and citizens, it also teaches them how to be socially "suave."[7] The crucial product of the educational process is "a personality,"[8] one that displays an appropriate degree of social sensibility.

Focus on social sensibility places a premium on the peer group. The roles of parents and teachers decline as peers become the "chief source of direction and sensitivity."[9] While this may be a central feature of the other-directed self, and an inescapable part of modern life, social scientists have long been concerned about the role of peers in academic settings. James Coleman's classic work on high schools documented the extent to which peer-driven cultures often place emphasis on nonacademic activities and perpetuate gender stereotypes.[10] Descriptions of college cultures today raise similar concerns.[11] However, Coleman also noted that variation in peer cultures across schools had significant consequences: some schools adopted institutional practices that served to promote academically oriented peer cultures and organizational climates conducive to academic growth, while others did not.

We begin this chapter by listening to college graduates reflect on how they experienced college and what they learned. These reflections illuminate the extent to which social life is valued in its own right, as it is expected to provide certain skills and attributes deemed important not only for success among peers, but also for life after college. The importance of the social thus goes much beyond the party scene; it goes to the core of how students define the college experience, understand their purpose in college, and value different dimensions of their college lives.

The centrality of the social sphere naturally raises questions about academics. While the purpose of college may not simply be to teach academic skills and competencies, but rather to develop "competent social actors,"[12] academics provides legitimacy to the enterprise and is broadly understood as a necessary and important component of what college has to offer. We thus listen to how students describe academic life in college, considering how they use their time as well as how they talk about their academic and social experiences. We then put college academic programs to a test: we examine how much students develop general collegiate skills, such as critical thinking, complex reasoning, and writing, during college. In addition to describing the overall patterns, we pay close attention to variation in learning both within and across institutions. Finally, we explore the extent to which graduates continue their education after college, and whether their college experiences and their performance on an assessment of general collegiate skills are related to their pursuit of graduate degrees. This portrait of academic and social life illuminates the promise as well as the limits of the dominant conceptions of the residential college experience.

Getting Along with Others

When asked what they learned socially, without missing a beat, college graduates emphasized learning how to get along with others. For many whom we interviewed, entering college was their first time being away from home and encountering people different from themselves. It was thus common for them to comment on diversity in college.[13] Summing up this theme, Beth reported, "I come from a very small town. . . . It's not diverse. So, I knew I needed to learn about other people and who they are and where they come from."

Opportunities to learn how to get along with others existed in all corners of campus, from the classrooms to the dorms, organized activities, and informal interactions. The classroom provided a new context, different from high school, as students were not "in classes with the same type of people, and people [were] from all over" (Melissa). While the classroom presented a relatively constrained environment, with faculty guiding the conversation and setting clear norms, group activities could be more challenging as students were left on their own to sort out their differences. As Julie recounted, "I can certainly remember some challenging group situations where, boy, were our styles different. Or maybe somebody else, maybe two other people in the group had big issues with each other and you had to sort of mediate; those lessons came in all fla-vors and types."

The lessons students learned outside of the classroom, including those related to interpersonal competency, arose from interactions with peers, whether in formal organizations or through informal socializing.[14] Stu-dents noted how engagement in clubs and campus organizations helped broaden their horizons. "I met a lot of people," Tanya commented. "I inter-acted with a lot of people that I probably wouldn't have interacted [with] if I wasn't as involved as I was." This exposure to difference taught Grant "about the variety of life in the US and the different ways that people—the outlooks people have." He went on: "It gave me the skills to interact with people who had all sorts of different ways of life." The exposure was ampli-fied when students studied abroad and their horizons broadened beyond the campus walls. Michael described it thus: "I feel like I became more globally connected and culturally understanding of other people."

Not surprisingly, students reported that the most contested environ-ment for dealing with others was the dorm. Classrooms and, to some ex-tent, group work could be mediated by the instructor, and students could choose to leave extracurricular activities or informal peer groups. How-ever, students are often assigned to dorms by their institutions and are required to live in them, at least for their first year. These spaces leave students with little choice but to figure out how to negotiate difference. Stephanie explained that dorm life taught her "how to live with people . . . with strangers" and how to "be conscious of other people's space and also with friends." Sometimes dealing with others could be mostly a nuisance, but at other times it could present more difficult situations, as experienced by Beth: "As a freshman, my roommate was a very interesting character. . . . She had a history of doing things like cocaine. That really just wasn't the norm for me. I didn't—I never saw that. My suitemate, she would cut her[self] and I had to deal with that. The girl across the hall from me, she stole from me. . . . I think I learned so much about people in my first year in college."

In *Paying for the Party*, sociologists Elizabeth Armstrong and Laura Ham-ilton portray similar conflicts between students on the all-female dorm floor they observed.[15] They note that these conflicts often had strong social class overtones, even though students did not necessarily interpret them in those terms. Given the variation in parenting styles across social class groups, it is not surprising that students enter college with different habits, predispositions, and· expectations.[16] They also arrive with different goals for higher education. Christine recalled, "A lot of people [weren't] there to learn as much as I was. They were there to have their experience and their social life and all that." Armstrong and Hamilton illuminate how students approach their studies, their social life, and even the essential purposes of education differently across social class groups. These differences often result in conflicts, particularly during final exams or at other stressful times that test students' tolerance levels.

Students credit social experiences with enabling them to acquire competence and become more sociable. Furthermore, students report learning about themselves in the process of learning about others. In many ways, encountering difference thus produces both engagement and reflection, as was aptly summarized by Kevin: "I think the act of going to social settings that I didn't go to in high school was really important socially. . . . Pushing boundaries, not because I ended up being a very different person than I was in high school—although I did—but because the act of exposing yourself to new things is going to make you think critically about who you are, who you want to be, in ways that you might not have before."

This personal transformation may not only change one's attitudes and dispositions, but also make one feel more fully developed. Dan related: "I learned about many different views in the world from many different people, then I became a *complete* individual. I am much more open now to many different things than I was before I went to college. So, religious-wise and business practices and just—every single aspect of my life has changed" (emphasis added). Social experiences can also help students engage with those who are different from themselves:

> It's about meeting people from different cultures, different backgrounds, being constantly *competent*, and respectful of other peoples' story. And that's quite frankly just their simple story of where they're coming from. So, socially I was always at all the little events around campus, the socials and hosting events, being the face and the voice of a lot of big events around campus. I've learned how to be *a better sociable person* (Brandon, emphasis added).

The Necessity of the Social

An institutional focus on personal development makes the social sphere of college indispensable. If students are to engage with others, and thus to learn both about themselves and about those different from themselves, colleges have to provide opportunities and students need to engage in a variety of experiences likely to produce these encounters. As Julie aptly noted, "College is certainly really good at providing you with all sorts of diversions, and you're always surrounded by events to go to, and sports, and music, and friends, and there's just—there are always a billion ways you can spend the next hour of your life." Through extensive social life, students can develop as "whole persons": well-rounded and well-adjusted. Riesman proposed that higher education plays an important role in this process, as college is meant to cultivate "the whole man."[17] Indeed, as much as the notion of getting along with others permeated students' discussions of college, so did the importance of being well-rounded, which was often discussed in terms of balance.

Julie explained that it was important to her to do well academically, but it was also important not to "disappear behind the mountain of books." What was really important was doing well academically while having a "healthy life" outside of the classroom: "I struck a really good balance between being involved in a lot of things outside the classroom, making a lot of really meaningful friends, and spending good time with them, but also leaving college with an academic record that I was very proud of." And even if students began college with their heads buried in the books, over time they opened their eyes to new opportunities and shifted their attention to the social. Chelsea explained that by the end of her first year she "discovered that there was so much more that [she] wanted to accomplish in college than just going to class, studying, and then getting all straight A's," so her priorities changed to "becoming an overall well-rounded person," which meant spending more time on extracurricular activities.

At times, social life became the core of one's identity. Academics were a given; classes, professors, and assignments gave legitimacy to the colleges students attended. But one could not allow those to trump the importance of the social experience, particularly when it was perceived as central to one's identity. Sharon described her college experience thus:

> I was very academically engaged in college. I balanced my social life with my academics, but I never neglected my work. I did well. I wasn't top of my class, but I graduated with a 3.6. . . . So, what it was is that I wasn't a 4.0 student, but I also maintained my social life. So, I think I was very academically engaged, but I did not let it sacrifice who I was. And, like, part of why I was in college is to make new friends, to have the experience (emphasis added).

When students had not engaged in social life, they occasionally looked back with regret. When asked whether they would have done anything different in college, some noted that they wished they had had more of a college experience, meaning more engagement in the social. For example, Valerie explained that she wished she had "enjoyed it more," because studying too hard limited her ability to participate in the social realm and learn about others. She recalled, "I didn't learn [about] a lot of people that I graduated with or didn't meet them until Senior Week, because I was always studying or in the library and not participating in fun activities because I had schoolwork."

Once students transitioned to the "real world" beyond the campus walls, they looked back with nostalgia for the missed opportunities, as reflected upon by Elizabeth:

> Well, basically now that I'm a professional and I need to go work eight to ten hours a day, I'm responsible for everything now. . . . All of my friends went through that party phase and they got it all out of their systems . . . but I feel like I was so dedicated in college to keep my grades . . . and I didn't really get my partying [out]. . . . I'm coming to terms with that, which is fine, but I kind of wish I would have been *the typical college student* for at least maybe a year or two (emphasis added).

And it was not only nostalgia but perceptions that life after college required social skills that gave the social sphere its cherished place. This did not preclude the importance of other academic or career-specific skills for labor market transitions, but it illustrates the extent to which the emphasis on sociability during college was perceived as benefiting students in their subsequent labor market pursuits. Chad explained, "I think a lot of what I've learned about being in a job is all that really matters [is] *how much people like you*, and how much you don't mess up. You can coast in some ways, like doing an above-average job and *being generally likable*. . . . It's not something I'm going to emulate, but . . . I wish I had spent more time like learning some of those social skills" (emphasis added).

Those who learned the appropriate social sensibilities during college were grateful for those skills. Courtney described it this way: "My main job is to support and build relationships and make [clients] feel like someone cares for them and they're not just another person to refer or send elsewhere." Thus, she perceived learning "empathy and the ability to build rapport with [people from] different cultures, different socioeconomic status [groups]" during college as being quite valuable for her current job. As some graduates moved to managerial roles, they witnessed the challenges of managing people and reflected on the benefits of having the "people skills" to do so. Nick explained: "I'm starting to see that managing people is more important than anything else, because a lot of times that's the biggest determinant on success—the people involved, not necessarily the situation. So, definitely the [soft] skills in working with people and communication were probably the biggest things I took away [from college that] prepared me for this [current job]."

While students' appraisals of their social experiences and the potential of those experiences to foster personal development were remarkably positive, several concerns could be raised that challenge this completely sanguine picture of social life. For example, researchers have documented that the simple act of placing students from different backgrounds in close proximity is not sufficient to generate thoughtful engagement with diversity. Diverse campuses can provide opportunities for engagement, but they do not inevitably create supportive environments.[18] Recent studies also indicate that students' interest in exploring diversity in culture, ethnicity, perspectives, values, and ideas actually declines during college,[19] and that negative diversity experiences are not uncommon and have consequences for academic outcomes.[20]

Indeed, while students in our study often reported that exposure to people different from themselves led to reflective thought and learning how to work with others, at other times it led to resignation. In those instances, students felt that some people were just different and would stay that way, and that the best one could do was to tolerate them. Illustrating this point, Joseph commented, "I also found out that there are a number of personality styles that I just kind of clash with or I need to stay away from. . . . I think over four years, I really learned to come to grips with that." Similarly, Vanessa noted:

> I guess I learned a lot socially then, because the first time you go in, you're friends with everyone—everyone is scared and everyone is this and that. By the time the years progress, I've been in a lot of arguments with a lot of those girls. I got into a lot of altercations with a lot of the girls. . . . By senior year it was, I guess, it wasn't that we were all friends; it was mutual understanding and mutual respect. "*You stay in your lane. I stay in my lane*" (emphasis added).

This resignation, which might be called the "tolerance of difference," highlights the fractured nature and contradictory practices associated with getting along with others. Riesman noted that peer groups, which modern individuals rely on as a moral compass, are typically comprised of individuals of the same age and class background.[21] Getting along with others thus may often mean getting along with similar others. Different others are not necessarily the source of social cues as much as a force to be, if not reckoned with, at least tolerated. This portrayal of an easygoing and tolerant self is deeply embedded in student culture. As Mary Grigsby noted in a recent study of college life, "This self is based in a polite, tolerant, superficial approach to interactions and requires little from the authentic person beyond conforming to a polite form of interaction with others."[22] While perhaps preventing open conflict, this approach can also lead to acceptance of racist and sexist behavior in the interest of getting along.

This highlights a second concern with the social sphere that is rarely attended to: a high degree of inequality. In the higher education literature, social integration is typically portrayed as a positive factor—one that is related to a range of desirable education outcomes, including persistence.[23] However, several scholars have noted that low levels of social integration may represent not a failure of the individual, as seems implicit in some scholarly accounts, but a shortcoming of the collegiate culture.[24] Indeed, social integration is not equally viable for students from all social backgrounds.[25] Middle-class parents cultivate their children's talents and abilities, including their social competence, from an early age.[26] Middle-class students thus enter college attuned to the social sphere and with an orientation toward sociability. While working-class students do not necessarily share the same orientations, and do not perceive the importance of or engage in extracurricular activities to the same extent, they are confronted with the dominant social practices of higher education.[27] Even more notably, institutions support and perpetuate the focus on the social, often making it difficult for students to avoid embracing what Armstrong and Hamilton have labeled the "party pathway" through college. It takes concerted effort, and often much knowledge about how higher education institutions operate, to find alternative pathways and secure adequate academic supports.[28]

Academic Engagement

Given students' emphasis on getting along with others and developing socially, it is not surprising that they spent a disproportionate amount of time participating in social activities as opposed to academic pursuits. Seniors in our sample reported spending fourteen hours attending class and lab, and an additional twelve hours studying outside of class. Overall, they were dedicating twenty-six hours to academic pursuits, or 15 percent of

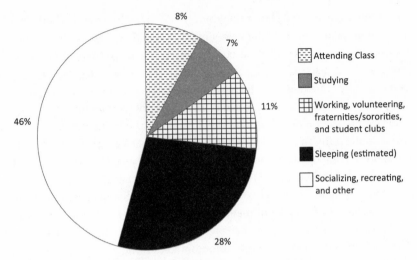

Figure 2.1 Time use by college seniors. Percentages are based on a full seven-day week totaling 168 hours.

the total time available in a week (figure 2.1).[29] Similarly, other recent estimates of time use reveal students' limited focus on academics. A study of University of California undergraduates reported that students spent only thirteen hours a week studying—three times fewer hours than they spent on other activities such as socializing with friends, using computers for fun, watching television, exercising, hobbies, and other forms of entertainment.[30] Effective study time may actually be lower, as the students in our sample reported spending only nine hours studying alone, with the other three hours spent studying with peers—which, as we showed in *Academically Adrift*, was not time well spent, at least not for developing general collegiate skills.

It is notable that students invested the same amount of time in academic pursuits as seniors as they had when they were sophomores.[31] Even though their junior and senior years were expected to include higher-level courses and more demanding curricula, they were not spending any more time on academics in their senior year than they had two years earlier. The National Survey of Student Engagement (NSSE), which over the past decade has surveyed more than two million students at more than one thousand colleges and universities, also reveals limited levels of academic engagement even among seniors. For example, 51 percent of college seniors reported that they had not written a paper during the current academic year that was twenty or more pages long, and more than half reported writing fewer than five papers that ran from five to nineteen pages in length.[32]

Surveys of seniors conducted by the Higher Education Research Institute at the University of California, Los Angeles (UCLA), provide another perspective on student engagement: among graduating seniors, less than half reported always completing homework on time, and only approximately one-third reported never coming to class late.[33]

While students spend substantially more time on social activities than on academics, that alone does not speak to what constitutes a desirable amount of time students should spend studying. Faculty members typically advise students to spend three hours studying outside of class for each hour spent in class—meaning that a student taking twelve credits of coursework would be expected to spend thirty-six hours on schoolwork outside of class. If faculty expectations are dismissed as unrealistic, one could turn to the federal definition of a credit hour, which includes the expectation that students spend "a minimum of two hours out of class" studying for each hour of classroom instruction.[34] This more lenient definition would still imply that a full-time student enrolled in twelve credits of coursework should spend at least twenty-four hours a week studying outside of class.

Indeed, twenty-five hours of studying per week used to be the average for full-time undergraduates. Combining several national surveys, economists Philip Babcock and Mindy Marks reported that students in the 1960s spent forty hours on academic pursuits: fifteen hours attending classes, and twenty-five hours studying.[35] By the early 2000s, the amount of time spent in classes and labs remained relatively stable, but the number of hours students spent studying decreased to between eleven and thirteen hours, depending on the survey. There are myriad reasons for these trends. Compositional change, technological innovation, and increased employment are often mentioned, but none of those factors can fully account for the observed patterns. In addition, while study time in college has declined in recent decades, the amount of time high school students spend studying has actually increased.[36]

Whatever the reasons for the decline, college students today spend less time studying than they did in the past, and less than either their faculty members or the federal government deem necessary. Moreover, college students in the United States dedicate less time to academic pursuits than do students in most European countries. In a recent EUROSTUDENT survey, students in all countries examined except Slovakia spent more time on academics (i.e., time spent in class and studying) than students in the United States.[37] The complexities of cross-national comparison notwithstanding, students' accounts of what it means to be academically engaged are quite telling. When asked whether they had been academically engaged during college, the majority of students reported being reasonably or very engaged, and this is how they defined academic engagement:

> I was a very good student. I did all my homework and studied for all my tests (Dan, business major at a selective educational institution).[38]
>
> Pretty committed. I went to 90 to 95 percent of all my classes, and I did all my homework and, for the most part, the readings (Caroline, psychology major at a more selective institution).
>
> Actually, like, I put forth a good deal of effort. I was great about going to class. I think I really only missed a handful of classes the entire time I was at college. I studied. Any homework I had to do, I did (Dennis, education major at a selective institution).
>
> I was fairly academically engaged in that I tried very hard not to fail most of my classes [laughter] (Eric, biological/life sciences major at a more selective institution).
>
> I was a good student. I did my homework on time (Cory, biological/life sciences major at a less selective institution).

What is remarkable about these definitions of academic engagement is their focus on fulfilling little more than minimum requirements. Moreover, the students quoted represent all school selectivity levels and span different majors, from the arts and science core to professional fields. Since our interview sampling was relatively small, we do not have adequate data to conduct a nuanced analysis of graduates' interview responses along fields of study. Other research has emphasized the importance of examining variation across fields of study in definitions of academic engagement—a topic that warrants further attention in future research.[39]

Defining academic engagement as minimal effort, the mere acts of showing up in class and turning in assignments, is consistent with a world of higher education in which many students do not even meet these low expectations. In this context, one may wonder whether even complying with the minimum is necessary. In reflecting on whether she would have done anything different during college, Beth remarked: "Maybe I should have relaxed a little bit more. I should have gone to more basketball games, a couple of more football games, things like that. I only skipped one college class ever. People right and left were skipping class and I was just like, 'How are you doing it?'"

When looking around and seeing students who are not working very hard but are still passing their classes, a student might be compelled to wonder what is really necessary and what it means to be a good student.

In this environment of low expectations, students often turn to faculty for guidance. Faculty, through assigning grades for student performance, provide an external (and thus supposedly objective) measure of students' academic achievement. Students internalize these signals and regard themselves as highly motivated because they "got good grades" and "worked very hard for them" (Jodie), or they claim to be good students because their "grades would say so" (Emma). Students thus look for external signals to evaluate their performance, but the challenge is that those signals are quite weak, as decades of grade inflation have eroded the power of grades to signal academic accomplishment. Despite low levels of academic engagement, our respondents graduated college with an average of a 3.33 cumulative GPA. Even those who reported studying alone five or fewer hours a week during their senior year still made it through college with a 3.22 cumulative GPA.

College students in our interview sample who defined academic engagement based on their GPA did not have meaningfully higher GPAs than did other students. Similarly, both groups of students—those who based their definition of academic engagement on hours studying and those who did not—reported studying the same number of hours during their senior year. Even an average level of academic engagement and performance may be considered an accomplishment when academics are regarded as painful. Rachel said, "I would say that I was a very hard worker. I wouldn't say that I was one of the very best workers. I certainly had other classmates who seem to have had a higher tolerance for homework pain than I did."

Limited Learning

Emphasis on personal development achieved largely through participation in college social life, combined with minimal definitions of academic engagement, raises questions about whether and to what extent these students were developing general collegiate skills, such as critical thinking, complex reasoning, and writing, during college. While general collegiate skills do not encompass all aspects of academic learning in college, they represent an important set of skills broadly endorsed both by higher education institutions and by employers.[40] Using an objective measure, the Collegiate Learning Assessment (CLA), we can identify the extent to which students improve their general collegiate skills during college.

Over the full four years of college, students gained an average of 0.47 standard deviations on the CLA.[41] Thus, after four years of college, an average-scoring student in the fall of his or her freshman year would score at a level only eighteen percentile points higher in the spring of his or her senior year. Stated differently, freshmen who entered higher education at the 50th percentile would reach a level equivalent to the 68th percentile of the incoming freshman class by the end of their senior year. Since standard deviations are not the most intuitive way of understanding learning gains, it is useful to consider that if the CLA were rescaled to a one-hundred-point scale, approximately one-third of students would not improve more than one point over four years of college.[42]

In addition to low average gains over time, it is valuable to note that improvement on the CLA was not significantly larger in the last two years of college than in the first two. *Academically Adrift*, which focused on the first two years of college, reported an average gain of 0.18 standard deviations on the CLA. One of the critiques of *Academically Adrift* rested on the expectation that students would improve their critical thinking, complex reasoning, and writing skills more during the last two years of college. General collegiate skills, such as critical thinking, are hard to practice in the large lecture classes that many underclassmen spend their first years attending. As students progress through college and advance to higher-level seminars, one might expect them to show marked gains in these complex skills. However, this expectation did not materialize. *Academically Adrift* covered three full semesters, from the fall of the freshman year to the spring of the sophomore year, implying an average gain of 0.060 standard deviations per semester. Considering all four years of college, there are seven full semesters between the fall of the freshman year and the spring of the senior year (i.e., between our observation points), implying an average gain of 0.067 standard deviations per semester. If one takes selective attrition into account, student gains were actually larger earlier in their college careers.[43]

Despite limited gains on an objective measure of critical thinking, complex reasoning, and writing, students overall believed that they had substantially improved their skills in these areas. In the senior-year survey (spring 2009), we asked students how much they believed they had developed different skills during college—including critical thinking, writing, using evidence to support arguments, and understanding charts and graphs. On a scale ranging from 1 ("not at all") to 7 ("a great deal"), the mean for each of the measures during the senior year was above 5, ranging from a high of 5.7 for critical thinking to a low of 5.1 for understanding charts and graphs. Few seniors thought that they had not learned much; only 4 to 7 percent of students rated different measures in the 1 to 3 range. Figure 2.2 shows

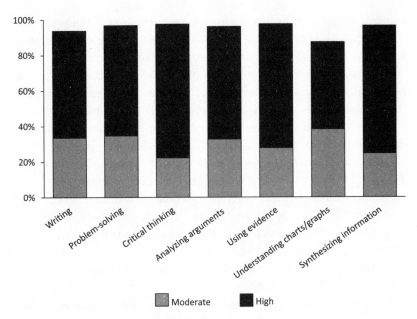

Figure 2.2 Percentages of college seniors who reported moderate and high levels of development of different skills during college.

the percentages of students who reported moderate (categories 4 and 5) and high (categories 6 and 7) levels of skill development. Students who rated their skill development as low (categories 1 to 3) are omitted from the figure. The only exception was the measure of understanding charts and graphs, for which 16 percent of students reported values in the 1 to 3 range. Across different skills, on average, almost one-third of students reported moderate levels of development during college. Almost two-thirds of seniors, however, reported that they had learned a great deal. Critical thinking led the way, with more than three-quarters of students reporting high levels of skill development in that domain. Students thus embraced the message, prominent in higher education rhetoric and college mission statements, that critical thinking was a key skill developed during college.

These findings may not be surprising, given that people tend to overestimate their own competence. Since the publication of research showing that most people believe they are better-than-average drivers, psychologists have documented individuals' tendency toward an overly positive appraisal of their own abilities across many domains.[44] In addition, social contexts provide cues that support overly optimistic conclusions. When academic engagement is defined in minimal terms and students are able to leave college with high GPAs despite limited academic engagement, they can only surmise that they have done well and learned much. These patterns raise caution about overreliance on students' self-reports of academic skills and personal development that have been reported in prior surveys. Gains in personal development are likely equally biased.

While an inflated sense of personal competencies may not be surprising, we also find that students' assessments of their learning gains increased with their distance from higher education. In 2011, which for the majority of our sample was two years after college graduation, ratings of how much graduates believed they had developed specific skills during college were even higher than in 2009. Depending on the measure, between 40 and 50 percent of survey respondents rated their learning during college higher in 2011 than they did in 2009 (their senior year). Moreover, this increasingly positive appraisal of college learning was observed for all groups, irrespective of college selectivity or subsequent labor market outcomes. The labor market thus did little to raise the students' doubts about their own academic engagement and learning during college. Instead, it helped to reinforce students' perceptions that they had learned a great deal in college despite low levels of academic engagement. This stands in contrast to what might be expected given employers' expressed dissatisfaction with graduates' low levels of general collegiate skills.[45] Employers may not have been happy, but they were not effectively conveying that message to these recent college graduates.

Variation in Student Learning

Although the average CLA gains over four years of college were limited, our data reveal substantial variation in learning both within and across institutions. With respect to cross-institutional variation, we highlight in particular the association between institutional selectivity and CLA gains. Before presenting results from our statistical analyses, figure 2.3 shows variation within and across institutions descriptively. For illustrative purposes, institutions are divided into three categories: less selective, selective, and more selective.[46] For each selectivity category, the black box represents the middle 50 percent of the distribution of CLA scores (i.e., between the 25th and 75th percentile). The lines above and below the boxes extend up to the 90th percentile and down to the 10th. The middle of the distribution (i.e., the middle of each black box, which represents the 50th percentile) shows that students attending less selective institutions started college with lower

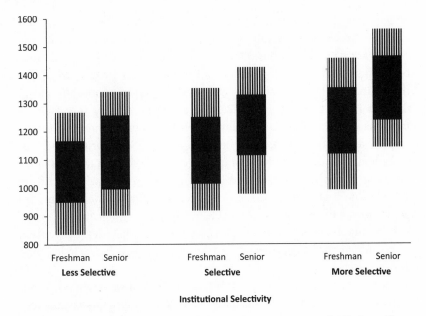

Figure 2.3 Distribution of freshman and senior CLA scores across institutions of varying levels of institutional selectivity. Black bars represent the 25th to 75th percentiles; vertical lines at the bottom of each bar represent the 10th to 25th percentiles, and at the top the 75th to 90th percentiles.

CLA scores than those at more selective institutions, and gained less between their freshman and senior years. However, there is substantial variation in CLA scores within each selectivity category, and there is a reasonable amount of overlap between institutions at different selectivity levels. Students who made substantial gains on the CLA between their freshman and senior years can be found across different institutional types, as can students with small or nonexistent gains. This finding implies the need to focus improvement efforts within institutions. While it can be useful to look at peer institutions, learn about their practices, and aim to emulate their organizational cultures, institutions can also learn a great deal from looking within themselves—identifying programs with students who learn more and those who learn less, exploring ways in which they may facilitate positive outcomes, and altering their practices to ensure that more students reach their full potential.

These descriptive patterns point to the importance of examining variation both within and across institutions. We begin by examining variation across institutions, focusing specifically on institutional selectivity. To examine this relationship, we compare senior-year CLA scores for students attending institutions of varying selectivity, controlling for their CLA performance at college entry (fall semester of their freshman year). In essence, we are asking: What is the difference in senior-year CLA performance between students attending schools of varying selectivity *if* we adjust for their initial level of general collegiate skills? We follow a convention from the sociological literature on K–12 achievement in referring to these estimates as growth. Researchers studying school sector differences, for example, have noted that "sector differences in senior test performance net of sophomore patterns reflect the impact of sector on *cognitive growth between the two administrations*, and in that sense, reveal how much of the 'added value' is attributable to school sector" (emphasis added).[47] This approach presents an approximation of learning growth when data are examined at only two points in time.[48] Thus, we adopt the rhetorical convention of simplifying the language to refer to these estimates as *growth* in learning during college.

Moreover, since students attending institutions of varying levels of selectivity differ, we adjust our estimates for a range of students' sociodemographic characteristics (including race, gender, and parental education) as well as their academic preparation (SAT scores and high school GPA; for a more complete discussion of the models and variables, see appendix A). We thus are examining the difference in senior year CLA performance between students attending schools of varying selectivity who entered college with similar levels of general collegiate skills, academic preparation, and background characteristics.

For a more intuitive representation of these model-based results, figure 2.4 reports predicted senior year CLA scores for students attending high- and low-selectivity institutions, where high and low selectivity refer to one standard deviation above and below the mean (for complete models, see table A2.2 in appendix A). The results indicate that students attending high-selectivity institutions improve on the CLA substantially more than those attending low-selectivity institutions, even when models are adjusted for students' background and academic characteristics. This association between institutional selectivity and CLA performance is consistent with findings for persistence and graduation in other research. A range of factors, from greater expenditures to unique peer environments at high-selectivity schools, may help to account for these patterns.

In the interviews, students attending more selective institutions remarked on the importance of academics at those institutions. Betty, a biological and life sciences major who attended a more selective institution, described her college experience as follows: "I think that academics in we formally examine the amount of variation in CLA gains between the freshman and senior years, only approximately one-quarter of that variation is across institutions, while the majority of the variation is within institutions. This pattern is consistent with research on a range of different educational outcomes.[49] Therefore, what students bring to educational institutions as well as what they do within them is crucial. We observed the types of comments noted above only at more selective institutions, but we also observed students at these same institutions who were less academically engaged and did little beyond the basics. Indeed, more or less academically engaged students, and those with high and low gains on the CLA, can be found across both more and less selective institutions.

These patterns indicate that the issues we have identified, namely weak academic engagement and limited learning, are widespread. They are not concentrated at a few institutions, or even at a specific type of institution. While students in more selective institutions gain more on the CLA, their gains are still modest, and while they spend more time studying alone, their average is still only slightly over ten hours per week. Data from the National Survey of Student Engagement similarly reveal that although students in the top 10 percent of institutions do indeed write more (and are more academically engaged across a range of measures), almost 40 percent of seniors at these institutions have not written a paper of twenty pages or more during their senior year, and more than a third have written fewer than five papers of modest length (five to nineteen pages). Concerns about academic engagement and learning, while varying across colleges and universities, also span institutions and represent challenges facing higher education as a whole.

Considering variation within institutions, we found that both academic preparation, measured by SAT scores, and sociodemographic characteristics (especially race/ethnicity) are associated with CLA gains (see the baseline model in table A2.2 in appendix A). Students who enter college with higher SAT scores gain more on the CLA. Conversely, African-American students gain less on the CLA over four years of college than do their white counterparts. These differences are somewhat reduced after adjusting for institutional selectivity, but are still large (see model 1 in table A2.2 in appendix A). Therefore, part of the explanation for the association of SAT scores and race/ethnicity with CLA gains is that less academically prepared students as well as African-American students were more likely to attend less selective institutions. However, even when students attended similarly selective schools, the differences in CLA performance associated with academic preparation and race/ethnicity remained.[50]

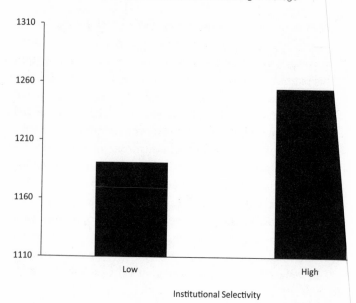

Figure 2.4 Predicted senior CLA scores, by institutional selectivity; based
model 1 in table A2.2, with all other variables held at their mean. Low and
institutional selectivity are defined as one standard deviation below and a
the mean, respectively.

general were pretty highly regarded at [the institution]. I was, at on
talking to people and people come here not because we have great a
or something. Most of the student body was pretty academically
and I certainly fell in that category and I've always been pretty ac
cally driven." Similarly, Joseph, a history major who graduated fro
other more selective institution, offered the following comments r
ing social engagement on his campus:

A social life [at that] time would be, "Hey, let's go to the library, and we
study for three hours together." Library dates were very common. As I g
out there more, I think I ended up realizing the value of kind of experie
learning a lot, going out and meeting new people and seeing the real val
in that. But again, I guess it's fairly jaded when I think back on it, becaus
much of the context for our socializing was around our school work, whi
is incredibly nerdy [laughter], but [it was great].

While schools may facilitate learning, variation in CLA performan
within institutions is much greater than variation across institutions.

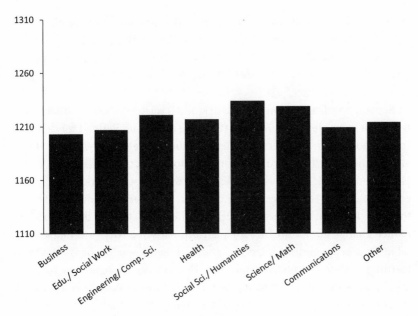

Figure 2.5 Predicted senior CLA scores, by field of study, with all other variables held at their mean, based on model 2 in table A2.2.

In addition to students' sociodemographic and academic background characteristics, we considered whether college major was related to CLA performance. Figure 2.5 reports the predicted senior CLA scores for different fields of study, adjusted for students' background characteristics and academic preparation (for complete results, see model 2 in table A2.2 in appendix A). The results indicate that students who majored in traditional liberal arts fields—social sciences, humanities, natural sciences, and math— demonstrated greater improvement on the CLA than did students who majored in business. The relationship is of similar magnitude for both social sciences/humanities and natural sciences/math, although the coefficient for natural sciences/math does not reach the conventional level of statistical significance.

Examining the relationship between college major and CLA performance is complicated by several factors. First, students change majors during their time in college. If we compare students' intended majors in their freshman year to their majors at the end of college, only approximately half of the students stay in the same major.[51] Moreover, changes across majors are not random. Students are more likely to leave certain fields, and certain types of students are more likely to change majors. Therefore, both the percentage of students leaving and the SAT scores of those who leave vary across fields. It is also valuable to note that not only the likelihood that students will change their majors but also the majors they finally choose are strongly related to their SAT scores, and that this association explains a substantial portion of the bivariate relationship between college major and CLA performance.

Second, the distribution of fields of study is related to institutional selectivity. For example, if we consider the three categories defined for descriptive purposes as more selective, selective, and less selective, traditional liberal arts fields are highly concentrated in more selective institutions, while professional fields (such as business, education, social work, health, and communications) are more prevalent in less selective institutions.[52] Therefore, the relationships between different fields of study and CLA performance change after adjusting for institutional selectivity (see model 3 in table A2.2 in appendix A). Understanding how college major is related to learning is thus complicated not only by students changing majors, but also by the distribution of majors across institutions. A detailed examination of these complexities is beyond the scope of our analysis, but the patterns reported here highlight the importance of careful attention to these issues in future research.

Reflecting on College and Moving on to Graduate School

Developing social sensibilities and, above all, being likeable and getting along with others emerged as an important outcome of college education. Students believed that they had grown in these areas in important ways. They also believed that they had substantially improved their general collegiate skills, such as critical thinking and writing. It is thus not surprising that students looked back on their college experiences quite fondly. In a recent survey conducted by the Higher Education Research Institute at UCLA, more than 90 percent of seniors reported being satisfied with their college experience.[53] When asked whether they wished they had done anything differently in college, 20 percent of students in our interview sample said that they would have done nothing differently. Most of the others focused on a specific class or a particular instructor. Some said they wished they had studied abroad, and others, as noted above, said they wished they had balanced their academic commitments with a robust social life. Among the eighty students interviewed, only three provided any indication of serious displeasure with college; the focus of their reservations rested with the cost. While she had "loved every minute of college," Carrie wondered whether those great academic and social experiences were "worth the huge cost." And although Tim felt that perhaps he had learned something during college, he also felt as though "there's nothing that they really gave me that's worth $25,000 of debt."

Given that the graduates were saddled with heavy debt and less-than-optimal labor market prospects (which we describe in the next chapter), it is surprising that more of them did not raise this issue. This lack of expressed dissatisfaction with college may reflect the psychological effect of effort justification as well as the graduates' personal attachment to college. Since the early research by Elliot Aronson and Judson Mills, psychologists have documented the pattern of effort justification across different contexts, indicating that people attribute greater value to outcomes in which they have invested effort.[54] College graduates have invested four years (and often more) of their time, energy, and effort, not to mention financial resources, into their college degrees. Thus it is not surprising that they would regard college as being valuable.

In addition, financial realities have to coexist with the strong sentiments students develop about their institutions during their college years. If college were simply an academic project, difficult financial conditions might have a greater effect on graduates and cause them to reflect more about its value. However, the intensity of college social life, with its new experiences and friendships, leads students to develop a strong sentimental attachment to their college years, notwithstanding their price.

Despite their sentimental attachments, and despite their belief that college had facilitated the development of their personal and academic skills, many students found their degrees to be inadequate for their labor market aspirations, and so they turned to graduate school for further education. Figure 2.6, drawing on longitudinal data from the Baccalaureate and Beyond (B&B) Longitudinal Study, reports the percentages of college graduates nationally who entered graduate or professional school within approximately one year of their acquisition of BA degrees.[55] The percentage of graduates who proceeded to graduate school within this time frame has increased notably over the last fifteen years, from 17 percent in the 1992–93 cohort to 27 percent in the 2007–8 cohort. In our sample, 32 percent of respondents were enrolled in graduate school in 2010, which for most was within approximately one year of their college graduation. The proportion of graduates in our study who pursued post-baccalaureate education increased over time. By 2011, almost 40 percent were enrolled in graduate programs; 30 percent were enrolled in full-time master's, professional, or doctoral programs, and another 10 percent were enrolled in part-time or other types of programs.

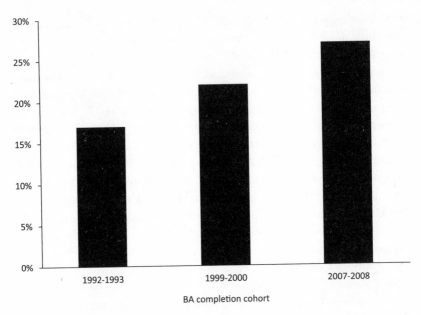

Figure 2.6 Percentages of graduate/professional school enrollment within approximately one year of BA completion (source: Baccalaureate and Beyond Longitudinal Study)

We explored the extent to which graduates' decisions about whether to pursue education after college were related to their undergraduate experiences, and, more specifically, to their senior year CLA performance and college major.[56] To examine these relationships, we estimated statistical models that adjusted for students' sociodemographic characteristics, thus asking whether CLA performance and college major were related to enrollment in graduate programs among students who shared similar sociodemographic characteristics (for complete models, see table A2.3 in appendix A). For this analysis, we divided graduate programs into two categories: (1) full-time master's, professional, and doctoral programs; and (2) part-time and other programs. To illustrate the patterns, figure 2.7 shows the probability of attending different types of graduate programs for students with high and low CLA scores, compared to not attending graduate school.[57] These findings indicate that graduates with high CLA scores were more likely to enroll full-time in master's, professional, or doctoral programs. At the same time, CLA performance was not related to whether students entered part-time and other programs.

One of the challenges encountered in estimating the relationship between CLA performance (or other college experiences) and graduate school attendance is the variation across graduate programs.[58] Due to the small sample size, we had to combine a variety of graduate programs into only two categories and could not conduct more nuanced analyses of different types of programs. Interview data, however, point to large variations in graduate programs along many dimensions, including respondents' perceptions of academic rigor. Many graduates responded ambiguously, noting that graduate education was different from undergraduate experience, but not taking a stand on whether it was harder or easier. Some claimed that graduate school was definitely easier, that the "the caliber of our classes [in undergraduate college] and everything was more rigorous," and that the grading was "a little easier" in graduate school. Other students noted that graduate school was definitely harder and more demanding, required more critical thinking, and, for those pursuing law degrees, required "a new way of thinking." Future research, focusing more closely on the character of specific graduate programs, is needed to provide further insights into the relationship between college performance and graduate school enrollment.

In addition to CLA performance, the rate at which students attend graduate school is related to their college majors. Figure 2.8 reports the

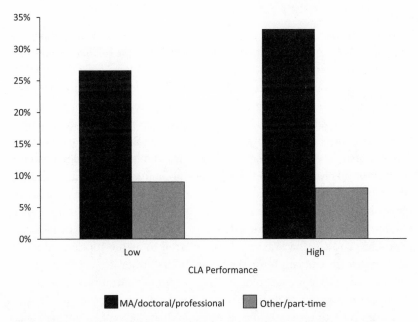

Figure 2.7 Probability of graduate school attendance, by senior CLA performance; predicted with all other variables held at their mean, based on model 1 in table A2.3. Low and high CLA performance are defined as one standard deviation below and above the mean, respectively.

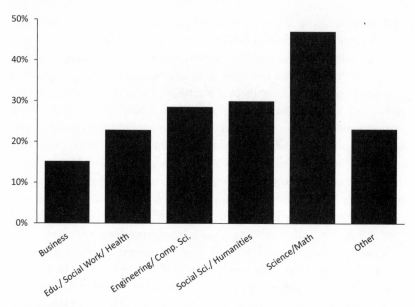

Figure 2.8 Probability of graduate school attendance, by field of study; predicted with all other variables held at their mean, based on model 3 in table A2.3.

predicted probability of enrolling in full-time master's, professional, or doctoral programs for students majoring in different fields of study (for complete models, see table A2.3 in appendix A).[59] Even after analyses adjust for background characteristics and CLA performance at the end of college, students who had graduated with degrees in traditional arts and science fields, and especially those who had majored in natural sciences and math, were substantially more likely to enroll in full-time master's, professional, or doctoral programs. Students who had majored in business were least likely to enroll in these types of graduate programs, although their probability of graduate school attendance was statistically indistinguishable from that of students in other professional fields, including education, social work, and health. These patterns illustrate what economists Eric Eide and Geetha Waehrer have referred to as the "option value" of undergraduate education, or the value of the option to attend graduate school and receive greater returns from increased educational attainment than an undergraduate degree. Many undergraduates choose their majors with the intention of later enrolling in graduate or professional schools. The "option value" of attending graduate programs is greater in liberal arts and science fields, such that students choose to major in those fields in part due to their expectations of attending graduate school.[60] This differential distribution of graduate school attendance illustrates the challenges of evaluating wages across different fields of study in the years immediately following bachelor's degree completion.

Preparing for Life after College

Over the course of the twentieth century, colleges increased their focus on the personal development of students. During the 1920s higher education began to endorse a focus on personal adjustment, driven by the emergence of new psychological sciences. Colleges became increasingly concerned with students' well-being, and tried to "make the total environment more flexible as well as fun."[61] At the same time, research reporting that social engagement was related to outcomes such as persistence further fueled higher education's attention to extracurricular activities, thus providing ample opportunities for social engagement on college campuses.[62]

Our graduates have deeply internalized the personal development message about the purpose of higher education. As college students, they placed emphasis on the social, which was the realm that provided opportunities for them to learn about themselves and about how to get along with others. This emphasis on personal development and social engagement at least partly reflects the role of schools in socializing students for membership in society. As agents of socialization, schools are expected to structure their academic and social activities in ways that facilitate a specific type of socialization that is valued at a particular historic moment. Graduates repeatedly emphasized how college was meant to develop a particular kind of sensibility—one that was attuned to others, able to read social cues, and able to act appropriately across a range of social situations. This social sensibility is what sociologist David Riesman called the "other-directed" character type in his seminal 1950 book *The Lonely Crowd*.[63]

Even if higher education today is appropriately socializing students for engagement in the modern world and helping them to develop a specific type of sociable personality, this leaves open the question about academic skills. Focusing on the social sphere can push academic learning to the fringes, helping to make the overall social enterprise legitimate while lacking the power to define the collegiate experience. Indeed, students feel they have learned most in their social lives during college. A senior cited in a study by George Kuh noted, "It is funny that we are talking about things outside the classroom because I feel like that is the place that I have done most of my growing."[64] Given this context, it is perhaps unsurprising that we find evidence of limited development of general collegiate skills, such as critical thinking, complex reasoning, and writing, over four years of college.

If not in school—and in college, in particular—where are students going to learn how to analyze evidence, solve challenging problems, and convey complex ideas? Echoing a long-standing human capital argument that employers have little incentive to provide general skills that can be transferred to other companies,[65] employers in a recent survey claimed that "many of the skills and abilities they seek can—and should—be taught on campus."[66] The kinds of skills needed are generic higher-order skills, with more than 90 percent of employers rating written communication, critical thinking, and problem solving as "very important" for the job success of new labor market entrants.[67] And indeed, this is one area where employers and faculty agree, with a virtually unanimous consensus among faculty that teaching critical thinking is a central aim of undergraduate education.[68] Social sensibility may be valuable, but focusing on general collegiate skills is thought by many to be increasingly necessary in this competitive market of labor and ideas.

3

Making It in the Labor Market

Over the past few years, the question of college value has gar-
nered increasing attention. In the public discourse, these discussions of value are largely focused on the economic—as opposed to
social, cultural, or civic—returns to schooling. For example, mainstream media headlines have encouraged readers to ponder "The
Dwindling Power of a College Degree," "Saying No to College,"
and "Is College a Lousy Investment?"[1] This growing concern is
not surprising, given both the increasing costs of college and the
difficulties that recent graduates have encountered in paying off
their college loans and finding economic positions that meet their
individual expectations. In chapter 4, we will examine some of
the social, cultural, and civic outcomes associated with college
graduates' education. Here, however, we focus more narrowly on
early labor market returns and the extent to which different aspects of undergraduate education are related to more or less desirable outcomes.

While it is not surprising that public discourse is increasingly focused on college value, often the wrong questions are being asked. Specifically, journalists often ask, "Given increasing
college costs, does it still pay to go to college?" instead of inquiring
about how returns vary with respect to different components of

Amanda Cook and Jeannie Kim coauthored this chapter.

undergraduate education, how college graduates find jobs, and what kind of jobs they find. Indeed, there is no real debate among the vast majority of social scientists on whether it "pays" to go to college. By and large, social scientists agree that, for a typical college graduate, the increased lifetime wages associated with college attendance not only cover the price of college but also cover the opportunity costs inherent in forgoing income to pursue a degree. College is a good investment for most students—particularly for those from disadvantaged backgrounds.[2]

Although social scientists and others have clearly established the general economic value of going to college, the reasons why college matters are complex. The dominant view in the social sciences, shared by policy makers who are focused on improving schooling to enhance individual and societal productivity, assumes that the value of school is primarily realized through the development of cognitive capacities—that is, "human capital." Although there is some debate about the relative value of generic and specific competencies, skill development is thought to make students more productive, and thus more valuable, employees and citizens.[3] A second approach, "credentialism," is skeptical that individual productivity is the central driver of returns to education. Scholars in this tradition argue that the value of college is derived largely from its ability to sort, select, and certify preexisting differences in individual ability and motivation, not from its development of new skills or knowledge. College in this view is largely understood as a *signal*. The degree—a symbolic sheepskin—matters more than the academic substance it is meant to represent. A third line of thought holds that the value of college is found in the social or institutional relationships developed by being on campus.[4] While formal instruction is seen to have little value, the broadening of one's social network and the development of cultural dispositions that facilitate social interaction and collaboration are thought to be at the core of the enterprise. In addition to individual social networks, scholars in this tradition examine organizational relationships—specifically, school-employer ties. This network-based view of college is widely held by many students and their families.[5]

What is it, then, about college that matters in terms of labor market outcomes? Assuming that one goes to college and earns a degree,[6] how significant are general collegiate skills such as critical thinking, complex reasoning, and written communication for early labor market outcomes? Our study extends prior research that has focused attention on college major and institutional selectivity by adding consideration of the extent to which general collegiate skills, as measured by the CLA, track with college graduates' labor market outcomes. We also explore how graduates found their employment, and the characteristics of those jobs in terms of skill requirements and job satisfaction. In addition, graduates' own accounts of and reflections about their experiences provide a deeper understanding of the processes underlying the patterns we observe in the quantitative data. Consideration of those accounts also provides insight into the meaning of these experiences for those who attempted to make the transition from school to work in historically difficult circumstances.

Labor Market Outcomes Two Years after Graduation

Our study focuses primarily on the college class of 2009. These students graduated during a time of particularly difficult economic conditions. The extent, historically, of how difficult these circumstances actually were is identified in figure 3.1, which reports unemployment rates from the Bureau of Labor Statistics's Current Population Survey of individuals aged twenty-two to twenty-seven who were not full-time students. Unemployment is defined here and throughout this chapter as the state of not having a job while actively looking for work. The trend lines illustrate two important points. First, our study focuses on school-to-work transitions for

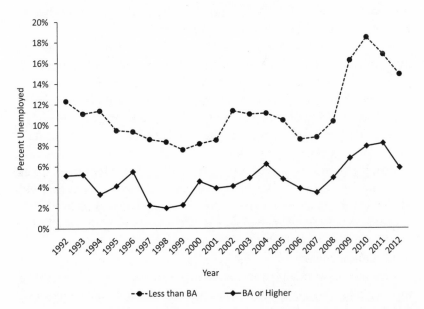

Figure 3.1 Percentages of adults aged 22 to 27 who were unemployed, by year and college degree (source: Bureau of Labor Statistics, Current Population Survey)

a cohort of graduates who experienced the most difficult circumstances in recent years: in 2011, the year we observed our cohort's labor market outcomes, 8.2 percent of young college graduates and 16.8 percent of young adults without college degrees were unemployed nationally.

Second, the figure shows that even in difficult times, college graduates in their early twenties maintain distinct advantages in the labor market, regardless of how difficult economic conditions may be. If one imagines a labor queue where individuals are lined up to compete for jobs, college graduates are more likely closer to the head of the line than non–college graduates. This again is likely due to multiple reasons, which include the following: college graduates are a more select group in terms of ability and motivation, they may have access to enhanced individual and institutional resources, and they may be more productive and potentially more valuable employees as a result of their additional learning. Over the twenty-year period from 1992 to 2012, young adults who did not attend college were approximately 2.5 times more likely to be unemployed than those who had finished college.[7] Contrary to some of the shrill public commentary of late, no matter how tough college graduates have had it, others have had it considerably worse. Tough times do not mean that it does not pay to go to college.

Figure 3.2 provides a snapshot of how college graduates in our study were doing economically in the spring of 2011, two years after the vast majority of them had graduated. Excluded from this analysis were the college graduates who were back in school as full-time students at the time of the survey. The figure highlights the extent to which a significant percentage of college graduates who attempted to make school-to-work transitions were struggling two years after graduation. Seven percent of these graduates were formally unemployed (i.e., they did not have jobs and reported that they were actively seeking employment). For many of these unemployed graduates, unemployment was not just a fleeting condition. Rather, for those unemployed at the time of the spring 2011 survey, the average number of months unemployed during the prior year was five, with 40 percent unemployed for six months or more. Almost a quarter of the respondents who were unemployed in 2011 were also unemployed when surveyed in the spring of 2010.

In addition to unemployment, other graduates were underemployed—4 percent were working fewer than twenty hours per week. While the remaining 89 percent of graduates had found either full-time employment (working thirty-five or more hours per week) or close to full-time em-

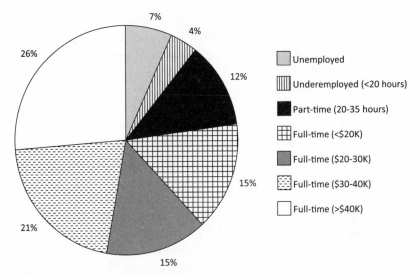

Figure 3.2 Employment outcomes and incomes of college graduates two years after on-time graduation

ployment (working twenty hours per week or more, but not full-time), large numbers of these individuals were in jobs with relatively low pay. Fifteen percent of college graduates were in full-time positions that paid less than $20,000 per year, and 15 percent were in positions that paid between $20,000 and $30,000 per year. Considered as a whole, 53 percent of the college graduates who were not re-enrolled full-time in school were unemployed, employed part-time, or employed in full-time jobs that paid less than $30,000 annually.[8]

Another way to get a sense of the difficulties many college graduates were facing is to shift the analysis from income to other occupational characteristics. Sociologists have long preferred analyzing individual occupational attainment as opposed to income for several reasons. First, annual income often varies in response to local labor market conditions or idiosyncratic fluctuations in individual or firm-specific situations, whereas reports of occupations and job titles tend to provide more stable outcomes. Second, rewards to occupations are related not just to income, but also to occupational status and prestige. In social settings, individuals are typically asked about what they do, not how much money they earn. Occupational status is a significant resource that individuals draw on in social interactions; their jobs can affect how they fare at a singles bar, a holiday dinner with extended family, or when meeting their future in-laws. Third, colleges and universities often explicitly promote the idea that graduates should find meaningful and satisfying employment, not just optimize their income. In considering the employment outcomes of college graduates, it would be a grave mistake to devalue those who chose to pursue jobs that drew on their education and were meaningful or were apprenticeships that were future-oriented, but were not associated with high income. Finally, consideration of occupations attained in "first jobs" after completing schooling have long been demonstrated by social scientists to be associated with labor market outcomes decades later.[9]

In order to distinguish between the educational skill requirements of occupations, we apply a coding scheme developed by sociologists Robert Hauser and John Robert Warren. Hauser and Warren's seminal work analyzed the educational attainments of individuals in every occupational title used by the US Census. We identify unskilled occupations by choosing a cutoff that demarcates a group of graduates whom, most would agree, are clearly not in jobs appropriate to their educational attainment. Specifically, we classify as unskilled occupations all jobs where the majority of occupants have completed *less than even one year of college*.[10] In the Hauser and Warren classification scheme, bank tellers are right at this cutoff, and receptionists fall just below. As an example, unskilled occupations include waitress, school bus driver, shipping dock loader, and nanny. These jobs are categorically distinct from the occupations of other graduates, such as teacher, business analyst, financial advisor, registered nurse, and product engineer.

Applying this conservative cutoff, we are able to identify the percentages of college graduates in our sample who had jobs that were typically filled by individuals whose education ended in high school. Figure 3.3 shows that 13 percent of graduates were employed in occupations requiring only minimal education: 1 percent in jobs where they were working fewer than twenty hours per week and 12 percent in jobs that were either full-time or part-time (twenty or more hours per week). The proportion of college graduates in the labor market in unskilled occupations is over and above the 7 percent who were unemployed and the 3 percent who were working twenty or fewer hours per week in occupations that required more skills than this cutoff.[11]

Although struggling college graduates who were experiencing negative labor market outcomes remained largely optimistic, they were typically keenly aware of their less than ideal occupational circumstances. For example, Lucy, a biology major from a less selective college,[12] who was

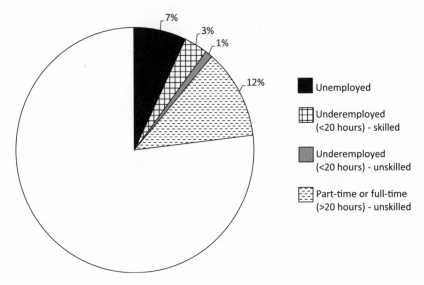

Figure 3.3 Occupational outcomes of college graduates two years after on-time graduation

working as a temporary receptionist, described her employment in the following way: "Well, I work as a temporary receptionist so, like, [laughter] technically, yes, I am employed, but I don't know. I don't consider it like a 'real job,' but it pays the bills, and therefore it counts as being employed."[13] Linda, a psychology major from a selective college, who was unemployed at the time of the interview, had this to say about her prior employment: "Jobs, yes. Like basic jobs that don't really pay much. Careers, no. Nothing I [could stay in] long-term."

These less than optimal labor market outcomes span different fields of study. There are, of course, liberal arts graduates with poor outcomes, such as Alice, a foreign language and literature graduate from a selective college who was working as a cashier: "I work at a cooperative food grocery store. So it's pretty much your basic grocery store cashier job. Sometimes I also work in the backroom, so just [stacking]. So it's nothing too exciting, but just something for now." But the same fate is encountered by graduates in other fields, including Leann, a business major from an equally selective college, who was also working as a cashier in a grocery store: "I'm happy to say that all of us just found employment now even though we graduated two years ago. . . . I'm depressed [laughter]. I'm a cashier now, but I did let them know that I am interested in becoming a manager since I got my degree. I'm working really hard to try to advance."

Factors Associated with Negative Early-Career Outcomes

In an effort to disentangle the extent to which negative employment outcomes are associated independently with graduates' performance on the
CLA, their college majors, and the selectivity of their educational institutions, we conducted analyses that simultaneously control for all three of
these factors in addition to respondents' sociodemographic characteristics
(including gender, race/ethnicity, and parental education).[14] These types of
analyses, which are descriptive in character, can isolate specific relationships—estimating particular associations between measures, independent
of other variables that are "controlled" for in the models. Because of our
limited sample size and the imprecision of our measurement, we are unable to attempt more complex econometric analyses that would strive to
produce enhanced causal inference from observational data. Nevertheless,
since the US federal government has not facilitated this line of research by
including individual-level measures of collegiate performance on objective
student assessments in large, nationally representative longitudinal datasets,[15] there are no other existing data that can link objective graduate skill
assessments (such as the CLA) with early labor market outcomes. Thus,
the findings in this chapter are of significant interest.

Our exploration of early-career outcomes begins with an examination
of whether a college graduate two years after on-time college graduation is
without employment and is actively looking for work (for complete models, see table A3.3 in appendix A). Figure 3.4 highlights the association of
unemployment two years after graduation with graduates' college majors
and CLA performance, controlling for differences in their individual sociodemographic characteristics. Both the choice of college major and the observed differences in general collegiate skills (as measured by the CLA)
track with the likelihood of experiencing unemployment two years after
undergraduate education. Graduates with business degrees were less likely
to be unemployed than graduates with degrees in many liberal arts fields.
Business majors, controlling for other factors, had a 2 percent unemployment rate—much lower than the rates for social sciences and humanities
(7 percent), social work (8 percent), communications, and other majors
(9 percent). These findings are generally consistent with Anthony Carnevale's recent research on post-graduation employment outcomes.[16]

College institutional selectivity is not significantly associated with early-
career unemployment in our analysis, nor is gender, race/ethnicity, or
parental education. We find this pattern of nonsignificant associations between employment outcomes and parental education as well as race/eth-

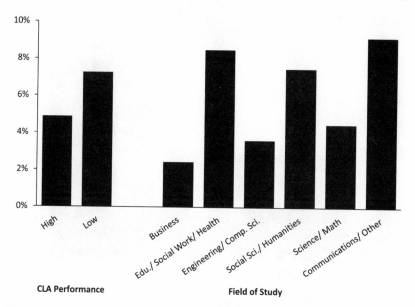

CLA Performance   **Field of Study**

Figure 3.4 Probability of unemployment two years after on-time graduation, by CLA performance and field of study; predicted with all other variables held at their mean, based on model 2 in table A3.3. High and low CLA performance are defined as one standard deviation above and below the mean, respectively.

nicity (after controlling for college major, institutional selectivity, and CLA scores) repeatedly in the analysis of labor market outcomes reported in this chapter. While one must be cautious not to overinterpret the absence of racial differences in early labor market outcomes of college graduates—given the small number of nonwhite graduates in our sample, as well as the early career stage of these individuals—the finding that social background is not associated with college graduates' labor market outcomes is largely consistent with sociologist Michael Hout's "expanded universalism" thesis. Specifically, Hout argued that the effects of a college degree are so great that if one restricts analysis solely to those with college degrees, social class background has little or no remaining association with labor market outcomes.[17] Although parents' level of education remains a strong determinant of who goes to and ultimately graduates from college, once these educational milestones have been attained, the education or occupational position of the parents of college graduates is not a strong predictor of how those graduates are sorted into occupations.

Interestingly, however, figure 3.4 shows that CLA performance is significantly associated with the likelihood of experiencing unemployment. Comparing college graduates who performed well on the CLA to those who

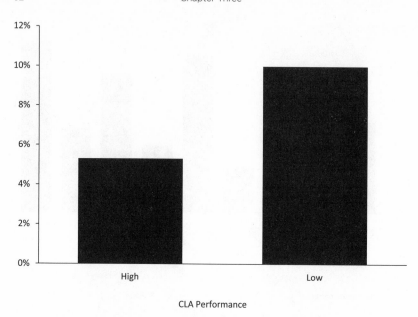

12%
10%
8%
6%
4%
2%
0%

High   Low

CLA Performance

Figure 3.5 Probability of having experienced job loss in the preceding year, by CLA performance; predicted with all other variables held at their mean, based on model 2 in table A3.4. High and low CLA performance are defined as one standard deviation above and below the mean, respectively.

performed less well (defined as one standard deviation above or below the mean of the senior-year CLA scores), the likelihood of experiencing unemployment increases from 5 to 7 percent. CLA performance might be related to unemployment for many reasons. For example, graduates with low CLA scores might have greater difficulties in successfully navigating structures associated with securing employment opportunities (e.g., search, application, and selection processes). Another potential mechanism, which we are able partially to examine with our data, is that employers determined that these graduates were unable to perform at adequate levels, and thus they lost their jobs.

In the spring of 2011 we asked graduates if they had lost a job in the past year. While one could be unemployed for various reasons, having "lost a job" implies that the individual has been fired, laid off, or denied a contract renewal.[18] This analysis is restricted to graduates who held a job at some point in the year prior to the survey, as other individuals were not at risk for job loss (for complete results, see table 3.4 in appendix A).[19] Figure 3.5 illustrates the relationship between job loss and CLA performance, revealing that graduates who performed well on the CLA had a 5 percent likelihood of having lost a job, compared to a 10 percent likelihood if they performed less well.[20] This finding suggests the possibility that employers made judgments about keeping these employees on the basis of factors that track closely with their performance on the CLA. Of course, other factors might also be at play (e.g., graduates with lower CLA scores might have been placed in less stable employment positions), and thus additional research is required to better identify the mechanisms associated with this important finding.

In addition to the negative outcomes of unemployment and job loss, we examined two characteristics of the jobs individuals attained if they were employed: income and the education level required. Both analyses adjust for institutional selectivity, graduates' CLA performance, and socio-demographic characteristics. Examining factors associated with college graduates' income two years after their on-time graduation, little can be said other than what is already widely known: fields of study vary in the extent to which they are associated with higher initial earnings (for complete models, see table A3.5 in appendix A).[21] While college graduates in our study with full-time employment made $34,200 per year on average, graduates who had majored in arts and science (controlling for other factors in our models) earned considerably less than those who had majored in business. For example, those in humanities and social science fields earned $6,400 less per year than those who had majored in business. Graduates who had majored in science and mathematics had earnings similar to those in humanities and social sciences. As noted in the previous chapter, however, arts and science majors were more likely to be enrolled in graduate school two years after graduating college, so these early-career outcomes are estimated for a narrower and more negatively selected group of graduates in those fields than for those with business majors. Only engineering and computer science majors out-earned business majors—on average, they earned $11,600 more per year. In 2011, male college graduates were paid $6,000 more per year than their female counterparts. However, 61 percent of this difference in wages was attributable to the graduates' choice of college major. After we controlled for college major in our analysis, the difference in earnings was no longer significant. Female graduates were thus disadvantaged in their early labor market outcomes primarily because they were disproportionately concentrated in fields of study with lower earnings.

It is worth emphasizing that senior CLA scores and the selectivity of the colleges attended were not significantly associated with the income of college graduates who were in full-time employment two years after

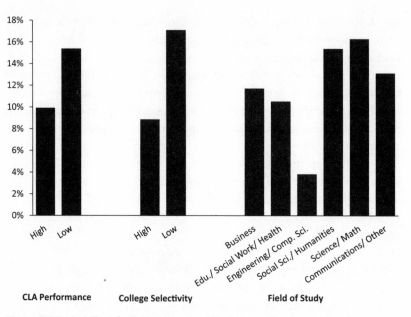

Figure 3.6 Probability of working in an unskilled occupation two years after on-time graduation, by CLA performance, college selectivity, and field of study; predicted with all other variables held at their mean, based on model 2 in table A3.6. The bars depicting high and low categories represent one standard deviation above and below the mean, respectively.

graduating. Parents and the general public might be surprised that graduates' earnings often do not closely track with the types of institutions they attended, but a significant body of social science research is consistent with this result. While college graduates have very different labor market experiences than do high school graduates, income differences across institutions were relatively small once individual characteristics were taken into account.[22] Although there is ongoing research and continued debate on this issue, as well as evidence that attendance at the most elite institutions is associated with attainment of the most privileged positions in society, in general it is not as important to labor market outcomes as is graduates' field of study. This is important, given recent policy discussions around building institutional accountability systems based on graduates' early-career earnings. We will return to this issue in chapter 5.

Analyses of whether or not graduates found themselves in unskilled occupations (i.e., positions where the majority of incumbents had not completed even a year of college) reveal different patterns (for complete models, see table A3.6 in appendix A). Figure 3.6 shows that business majors did not distinguish themselves from other fields of study when the analysis focused on this dimension of labor market outcomes. Only engineering and computer science majors had significantly improved chances of avoiding unskilled occupations. Indeed, only 4 percent of graduates from those fields of study, net of other factors, were in unskilled occupations. However, both CLA performance and institutional selectivity were related to this labor market outcome. As shown in figure 3.6, graduates who had attended a highly selective college had a 9 percent likelihood of working in unskilled occupations two years after their on-time graduation, compared to a 17 percent likelihood if they had attended a low-selectivity college. Graduates who had performed well on the CLA had a 10 percent likelihood of being in unskilled occupations, compared to a 15 percent likelihood if they had performed less well on the assessment as seniors.[23]

While preceding analyses considered unemployment separately from employment in unskilled occupations, figure 3.7 combines the two outcomes and compares them to those of graduates who were working in occupations that required at least minimal skills (i.e., occupations where at

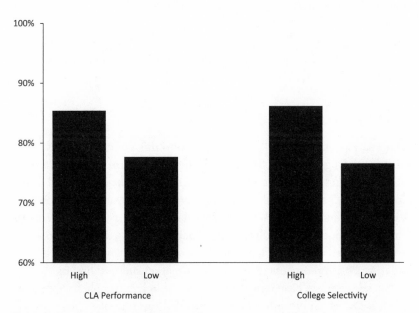

Figure 3.7 Probability of a positive employment outcome (defined as avoidance of unemployment and unskilled employment) two years after on-time graduation, by CLA performance and college selectivity; predicted with all other variables held at their mean, based on model 2 in table A3.7. High and low categories are defined as one standard deviation above and below the mean, respectively.

least half of those employed had completed at least one year of college; for complete models, see table A3.7 in appendix A).[24] In essence, these analyses examine whether graduates were able to secure good employment outcomes by avoiding both unemployment and employment in unskilled occupations. The results indicate that college majors were not related to whether graduates were employed in jobs where at least some college education was the norm. However, both college selectivity and CLA performance were associated with graduates having found jobs in which most workers had at least some college education. Graduates who had attended highly selective colleges had an 86 percent likelihood of working in jobs where at least some college education was the norm, compared to a 77 percent likelihood if they had attended colleges that were less selective. Graduates who performed well on the CLA had an 85 percent likelihood of reporting employment in jobs that were not unskilled, compared to a 78 percent likelihood if they had performed less well on the CLA.[25]

While there is some statistical fluctuation across models, the overall pattern of these results is generally consistent with the conclusion that graduates' CLA performance at the end of college is associated with the likelihood of their success in the labor market two years after their on-time graduation (with the exception of income, which also does not vary systematically in relationship to the selectivity of colleges). Depending on the particular outcome examined, field of study and college selectivity are also more often than not associated with early labor market success.

Finding a Job

Our analysis of labor market outcomes up to this point has largely relied on considering graduates at one point in time, approximately two years after their on-time college graduation. The results have provided a useful "snapshot" of how students were faring and the extent to which their experiences and competencies, measured in college, were associated with early-career success and failure. Additional insight into the extent to which college shaped these early labor market experiences can be gained by considering a critical process related to labor market success: finding a job.

Social scientists have long been interested in how people find jobs. Sociologist Mark Granovetter, who researched the role of social networks in job searches, found that 56 percent of his sample of mid-career professional men had found their most recent jobs through personal contacts (i.e., relatives, friends, or acquaintances). The rest found jobs through

formal means (i.e., using employment agencies or responding to advertisements) or direct application (i.e., visiting or writing to firms without
having heard of a *"specific* [job] opening").[26] Subsequent studies have revealed that, depending on the population, about 40 percent of jobs are
found through personal contacts.[27]

Recent college graduates differ from most other job seekers in that they
have access to college career resources.[28] To varying degrees, colleges prepare students for the labor market by helping them to develop career goals,
to polish their resumes and cover letters, and to practice their interviewing
skills. Colleges also attempt to match qualified students with employers.
To do this, colleges must cultivate "mutually beneficial" relationships with
potential employers—relationships in which "schools place students into
good jobs and guarantee corporations [and other employers] dependable
workers."[29] In theory, these relationships should promote social mobility
by providing qualified students from all backgrounds with equal access to
promising job opportunities.[30] With the exception of one or two small-
scale qualitative studies, however, there has been little empirical research
on this topic, so we know relatively little about the role colleges play in
their recent graduates' job searches.

Although the research on relationships between colleges and employers is sparse, the literature on linkages between high schools and employers can offer some important insights. Sociologist James Rosenbaum has
documented that, compared to schools in countries like Japan and Germany, high schools in the United States do little to link their graduates
with jobs. However, when US high school graduates do receive such institutional assistance, they find good jobs with potential for advancement.
That is, "School placement leads to vastly superior earnings trajectories
over the first decade [after graduation]."[31] Since we only track our sample
of recent graduates for two years after graduation, we cannot definitively
determine whether the graduates who found jobs through their colleges
were on career trajectories superior to those of their peers. Nevertheless,
it is relatively safe to assume that graduates who avoided unskilled occupations (i.e., graduates who found jobs in which the majority of workers had
at least one year of college) were on brighter career trajectories than those
who did not. Thus, if college-to-work linkages function like high school-to-
work linkages, we would expect recent graduates who found jobs through
their colleges more likely to avoid unskilled occupations than their peers.

In 2011 we asked the *Academically Adrift* cohort whether they had found
their most recent jobs through employment agencies or advertisements,

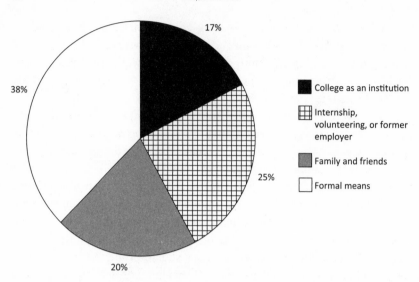

Figure 3.8 How graduates found full-time employment

their college career resources, internships or volunteer opportunities, former employers, college friends, or other personal ties.[32] As shown in figure 3.8, the graduates found jobs by using a wide range of strategies.[33]

Formal Means

A plurality of respondents, 38 percent, reported finding their most recent jobs through employment agencies or publicly available job advertisements. Following Granovetter, we call this strategy "formal means." For those pursuing formal means, according to our graduates, persistence was often helpful, as was leaving good impressions on potential employers. Michael, an engineering major from a selective institution, relied on online job postings to find employment as a product engineer. He recalled, "I searched all over. I made profiles on Monster.com, CareerBuilder, with [my college's] career center . . . and just kept looking and looking." Amanda, a business major from a selective institution, who was without a job but actively looking for work, maintained contact with an employment agency even after it initially rejected her application:

> I heard about [my job] through a temp agency. I had initially applied a
> couple of months before with that same agency for another job. I wasn't
> hired for that job, but then they called me a couple of months back. I sent a
> thank-you letter to the person that interviewed me. . . . I think it may have

helped. She called a couple of months later, and she's like, "Hey, if you're still looking, this company is hiring for a mortgage specialist." I'm like, "Well, sure." I was just ready to have anything at that point.

Some respondents found their jobs by combining formal means with personal ties.[34] Gillian, a health major from a selective college who was employed as a registered dietician, successfully coupled formal means with the use of her personal network: "I had seen the job on MD.com and I applied, but then I found out that a friend of my fiance at the time, his friend's father-in-law, worked for the same hospital, and he's pretty high up. So I got in contact with him and he kind of passed along my résumé to the director of our department. So I think that definitely had an impact on my getting the job." By contrast, those who did not use personal ties to raise the visibility of their applications were often overlooked by potential employers. Maya, an unemployed communications major from a less selective college, tried unsuccessfully to find a job through formal means:

> For the longest time I was just strictly looking on different companies' websites, looking for advertisements, looking on Craigslist—but the more and more I talk to people, I realize I'm not going to find a job that way, because a lot of companies usually post internally, or the way you get a job is through your connections. So that's what I've been trying to do: build my network to make connections so I can get a job.

Because our survey did not allow respondents to select more than one job search method, we are unable to say exactly how common this dual strategy was. Future research should explore the extent to which job applicants supplement formal applications with the use of personal ties.

On-Campus Resources

Seventeen percent of recent graduates reported finding their job through their colleges' formal and informal career resources.[35] Formal career resources include career counseling, résumé and interview technique workshops, job fairs, internship and volunteer opportunities, and exclusive job postings. Informal career resources include faculty and other on-campus mentors who alert students to job opportunities. Institutional reputation may be another informal career resource that colleges offer their graduates.

One of the primary means by which colleges helped their students find jobs was by organizing career fairs and other on-campus recruiting events.

These events gave the students and recent graduates the opportunity to learn about job openings and meet employers who were specifically interested in hiring recent graduates. Our interview data suggest that finding a job through career fairs and on-campus recruiting events can be a more direct process than finding one by other means. Tiffany, a computer science major from a less selective college, found a job as a computer network administrator with relative ease: "We had a career fair at school and I turned in my résumé to a couple of people. Then they got back to me and told me to apply for several different positions there. When I came down for the interview, they noticed on my résumé that I have experience in volunteering in information technology. They asked me if I would like to work there."

In addition to the concrete ways in which college graduates recounted obtaining assistance in the job search process from their institutions, a number of graduates also had a sense that institutional reputation worked in their favor. If we use institutional selectivity as a proxy for institutional reputation, there is moderate evidence that college selectivity is associated with better labor market outcomes. In other words, as demonstrated earlier in this chapter, when we control for student characteristics, graduates from highly selective institutions fared slightly better than those from low-selectivity institutions in avoiding unskilled employment as well as negative employment outcomes (defined more broadly as unemployment, underemployment, or unskilled employment).[36]

Supplemental analyses show that engineering and computer science majors, science and math majors, and business majors were significantly more likely to find jobs through their colleges than were other majors. Whereas 23 percent of the first group obtained jobs through their colleges, only 12 percent of the second group did so. This may be due to unobserved differences between students' job search styles: students in science, engineering, and business might be more job-oriented than other students, and thus more likely to take advantage of on-campus career resources. Institutional reputation may also be a factor behind colleges' tendency to focus their career services disproportionately on engineering, science, and business majors. At many colleges, business, engineering, and science programs are touted as elite programs for the highest-achieving group of students. High-performing high school students (and their families) often focus on these programs' reputations when deciding where to go to college. As sociologists Elizabeth Armstrong and Laura Hamilton note, these programs' ability to match their students with jobs upon graduation "reflects on their respective programs, raises the national profile of the school, and facilitates recruitment of high-achieving high school students willing to cross state lines [and pay out-of-state tuition] for the right academic curriculum."[37] Thus, universities have an incentive to focus disproportionate resources on career services for high-performing (and high-tuition-paying) students. Armstrong and Hamilton argue that "providing this help only for those in select programs . . . gives an edge to those who least need it."[38]

These examples illustrate a complex web of activities through which institutions have assisted their students in transitioning to the labor market. While the direct ties between the educational system and the labor market in the United States are weak compared to those in other nations, US colleges nonetheless play an important role in linking students to labor market opportunities. The influence is often indirect, through résumé and interviewing workshops, or possibly though institutional reputation. At other times the assistance is much more direct, linking students to specific employers through job fairs and other on-campus recruiting events. While the United States may lack tight coupling between educational and labor market institutions, colleges and universities are actively engaged in creating a range of institutional supports for transition into the labor market.

Internships, Volunteer Opportunities, and Former Employers

Twenty-five percent of graduates claimed to have found their most recent job through an internship, volunteer opportunity, or former employer. In the interviews, graduates described how they managed to convert their internships, volunteering stints, and part-time jobs into full-time employment by staying in touch with their former supervisors and employers, sometimes working for them on a part-time basis before transitioning into full-time positions. Chelsea, a communications major from a more selective college, successfully converted her internship into a full-time job as a programming coordinator for a local television station:

> I initially became introduced to the company through my internship. I found out about the internship through [my college]. . . . Once you're kind of in the door . . . then you are able to find out more about job opportunities. . . . So once I was an intern and I started to make contacts there. I kept in touch. I worked part-time when I was in school, and when I graduated there wasn't anything available immediately, so I stayed on part-time for about five months. Then a full-time position, a newsroom coordinator position, opened up in October of '09 and I was selected to take that position.

While some graduates found their internships, volunteer opportunities, and part-time jobs without the help of their colleges, our interview data suggest that many respondents, Chelsea included, located them at least in part through college resources. In light of this finding, we would argue that colleges are responsible for matching significantly *more* than 17 percent of graduates with jobs. Indeed, if these patterns reflect broader trends, college-to-work linkages in the United States may be much stronger than has previously been imagined. Further research is needed in order to obtain a more precise estimate of colleges' role in linking students with internships, volunteer opportunities, and part-time jobs that eventually turn into full-time jobs.

Personal Ties

Twenty percent of graduates claimed to have found their most recent job through college friends, relatives, or other personal contacts. This low figure is somewhat surprising, given that existing research on job search methods suggests that younger, less experienced, and less skilled workers are more likely to find jobs using personal contacts than their older, more experienced, and more skilled counterparts.[39] Low levels of reliance on personal contacts might be related to our exclusive focus on recent college graduates who have access to college career resources (i.e., job fairs, internship opportunities, and exclusive job postings) which may reduce their need to rely on personal contacts. It is also possible that the figure of 20 percent is artificially low, as some respondents who claim to have found their jobs through formal means most likely supplemented their formal applications with the use of personal ties.

Graduates used personal ties in a variety of ways, some of which were more overt than others. As the following two interview excerpts illustrate, some graduates used personal ties to gather inside information about job openings, whereas others had network contacts explicitly advocate on their behalf:

> Yes, she [family friend] said that the position would become available. It's actually something that I wanted to do in school so she told me that this position would become available. I checked the website frequently, [then] I faxed them my application. (Tanya, business major, less selective college, financial investigator)
>
> My father-in-law as well as my father helped me distribute or get conversations started for résumés, and that's actually how I got my job. I guess

my father had spoken with the president of the company. He told him to contact me and passed along my résumé. (Peter, architecture major, selective college, product engineer-manager)

Less than half of recent graduates who used personal ties to find jobs relied on college friends to do so. As the following interview excerpts illustrate, many of their college friends were in the same boat—having a difficult time finding work:

> Honestly, no. Just from the fact that I'm class of '09. We all graduated right at the heat of the recession. Pretty much everyone was in the same boat. Like we were all trying to find a job. We all just went to a master's degree. It might have been what we wanted to do, or some people just did it because they knew there wasn't going to be a job until maybe when it came out after their degree. They weren't super helpful, unfortunately (Chad, psychology major, more selective college, market researcher).
>
> Especially since I have so many friends that were still looking for jobs too, or trying to find a new job. So we were all kind of in it together (Irene, nursing/physical therapy major, more selective college, nurse).

This finding challenges the idea that extensive participation in social activities during college will necessarily help smooth the transition from college to work. However, the possibility remains that these college ties will prove useful later on in graduates' careers. Future research should explore the extent to which that actually happens.

Search Method and Job Quality

Preceding analyses in this chapter have shown how graduates' fields of study, CLA performance, and the degree to which their colleges were selective in admissions were associated with whether or not they were employed in unskilled occupations (i.e., positions in which the majority of workers had not completed even a year of college). Building on this analysis, we consider whether graduates who found jobs through their colleges or through internships were significantly less likely to have negative labor market outcomes than were graduates who found their jobs through other means (in analyses that controlled for institutional selectivity, field of study, CLA performance, and sociodemographic characteristics; for complete models, see table A3.6, model 3, in appendix A). The results indicate that graduates who used college resources or internships to find jobs were indeed significantly less likely to be working in unskilled occupations than were other graduates (3 percent compared to 16 percent).[40] This makes intuitive sense, as most college career centers would be likely to exclude unskilled jobs from their online job portals and career fairs.[41] This finding suggests that college-to-work linkages function like high school-to-work linkages, in that they place graduates in jobs with more desirable job characteristics.[42] In supplementary analyses we found that graduates who located jobs through formal means or personal ties fared significantly *worse* than graduates who found jobs using college career resources.[43]

If we assume that essentially all of our college graduates wanted skilled employment and could distinguish between job opportunities along this dimension, it follows that those who ended up in unskilled jobs had tried but failed to obtain such employment. This could mean that employers deemed them unsuitable for jobs requiring college degrees, or it could mean that the graduates had a difficult time locating job openings for which they were qualified. If the latter is true, and the positive effects of finding jobs through college are not simply artifacts of students who self-selected into successfully using these programs, then an expansion of college career services might help reduce the number of college graduates with unskilled occupations.

In addition to identifying how they had found their most recent jobs, graduates reported on whether their employers had asked to see their transcripts during the hiring process. Just over a third of respondents, 37 percent, reported having been asked to show their transcripts. This suggests that the majority of employers apparently do not see college transcripts as being particularly useful in sorting among job candidates. Indeed, there is anecdotal evidence that some employers are eschewing college transcripts in favor of alternative measures of qualifications, such as formal assessments of applicants' skills and competencies.[44] Having attempted to examine closely and make analytical sense of college graduates' transcripts in this study, we can well understand employers' apparent lack of interest in that information. The titles and numbering of college courses and the credits assigned to them vary so widely that the meaning of transcript coursework is quite difficult to decipher. In addition, grade inflation—which is rampant throughout higher education, but varies widely within and across colleges—further complicates the meaning of official transcripts. Have the students received high grades from attending lenient institutions, from selecting easy courses, or from applying themselves and excelling? Employers' lack of interest in college transcripts is also likely associated with their implicit reliance on other, more readily observable indicators to sort across applicants, such as the reputations of the institutions they have attended and the occupational relevance of their majors, as well as their work and internship experience. More research is needed to gain a clearer understanding of how employers determine whether recent graduates have the necessary skills for particular jobs.

Where College and the Labor Market Meet

Before concluding our analysis of college graduates' early labor market outcomes, we take a closer look at how they feel about their jobs and how they think college has contributed to the development of their professional skills. First, we look at the relationship between job satisfaction, CLA performance, and the matching of education with occupation. Do graduates with better CLA performance and graduates with jobs that "match" their level of education have higher levels of job satisfaction? Second, we examine how graduates draw connections between their college experience and their professional success. In other words, returning to the question of how the value of college varies for individuals, we look at how graduates think about the professional "value" that college has added to their lives.

Job Satisfaction

Prior research has amply demonstrated that on average, college graduates are more satisfied with their jobs than are their less-educated counterparts. This gap in job satisfaction has been attributed to a variety of factors, although pay is the most powerful explanatory variable.[45] As we have seen throughout this chapter, however, not all post-college jobs were highly desirable. One would thus expect significant variation in levels of job satisfaction *within* the college-educated population. Some of that variation may be associated with what sociologist Arne Kalleberg has termed "work values," and the extent to which individuals are able to obtain "job rewards." Kalleberg has defined work values as the "wants and expectations" people have for their jobs, and job rewards as the perceived benefits they receive from their jobs, such as intrinsic satisfaction, financial rewards, and opportunities for advancement.[46] Kalleberg found a close correlation between job rewards and job satisfaction. He also found that the extent to which people could obtain job rewards depended upon their individual characteristics (including educational attainment) and the broader conditions of the labor market.

In light of our finding that graduates with higher CLA scores fared better in the labor market than their lower-performing peers, we examine whether general collegiate skills were positively correlated with the attainment of more satisfying jobs. A descriptive bivariate analysis revealed that graduates with CLA scores in the top quintile had moderately higher levels of job satisfaction than graduates with CLA scores in the bottom quintile. On a seven-point scale, those with the highest CLA scores rated their overall job satisfaction slightly more than a quarter standard deviation higher than did those with lower CLA scores (5.3 versus 4.9).[47] Thus, in addition to being able to obtain jobs with better *objective* characteristics (i.e., jobs that required a college degree), graduates with higher general collegiate skills had jobs with better *subjective* characteristics (i.e., jobs that they found more satisfying).

While this is certainly an interesting finding, it says little about the specific character of job satisfaction. An alternative theory, one that focuses on educational matching, hypothesizes a relationship between job satisfaction and the extent to which a job matches one's educational credentials. Using national survey data, sociologist Steven Vaisey found that "overqualified" workers (those who had more education than their jobs required) were consistently less satisfied with their jobs than were workers whose level of education matched their jobs. Vaisey and others have theorized that overqualification leads to lower levels of job satisfaction because "actors desire to achieve consonance between their various social statuses and . . . social and cognitive discomfort can result when they are not successful."[48] In other words, if people find that their educational attainment is failing to yield the kind of professional rewards they have anticipated, they are likely to experience some degree of disappointment or dissatisfaction.

Consistent with the educational matching theory, graduates in our sample who avoided unskilled occupations had significantly higher levels of overall job satisfaction than did graduates in unskilled occupations, who rated their job satisfaction slightly more than half a standard deviation lower than did graduates with other jobs (4.4 compared to 5.1).[49] Another way to examine the relationship between educational matching and job satisfaction—one that does not require relying on our occupational coding metric—is to compare self-reported job skill requirements to self-reported levels of job satisfaction. The correlation between respondents' reports of how frequently their jobs required their use of a range of higher-order skills (e.g., writing, complex problem solving, critical thinking, analyzing arguments, and data analysis) and their overall level of job satisfaction confirmed that job satisfaction was closely related to the kinds of skills that graduates exercised at work.[50] When college graduates used generic higher-order skills, particularly problem solving and critical thinking, in their jobs, they were more satisfied with those jobs overall.

Indeed, returning to our earlier question, we found a strong relationship between CLA performance and self-reported job skill requirements. Graduates with higher CLA performance held jobs that gave them greater opportunities to exercise general collegiate skills. What all of these findings suggest is that college graduates with varying levels of general collegiate skills have significantly different levels of success in obtaining and holding onto more satisfying jobs. These findings underscore the importance of holding college students to a higher standard and helping them develop the skills they need to qualify for jobs they will find satisfying.

Perceptions of College Relevance

A look at graduates' personal reflections on the link between college and post-college success can further illuminate our understanding of how they experience college-to-work transitions. Their responses to a question about how college contributed to their professional success were wide-ranging. Some reflected a "credentialist" orientation towards education. Christine, who was working as a nurse two years after college, remarked: "The nursing degree makes a big difference. I certainly couldn't have done it [gotten this job] without the RN after my name." Candace, who was employed as a business analyst, echoed the sentiment: "Most importantly, a four-year degree is required for the job that I do, so I . . . wouldn't be specifically in this role without it." Most graduates, however, linked the acquisition of general collegiate skills, field-specific skills, and "soft" interpersonal skills to post-college success. Interestingly enough, very few remarked on the "social capital" (social network) benefits of attending college. This could be because, as noted earlier, the social networks our respondents developed in college had not yet yielded any significant career-related benefits.

Most graduates who couched their post-college success in terms of competencies mentioned multiple forms of general collegiate skills, along with field-specific and interpersonal skills. Ashley, a program coordinator at a senior center, remarked on how the interpersonal and general collegiate skills she acquired in college helped her do her job: "The ability to interact with people. To work in groups, to learn how to deal with people and to think critically and be able to solve problems. It's an interesting population to work with. I work with seniors, and so the ability to understand the different perspectives and be able to [have an] edge [at] this job and do it with the best of my abilities."

By contrast, Paul, who was working as a research analyst at an investment firm, reflected on field-specific and general collegiate skills:

> I majored in math and finance at [my college], so that's kind of right in with what I'm doing. . . . Let's see, definitely some of the investment—specifically one investments course at [my school] that's been pretty helpful. In addition, probably some of the math classes as well as the finance classes. Really, the critical thinking skills, I guess, kind of, that were refined while at [my college] have been pretty important. Not necessarily all of the book knowledge. While that is important, I think kind of more along the lines of problem solving and kind of having an inquisitive mind to go about knowing which questions to ask and that sort of deal has probably been most beneficial.

Other respondents, such as Courtney, noted how field-specific knowledge had facilitated the development of a set of interpersonal skills she was using as a support advocate counseling women who gave up their children for adoption:

> I had to take English and writing, and then we would study diversity and racism, and then in sociology we would do the same thing. So I had a lot of overlapping, and a lot of emphasis on segregation and just the different problems our nation has with regards to that. That really helps with how I treat people, how I work—it really overflows into my work ethic, I think, too, and meeting people where they're at and just having that knowledge. I don't know; once you learn something, it changes everything.

Finally, some respondents adopted a blended human capital–credentialist perspective. Patrick reflected on the field-specific knowledge he had gained in college, but also admitted that having the proper credential helped him get a foot in the door as a lab technician:

> I was a geology and environmental science major, so it's pretty darn close [to what I'm doing now]. . . . General lab work knowledge, I guess, has been the most useful thing. Just kind of—some training, and being careful, and going through procedure and protocol lists. I mean, to be frank, there's not a whole lot of direct crossover with the stuff I'm doing, but I don't think I

would have gotten the job without the demonstrated geology or environmental science background; so it helped in that way.

Given students' focus on social and extracurricular activities during college, we may have expected most respondents to emphasize soft-skill development above all else when discussing how college helped them perform their jobs. However, the soft-skill perspective was not significantly more prevalent than other perspectives, and most respondents mentioned more than one skill type in their responses. This suggests that college graduates view the professional benefits of college in a variety of ways. Graduates may have adopted a variety of different perspectives, but most would agree that college gave them a range of career-relevant skills.

Thus, in spite of evidence of limited learning—at least with regard to general collegiate skills—many graduates came away from college with a sense that in fact they had learned a considerable amount, and that their learning was helping them excel at work. We also observed this pattern when these same people were still in college: many claimed they were learning a great deal even as they reported not applying themselves, not being academically challenged, or not showing significant progress on the CLA. For example, the 35 percent of our sample who reported in their senior year that they studied alone less than five hours per week also reported that college had helped them develop generic competencies. Of this subset of students, 81 percent reported positively that college contributed to the development of their critical thinking skills (21 percent reporting "a great deal," the highest rating in a seven-category scale), and 65 percent reported positively that college contributed to developing skills around written communication (15 percent reporting the highest category).[51] At one level, these inconsistencies are troubling. After all, if students fail to recognize the deficiencies in their own education, they are unlikely to change their study and course selection habits. Alternatively, we might interpret this as a sign that most college students have not become overly cynical about higher education. While some students view college through primarily a credentialist or social capital lens, most maintain that college was an opportunity to develop important generic, field-specific, and interpersonal skills.

Improving College Graduates' Labor Market Success

One of the goals of this book is to bring data to bear on the following questions: What is it about college—or college students themselves—that makes some graduates more successful than others? Why, and under what circumstances, are early labor market outcomes positive? Our multivariate analysis demonstrates that graduates' CLA scores—as well as their college majors and the institutions they have attended, to some extent—track closely with the avoidance of unemployment, underemployment, unskilled employment, and job loss (i.e., with early labor market success). This correlation between CLA performance and post-college success suggests that college, at least to a certain extent, is not just about signaling and social networks, but also about what students in general can do at the time of their graduation. In short, those who leave college with greater demonstrated performance on an assessment of critical thinking, complex reasoning, and writing fare better than those who fail to do so.

In addition to general collegiate skills, one's choice of field of study has a significant impact on post-college success, at least two years after on-time college graduation. Some of the differences that exist across majors do not fit neatly into the arguments made by some liberal arts proponents that academic investments focused on the development of generic competencies will translate directly into positive employment outcomes. While generic competencies do matter in general, these are not the only skills that are relevant. For example, consider the early labor market success of business majors, who as a group had relatively low levels of academic engagement (measured in terms of hours studying and number of courses with significant reading and writing requirements) as well as relatively low gains on the CLA while in college. How can one account for these apparently anomalous findings? Multiple factors likely are at play. Many business majors were likely involved in internships and apprenticeships in college that could have facilitated successful school-to-work transitions after graduation while simultaneously decreasing the time spent on traditional academic coursework. Business graduates also were in some ways positively selected for occupational success, as potentially they were more focused on occupational outcomes and, when at the top of the ability distribution, more likely than arts and science majors to forgo graduate school for labor market opportunities. Other researchers have also observed this relationship and have offered other explanations for the success of occupationally focused majors. Some have argued that certain majors impart more valuable (or more marketable) field-specific skills than others. This is a human capital argument: higher education imparts career-related benefits insofar as it increases graduates' occupationally useful knowledge and skills. Others have argued that some majors serve as better signals of employability than others, regardless of whether those degrees are underpinned by actual field-specific knowledge and skills. This is a credentialist (or signaling) argument. Because our data on skills and competencies only focus on general collegiate skills and not also on subject-specific competencies, we are unable to make much of a contribution to this particular debate. We will say, however, that employers' increasing propensity to assess job applicants' generic and field-specific skills before extending a job offer suggests that *both* generic and field-specific competencies likely matter in the job market. We also provide clear evidence that generic skills provide labor market returns over and above the differing outcomes that are associated with fields of study.

4

Parents, Partners, and Optimism about the Future

The early twenties are an age of exploration. They are part of what psychologist Jeffrey Arnett has termed "emerging adulthood."[1] Arnett argues that individuals in their late teens and early twenties, no longer youth and not quite adults, exist in a unique space characterized by both instability and possibility. This is a time when options can be tested and various interests, from vocational to romantic, pursued; a time when responsibility may linger on the horizon but commitments do not yet have to be made.

"Emerging adulthood" is a recent phenomenon, embedded in broader structural and cultural changes that have transformed traditional understandings of adulthood. In preceding decades, adulthood was characterized by specific transitions such as completing school, entering the labor market full-time, leaving the parental home, getting married, and having children. One became an adult as one completed these specific transitions. There were objective ways to assess progress: one could observe specific markers and infer the attainment of adult status.

In recent decades, the notion of adulthood has shifted toward a more subjective or psychological definition, with young adults reporting that taking responsibility for one's actions, having the

Karly Sarita Ford and Esther Yoona Cho coauthored this chapter.

ability to make independent decisions, and becoming less self-oriented (self-centered) are central markers of adulthood.[2] This psychological orientation nonetheless signals the importance of independence. In addition to being independent in one's thoughts and actions, young adults recognize the importance of the more practical form of independence: financial. Three-quarters of young adults report that being financially independent from parents is necessary for being considered an adult.[3] More generally, 95 percent of Americans still believe that completing school, being employed full-time, and establishing an independent household are important markers of adulthood.[4]

Independence, of course, is an imprecise term. None of us are ever truly independent; our lives are marked by interdependence, from the early days of childhood to the final days of our lives. It is nonetheless a cultural value towards which we often strive—a value that is particularly strong in the United States, where independence is a cornerstone not just of adulthood, but of our national identity.[5] In recent decades, however, as material independence in the form of a stable full-time job that allows one to support an independent household has become increasingly elusive, the subjective or psychological definition of adulthood has gained more appeal. In the process, traditional markers of adulthood have receded to the background.

Nevertheless, examining traditional markers of adulthood can be valuable in illuminating the unique structural and cultural contexts in which young adults are making their transitions at the turn of the twenty-first century. In this chapter we focus specifically on two dimensions: living arrangements and partnering outcomes. Where young adults live—and in particular whether they live at home—as well as whether they have romantic partners has changed notably over recent decades. In spite of their changing, and arguably contested, role in the transition to adulthood, these markers continue to offer a useful lens into the lives of young adults today. In addition, examining these dimensions of young adults' lives draws attention to often-neglected forms of social inequality. Expectations that parents will support children further into their adulthood places increasing pressures on families, especially those with limited resources. And as marriage becomes delayed, whether one attends college and what type of college it is can become increasingly consequential in the process of finding a partner.

Beyond living arrangements and romantic relationships, we examine graduates' engagement in the broader world as well as their hopes for the future. We find that in general, college graduates' engagement with current events, through either reading newspapers or discussing politics and public affairs, was remarkably limited. Even this limited engagement, however, has produced a pessimistic picture about the future of the country. At the same time, graduates were highly optimistic about their own futures, with the vast majority expecting their lives to be as good if not better than those of their parents. How graduates aimed to attain that goal was often vague, as four years of exploration during college had not necessarily produced a clear path forward.

Elusive Independence: Living at Home and Parental Support

In a seminal commentary on American society, Robert Bellah and his colleges described American parenting in the mid-1980s as being focused on producing independent children who would leave home.[6] According to this standard, many parents are not being successful today: one year after college, a third of the college graduates in our sample were living at home, and two years after college, almost a quarter were still in this situation (figure 4.1). For many, living with parents or other relatives was not just a temporary condition: 70 percent of those who were living at home two years after graduation had been in the same situation a year earlier.

Times have changed, however, as have cultural expectations about parenting and young adulthood. New results from the Culture of American Families Survey highlight the extent to which parents' attitudes have changed since Bellah's research. Two-thirds of the parents said they would encourage a twenty-five-year-old to move back home if he or she could not afford housing, and that they would "willingly support a 25-year-old child financially" if needed. In addition, while parents hoped their children would attain financial independence, the same percentage hoped that they would maintain close ties with parents and family.[7]

Given these parental attitudes, it may not be surprising that a substantial proportion of young adults today spend some time living with family. National data presented in figure 4.2 indicate that the proportion of twenty-two- to twenty-four-year-olds living with parents has been increasing since the 1960s. Although it still represents a minority—less than 40 percent—the proportion of young adults living at home today is almost double what it was in the 1960s. Whether young adults leave for college and then return, or whether they never leave in the first place (by attending college either close to home or not at all), young adults are increasingly likely to spend at least some of their twenties in the parental home.

Remarkably, the overall trends in the proportion of young adults living

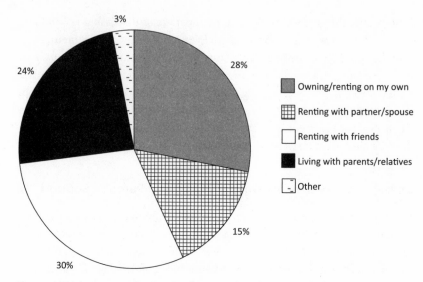

Figure 4.1 Living arrangements of college graduates two years after on-time graduation.

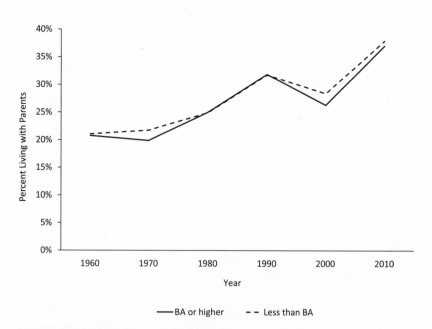

Figure 4.2 Percentage of young adults aged 22 to 24 living with parents, by year and educational attainment (source: Integrated Public Use Microdata Series, IPUMS, 1960–2000).

at home in figure 4.2 are similar for individuals with and without college degrees. Although college graduates are in a stronger economic position than those without college education, and although labor market prospects have particularly deteriorated in recent decades for those without college degrees, graduates and nongraduates are living at home at similar rates. This similarity among graduates and nongraduates, and the patterns of change in the overall proportion of young adults living at home since the 1960s, point to broad economic and cultural transformations that have occurred over this time period, as well as a corresponding shift in the understanding of adulthood. Cultural shifts described in the Culture of American Families Survey are accompanied by changes in economic realities for young adults, from the need for prolonged schooling to greater uncertainties faced by young adults in a globalized economy.[8] And the pattern is not unique to the United States. The rise of "accordion families" (families with adult children who are living with their parents) is a broad phenomenon observed across a number of nations in the developed world.[9]

While transitions to adulthood are embedded in broader cultural and economic contexts, we find that individual circumstances, and especially labor market difficulties, are related to whether college graduates return home. To illustrate how labor market conditions are related to the likelihood of living at home, figure 4.3 shows the probabilities of living at home for different groups of graduates: those who were employed versus those who were unemployed, and those who found employment in skilled versus unskilled occupations. These estimates are adjusted for graduates' sociodemographic characteristics, CLA performance, and college selectivity (for complete models see table A4.3 in appendix A).[10] The results indicate that unemployment is strongly related to living at home. The probability of living at home more than doubled when college graduates were unemployed. Unable to find work, they often sought refuge in the parental home. Parents also assisted graduates who were employed but were struggling to find jobs commensurate with their college degrees, although this association was weaker. The probability of living at home was about ten percentage points higher when respondents were employed in unskilled jobs as opposed to skilled ones.

Along with labor market conditions, other financial circumstances, such as carrying high college loan debt, may be anticipated to increase the chances that graduates would return home. As is the case for college graduates nationwide, debt was a feature of life for most of the college graduates in our sample. Two-thirds of our graduates had college loan debt, and

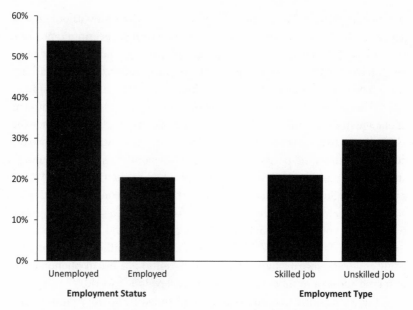

Figure 4.3 Probability of living at home, by employment conditions; predicted with all other variables held at their mean, based on table A4.3.

those in debt had an average of $27,000 to pay off as of 2011. Considering the labor market outcomes described in chapter 3, and especially considering the average annual income of those employed full-time, this amount of debt represents a substantial financial burden. In addition, this figure does not include the debt college graduates were incurring, or will incur, in graduate school. Although the graduates were indebted, sometimes heavily, our analyses indicate that college loan debt was not related to whether they returned to their parental homes. This was the case even when the debt burden was substantial; when graduates owned more than $30,000 of college debt, they were not more likely to live at home (see table A4.3 in appendix A).[11]

Moreover, labor market conditions were not the only factors related to whether college graduates lived at home—so were graduates' racial/ethnic and social class backgrounds. Although a large and increasing proportion of college graduates may be living at home, not all families were equally likely to assist their children in this way. Our analyses show that college graduates from Asian, Hispanic, and other nonwhite racial and ethnic groups were more likely living at home than their white counterparts (see table A4.3 in appendix A). Similarly, college graduates whose parents had only some college education were more likely living at home than those whose parents had college degrees. Notably, these patterns persisted even after graduates' employment status was taken into consideration. As noted in the previous chapter, sociodemographic characteristics did not have an independent relationship to labor market outcomes among college graduates. Racial/ethnic and family background differences in living at home were thus similar, whether or not labor market measures were included in the statistical models. These patterns in living arrangements illuminate the different ways in which families were trying to assist their children in the transition to adulthood.

Considering whether young adults live with their parents is important for understanding the contours of the prolonged transition to adulthood and the resulting challenges facing middle-class and working-class families that are becoming increasingly overextended.[12] Although living with parents is of central concern, we also briefly mention the patterns observed for other types of living arrangements. When the analyses were adjusted for background characteristics, senior-year CLA performance, and college selectivity, male college graduates were less likely to live at home than their female counterparts—instead, they were more likely to live with friends (see table A4.3 in appendix A).[13] While our sample of male college graduates is small, raising caution about the robustness of the findings, these patterns are consistent with other recent research on young male adults. For example, in his recent book *Guyland*, sociologist Michael Kimmel provides vivid narratives of young men struggling on the path to adulthood. These men often continue their college behaviors after graduation—including living with friends, whether they are friends from college or from elsewhere.[14]

Perhaps more notable than this small gender difference in male graduates' likelihood to live with friends is the *overall* prevalence of living with friends. The descriptive distribution of living arrangements in figure 4.1 shows that almost one-third of college graduates lived with friends two years after graduation. Among those, almost half were living with friends from college. A similar proportion (28 percent) of graduates had set out on their own, and about half as many (15 percent) were living with their partners or spouses. Those living on their own may be in this arrangement for the long haul, and many others may join them at some point in their lives, given recent trends depicted in *Going Solo*.[15] But for now, "going solo" was not the norm among young college graduates, nor was living with a partner or a spouse. Instead, graduates lived in a variety of arrangements, including a substantial proportion who returned home and many others who continued their college experience of living with friends.

When graduates lived at home, parental support went considerably beyond simply providing a place to sleep. In the interviews, when asked about their living and financial arrangements, college graduates who were living at home said that their parents were covering many of their living expenses. When asked if they contributed to covering these expenses, college graduates who were living at home often said no, or that they contributed "a very small amount," covering "gas for the car, sometimes some groceries I'll just buy, things like that" (Gabe). Some graduates also noted paying for their own personal expenses, such as car insurance and cell phone bills. Parents typically covered the majority of the expenses, including food. While accounting for expenses, few graduates discussed rent or mortgage payments, omitting explicit recognition of the single largest expense they avoided by living at home. It was thus possible for graduates to think about expenses as being equally shared between themselves and their parents: "They help me out with some things, but I pretty much pay for my student loans, for my car insurance, and they buy my food. I don't know; kind of 50–50, I guess" (Sara).

But graduates living at home were not the only ones who continued to depend financially on their parents. Figure 4.4 reports the percentage of graduates who had received financial assistance from parents over the previous year, separately for graduates in different living and financial circumstances.[16] Two years after college graduation, almost three-quarters of graduates reported having received financial assistance from parents, including 83 percent of those who were living at home and 71 percent of those who were not living at home. Similar proportions of college graduates benefited from their parents' generosity, regardless of whether they had college loan debt. When the graduates faced tough labor market conditions, their parents were more likely to assist them. This was particularly the case for those in unskilled employment. However, even when the graduates were not facing poor labor market outcomes, their parents were supporting them financially.

Even after analyses were adjusted for sociodemographic characteristics, CLA performance, and college selectivity, some graduates were more likely to receive financial assistance from their parents. More specifically, graduates living at home and those working in unskilled jobs were more likely to benefit from their parents' generosity (see table A4.4 in appendix A). Notwithstanding these differences, the overall continued dependence on parents was remarkably high. Regardless of the conditions, including living arrangement, debt, and labor market circumstances, descriptive data

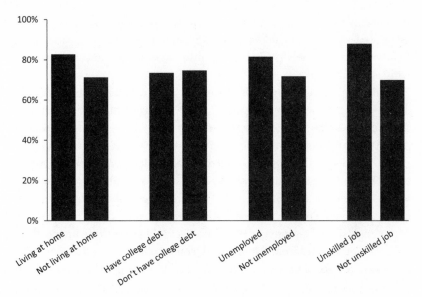

Figure 4.4 Percentages of college graduates receiving financial assistance from parents two years after on-time graduation, by financial and employment conditions.

indicate that at least 70 percent of graduates received financial assistance from their parents.

These high levels of parental assistance reflect national patterns. A recent study reported that 80 percent of eighteen- to twenty-five-year-olds who lived at home were receiving financial assistance—as were 75 percent of those who did not live at home.[17] According to prior research, parents provide an average of $38,000 in financial assistance to young adults in their transition to adulthood, in the form of housing, food, educational expenses, and cash assistance—averaging slightly over $2,200 per year.[18] In our sample, approximately half of the graduates reported receiving up to $2,000 from their parents over the previous year, while 15 percent reported receiving direct financial assistance in the amount of $10,000 or more.

The widespread dependence of young adults on their families implies that all types of families today are increasingly expected to assist their children during transitions to adulthood. This represents an upward trend of family dependence from prior decades. For young adults aged twenty-three to twenty-four, for example, the proportion receiving financial support from parents has increased from less than 50 percent in 1982 to almost 70 percent in 2011.[19] As Richard Settersten and Barbara Ray note in their recent work, "What is now striking are the significant flows—and associated strains—in middle-class [and, we would add, working-class] families at a time when families themselves have become increasingly stressed or fractured."[20]

While all families may wish to support their children, their ability to do so varies by their circumstances. Prior research shows that although dependence on families has increased over time for all social groups, the proportion of young adults who receive assistance varies by parental education.[21] In our analyses, which control for sociodemographic characteristics, CLA performance, and college selectivity, parental educational level was associated with the probability of providing assistance to children (see table A4.4 in appendix A). Parents with low educational levels (i.e., those with a high school diploma or less) were least able to provide financial assistance to their children. Parents with some college education were also less likely to provide assistance to their children than were parents with college degrees, although this did not reach the level of statistical significance. At the same time, as noted earlier, parents with some college experience were most likely to provide children with a place to live.

The *amount* of financial resources that families are able to pass onto their offspring varies even more than the act of providing assistance. As sociologist Frank Furstenberg notes, families at all income levels "provide roughly the same proportion of their earnings to support their young adult children," but this produces vastly disparate amounts of resources across the income distribution.[22] Recent estimates indicate that children whose families were in the top quartile of the income distribution received three times the amount of financial assistance during their transition to adulthood than did children in the bottom two quartiles.[23] Families at the top of the income distribution were more able to assist their children in all respects, from direct cash assistance to support for college. Supplemental models based on our sample indicate that even among college graduates, who represent a much more selected sample, parents who were highly educated (with graduate and professional degrees) provided higher amounts of financial assistance to their children two years after college graduation than did parents with lower amounts of education, including those with college degrees. Young adults' high level of dependence on their families in the protracted transition to adulthood has implications for long-term inequalities. Families' differential abilities to assist their children create vastly different starting points for young adults, which are likely to influence their overall socioeconomic trajectories and thus have notable consequences for social inequality over the life course.[24]

Finding a Romantic Partner

While marriage was once deemed a central marker of adulthood, today only about 50 percent of Americans consider it a necessary precondition for being regarded as an adult.[25] The decreasing role of marriage in the definition of adulthood is related to a range of macro-level forces, from prolonged schooling to high cohabitation and divorce rates. One factor that is usually not included in this discussion, but deserves to be, is college culture. Recent academic and popular accounts portray romantic experiences during college as transient and largely irrelevant to long-term commitment. Although college is still seen as a part of growing up, it is not necessarily considered a part of developing long-term attachments, whether in the form of serious romantic relationships or of marriage. Instead, romantic relationships in college are often described in the context of "hooking up."[26] For youth, the meaning of this term can range from making out to having sex. Regardless of the specific meaning, "hooking up" implies a certain degree of casualness and nonchalance. A hookup may turn into something serious, almost by chance, but it is generally not meant to imply any degree of commitment or long-term expectations.

Perhaps the most important consequence of describing college romance as essentially "hooking up" is that it obscures how colleges are implicated in structuring long-term romantic relationships, and particularly the ways in which they potentially contribute to growing inequality. Given the increasing prevalence of delayed marriage, particularly among the college-educated, it is not surprising that only 8 percent of college graduates in our sample were married two years after graduation. However, many more of our college graduates were in stable romantic relationships, with 9 percent cohabitating and another 32 percent reporting being in serious romantic relationships. Thus, although "hooking up" may increasingly be taking the place of formal dating,[27] and while it may be a defining feature of the college party scene,[28] nearly half of the graduates in our study found themselves in stable romantic relationships two years out of college.

Notably, among the graduates who were partnered (married, cohabitating, or in serious relationships), college was the most important source of potential partners. Forty percent of college graduates in romantic relationships reported having met their partners at college (figure 4.5). As Rachel described the process of meeting her same-sex partner:

> Well, we met in college. We were mutual friends. She was friends with one of my closer friends, so we have known each other through a network.

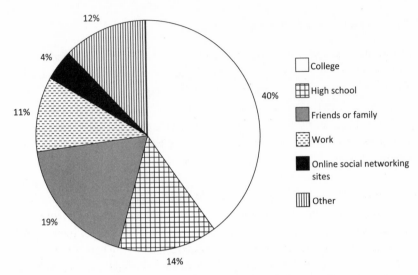

Figure 4.5 Percentages of college graduates meeting their romantic partners in different contexts.

Being in [college name] is such a tiny school. It's hard not to know all those people. And then in our senior year, in the winter, we took a . . . class together, and so then we started dating that spring and we have been since.

Other graduates met their partners in college but did not start dating them until after graduation, such as Julie:

We met in college and never dated in college but were relatively close friends. We had very close friends in common, and so sort of knew each other tangentially, and stayed in touch briefly—and I mean sporadically, I suppose, every once in a while after he graduated. He was two years older than me. Then this one really close friend that we had in common set us up about a year—a little more than a year ago, [which is when] we started dating.

Combining the percentage of graduates who met their partners in college with the 14 percent who remained with their high school sweethearts, we found that educational institutions were the primary source of graduates' romantic partners. Next to college, the most common way to meet a partner was through friends or family—but at 19 percent, this pathway to romance was not even half as common as college. Although the media have popularized the notion that online connections are an integral part of the dating landscape, only 4 percent of graduates in romantic relationships at this stage of their life course reported meeting their partners through social networking websites.

Inequalities in Partnering Outcomes

Given the importance of college for meeting partners, do graduates from different types of institutions have the same partnering outcomes? One of the most notable changes in American higher education in recent decades has been the reversal of the gender gap, with women surpassing men in both college entry and completion.[29] In addition to being of interest to social scientists as a unique example of the reversal of social stratification patterns, the increasing presence of women on college campuses has raised concerns among college administrators.[30] We thus examine the relationship between the proportion of women on campus and the probability of a college graduate having a partner. These analyses are adjusted for individuals' sociodemographic characteristics as well as their CLA performance and the selectivity of the institutions attended (for complete models, see table A4.5 in appendix A). The results indicate that graduates who attended institutions with higher proportions of women were less likely to have partners two years after college. To present the findings in a more intuitive way, figure 4.6 reports the probability of having a partner (i.e., being married, cohabitating, or being in a serious romantic relationship) for graduates who attended schools with low and high presence of women.[31] Graduates who attended institutions with a higher proportion of women had a substantially lower probability of being partnered than their counterparts who attended institutions with a lower proportion of women.[32]

The same models indicate that men were significantly less likely than women to have partners two years after college, with analyses adjusted for background characteristics, CLA performance, and the selectivity and gender composition of the institutions attended (see table A4.5 in appendix A). Whether this represents the pull of "Guyland"—men's tendency to move into committed relationships later in life than their female counterparts — or the uniqueness of our sample, it warrants further investigation. Similarly, African-American and Asian graduates in our sample were less likely to be partnered two years after college. This trend mirrors previous findings of racial and ethnic differences in romantic relationship patterns among teenagers and young adults.[33]

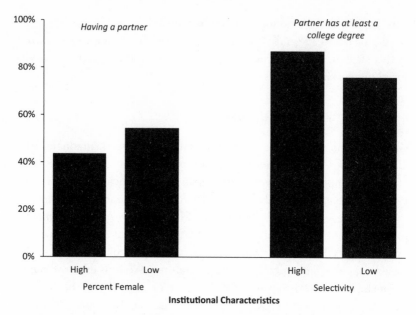

Figure 4.6 Probabilities of different partnering outcomes, by institutional characteristics; predicted with all other variables held at their mean, based on table A4.5.
High and low categories are defined as one standard deviation above and below
the mean, respectively.

When college graduates did find partners, they were often in relationships with individuals who were equally educated. While rates of homogamy among other educational groups have decreased since the 1980s, the
proportion of college graduates partnering with other college graduates
continues to increase.[34] If we consider college graduates in our sample who
were partnered (i.e., married, cohabitating, or in serious romantic relationships), the vast majority (81 percent) were partnered with individuals
who attended or completed college (70 percent were partnered with individuals who had completed a bachelor's degree or more).

To what extent do colleges contribute to their students' ability to find
partners with at least college degrees? To consider their role in this process, we examine whether institutional selectivity and the percentage of
women on campus were related to the extent to which graduates partnered with individuals who had at least college degrees. The proportion
of women on campus was not related to the partners' education level, but
institutional selectivity was. For simplicity, figure 4.6 presents selected results (for complete models, see table A4.5 in appendix A). The last two
columns show the probability of having a partner with at least a college

degree for graduates who attended institutions of high and low selectivity.[35] The findings indicate that institutional selectivity helped graduates find similarly educated partners: graduates who attended schools of high selectivity were more likely to have partners with at least college degrees than were graduates who went to low-selectivity schools. Considered in reverse, the findings indicate that college selectivity plays a protective role in the partnering process by reducing the probability that a graduate will partner with an individual who has less than a college education.

The importance of colleges reaches beyond the partner's education level. College is related not only to how educated the partner is, but also to where the partner was educated. When college graduates in our study were in romantic relationships with other college graduates, the selectivity of their partners' colleges was highly correlated with the selectivity of their own institutions.[36] Figure 4.7 summarizes the distributions of partnering outcomes for our sample. The last two columns show that among graduates who were in relationships with individuals who attended or graduated college, 45 percent were with somebody from the same college, and 63 percent were with somebody who attended a similarly selective institution.[37] These descriptive relationships held even after models were adjusted for

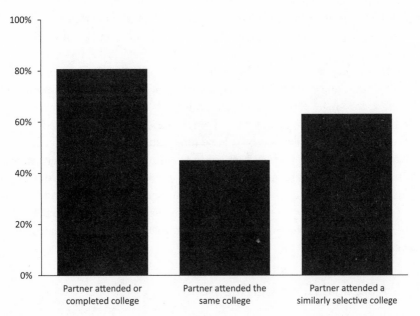

Figure 4.7 Percentages of partnered college graduates with different relationship outcomes

graduates' sociodemographic characteristics, CLA performance, and the representation of women on campus (for complete results, see the final model in table A4.5 in appendix A). While much research has focused on estimating the effects of college selectivity on labor market outcomes, these results point to another important dimension of college influence that deserves careful attention in future research: romantic relationships.

These patterns of association between the educational levels and school types of our respondents and their partners are often referred to by social scientists as homophily—or, more colloquially, the notion that "birds of a feather flock together." In all forms of social networks—from friendship to romance, and from work to support—similarity breeds connection. Many social networks are thus relatively homogeneous.[38] Nonetheless, the strength of these college associations is quite remarkable. While the intensity of college influence is likely to wane over time, as graduates get further away from college graduation, national data that include a wide age range still demonstrate a substantial likelihood that graduates will find partners who went to the same or institutionally similar colleges. A recent study using national data reported that approximately 30 percent of partnerships between college graduates consist of partners who attended the same institution.[39] Furthermore, when two partners in a relationship have not both graduated from the same institution, they have often attended similar types of institutions. For instance, graduates who attended highly selective schools were often partnered with others from similarly highly selective schools.[40]

Thus, while romantic relationships during college are often portrayed as transient and as lacking consequences, college presents an important context for longer-term romantic commitments. Many of the graduates in our sample met their partners at college. But even beyond this direct link, the influence of college was broad and long-lasting. Graduates' chances of being in a romantic partnership were related to the type of college they attended. Furthermore, and perhaps more significantly, the degree of selectivity of one's college was related to the level of educational attainment of one's partner, as well as to their institution's level of selectivity. Far from being irrelevant, colleges play an important role in shaping graduates' romantic relationships.

Lack of Engagement with the World

While marriage may no longer be considered one of the central markers of adulthood, research indicates that young adults today place a premium on responsibility: being an adult means taking responsibility for one's actions.[41] However, that personal responsibility does not necessarily translate into broader societal responsibility or civic engagement. Since the 1970s, civic engagement among young adults has decreased along almost all of the dimensions tracked by social scientists, from belonging to clubs and attending religious services at least once a month to reading newspapers and voting.[42] The only area of engagement that has not decreased over time is volunteering. Deliberate efforts by high schools, colleges, and community groups have kept young adults engaged in volunteering. Once young adults leave those institutions, however, their volunteering declines.[43] In our sample, over two-thirds of college seniors reported volunteering. That percentage dropped after students left college, with only half of college graduates reporting volunteering two years later. Moreover, only 43 percent were engaged in volunteer activities at both time points. Thus, while college may have facilitated volunteering by providing a rich context for easy access to volunteer opportunities, it did not necessarily facilitate the adoption of attitudes about volunteering that persisted after degree completion and led to long-term commitment.

College also did not appear to instill values regarding other forms of civic engagement. Arthur Levine and Diane Dean's recent portrayal of college students noted widespread disengagement from traditional politics. Approximately two-thirds of college students in their study reported that they were not politically engaged, and even if they supported a particular campaign, fewer than half would get involved, whether by attending rallies, displaying stickers, or joining Facebook groups.[44] These forms of engagement may increase as college students transition into adulthood and make more permanent family, work, and community commitments.[45] However, our findings reveal that college graduates were also disengaged in broader ways that were not tied to specific communities or adult commitments: they rarely read newspapers or discussed politics and public affairs. As the descriptive results in figure 4.8 show, only approximately one-third of college graduates were reading newspapers online or in print daily, and only 16 percent were discussing politics and public affairs with family or friends that frequently. The more disconcerting results were found at the other end of the spectrum: a large proportion of college graduates were minimally engaged, with over 30 percent reporting that they read newspapers online or in print once a month or never, and almost 40 percent reporting that they discussed politics and public affairs with family and friends that infrequently.

These patterns of low engagement are also apparent in national surveys.

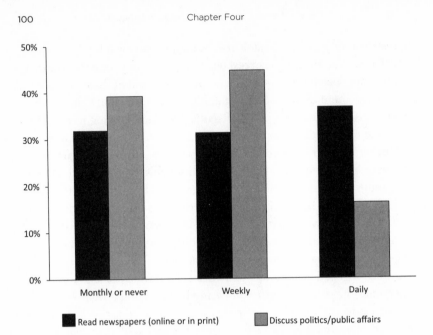

Figure 4.8 Percentages of college graduates who read newspapers and discuss politics/public affairs monthly/never, weekly, and daily

Figure 4.9 reports results from the Pew Media Surveys, restricted to young adults aged twenty-two to twenty-seven. Only approximately 40 percent of young adults in this age group reported reading newspapers regularly. Moreover, this percentage has decreased slightly even over the last decade. It is also worthwhile to note the overall similarity between the results for college graduates and for individuals without college degrees. The gap between the two groups is only five to ten percentage points over this time period, and the downward trend over time holds for both groups. Given that college graduates are a select group that may be expected to be more civically engaged and aware, and that they have spent four years (and often more) in college, where they may have been exposed to ideas about the importance of civic engagement, this relative similarity between college graduates and their non–college educated peers raises questions about the role of college in fostering civic awareness and engagement. As sociologist David Labaree has argued, education, and college in particular, is increasingly seen as a consumer good and as a tool to improve one's lot in the occupational hierarchy. Consequently, other purposes of education, including that of preparing citizens for participation in a democratic society, have faltered.[46]

While there may be doubts about college's effectiveness as an institution that facilitates civic and political awareness and engagement, the question remains whether some colleges are more effective in this regard than others. To consider possible variation across schools, we examined the likelihood of minimal civic engagement and political awareness (i.e., reading newspapers or discussing politics and public affairs monthly or never) for students who graduated from institutions of varying levels of selectivity. These analyses adjust for students' sociodemographic characteristics and CLA performance at the end of college (for complete models, see table A4.6 in appendix A). Figure 4.10 illustrates the findings by reporting the predicted probability of being minimally civically and politically aware for graduates from high- and low-selectivity institutions.[47] The results indicate that graduates who attended low-selectivity institutions were twice as likely to be only minimally engaged as were graduates who attended high-selectivity institutions, and that was the case for both outcomes (reading of newspapers and discussion of politics and public affairs). Supplemental analyses also reveal that graduates who attended high-selectivity institutions were substantially more likely to rely on newspapers (online or in print) as their primary source of news than to rely on either social media

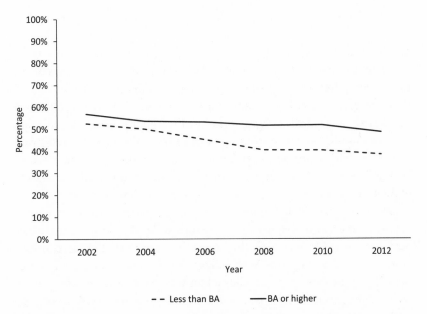

Figure 4.9 Percentages of young adults aged 22 to 27 who read newspapers regularly, by year and college degree (source: Pew Media Surveys 2002-12)

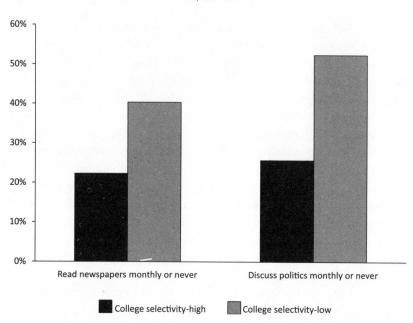

Figure 4.10 Probability of reporting low levels of civic/political awareness, by college selectivity; predicted with all other variables held at their mean, based on table A4.6. High and low college selectivity are defined as one standard deviation above and below the mean, respectively.

or television. These strong relationships between institutional selectivity and civic and political awareness highlight the potential of institutions to provide contexts that facilitate the development of attitudes and dispositions for greater civic awareness and engagement. Selective institutions may have a range of advantages, including their ability to attract a more select student body and gain access to more resources that can help cultivate civic and political engagement. However, other institutions may similarly be able to rely on their traditions, their missions, or other unique aspects of their environments to encourage long-term civic engagement.

School context is also important for understanding the relationship between different individual characteristics and civic and political awareness. Student performance on the CLA, a test of critical thinking, complex reasoning, and writing, was marginally related to civic and political awareness before the analyses were adjusted for school context. Adjusting analyses for college selectivity explains virtually all of the relationship between CLA performance and civic and political awareness (see table A4.6 in appendix A).[48] In other words, once we compared graduates who attended schools of similar selectivity, their CLA performance was not related to civic and political awareness.

However, even after school context was considered, some individual characteristics remained associated with the likelihood of civic and political awareness. For example, males were more likely to be civically and politically aware than were females (see table A4.6 in appendix A). While our sample of male graduates was small, this is worth noting and exploring in other datasets, particularly in light of recent concerns about male college matriculation, performance, and overall disengagement. Moreover, another consistent result across both models was lower civic and political awareness among students whose parents only completed high school or less, compared to that of students whose parents completed college. While college graduation decreased the impact of social background on labor market outcomes, as shown in the preceding chapter, it did not have the same relationship to civic and political awareness. The question of whether this is a product of college's focus on employability as opposed to civic engagement or other forces within and outside of college walls requires careful attention in future research.

Low levels of civic awareness and, in particular, low levels of conversation about politics and public affairs may stem at least in part from a lack of common news sources. What is remarkably different about the current generation of college students (and, by extension, graduates) from past generations is "an absolutely astounding array of choices for getting news. . . . The consequence is that there is no common source of news content or even what could be called common content."[49] The proliferation of blogs, e-mail alerts from websites or special-interest organizations, and tweeting allows for a constantly increasing differentiation of news sources. Without common or even related news sources, graduates are less likely to share common knowledge, making conversations perhaps that much more difficult, disconnected, or fragmentary.

Descriptive results from our survey provide some credence to this proposition. In addition to inquiring about how often respondents discussed politics and public affairs, we also asked about their primary sources of news. Figure 4.11 reports the percentages of graduates who were only minimally engaged (i.e., discussed political and public affairs monthly or never) by their primary source of news.[50] When college graduates relied on social networking sites or e-mails from organizations and websites as their primary source of news, they were substantially less likely to engage in discussion of politics and public affairs with family and friends. For respondents whose primary source of news was newspapers, only a quarter were

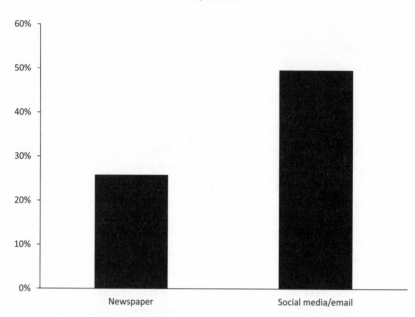

Figure 4.11 Percentages of college graduates who discuss politics/public affairs monthly or never, by their primary news sources.

disengaged. The percentage of disengaged graduates who rarely discussed politics and public affairs doubled for those who relied primarily on social media. This is perhaps the irony of online communication: it makes information easily accessible while reducing the amount of shared knowledge, and thus the opportunity for engaging with others.

Regardless of how they may have obtained the news, graduates had a negative picture of the current state of affairs in the United States. When interviewees were asked about their sentiments regarding the direction in which the country was heading, their responses were overwhelmingly negative. Only 17 percent of interviewees noted that the country was going in a positive direction.[51] The other responses were mixed or unclear, or distinctly negative—51 percent of graduates fell into this latter category. While graduates felt the country was not heading in a positive direction, a number also felt that there was not much they could do about it, or really much that anybody could do about it. These kinds of sentiments may have contributed at least in part to their lack of political engagement. As Gillian remarked, "It's not great but, I mean, I pay attention to what I hear on the news, but I guess I don't get all worked up about it. I mean, there's only so much that I could do or someone in charge could do." Another graduate, Steve, echoed those sentiments: "Well, I would guess I'd say I'm not very happy with it, but we really don't know how anybody could change it, because it's just such a large thing happening. And it just seems like [the littlest thing] can knock the whole house over sort of thing. So, I mean, yes, it's not the best [of] what's happening, the economy thing, but could it really be fixed? I don't know."

Graduates in our sample perceived that the country was not heading in a positive direction for many reasons. They worried about a number of issues, from health care to education and climate change, but the economy and the gridlock in Washington gained the most attention. John placed the emphasis on politics: "[The country is headed] in a negative direction, I suppose. Yes, it's, I think, that the intransigence of the political parties in Washington to compromise and the increasing gulf between the two extremes are detrimental to getting anything reasonably done." David concurred, and connected the political challenges with economic woes: "Well, from the last thing that I understand is going on with the national debt and the loss of the credit rating, it seems like we're in a state of crisis really, and it seems like we really need to get together or Congress needs to get together and solve this thing one way or another without worrying [more] about bashing each other than resolving this issue." Finally, Ken combined it all together into a bleak picture: "I mean, I guess we're in debt, we're in wars we can't afford, and we have domestic issues. So it seems to be a low spot in the country's history."

Although hardly positive about the current state of affairs or the future of the country, graduates also recognized the limits of their own knowledge. Catherine remarked, "I guess I have not been watching enough news to form a really solid opinion. I think that getting out of wars might help, but I guess I don't know enough to say very surely what would happen." Similarly, Dennis confessed, "I'm not sure. I don't think I've read up on it enough to really give a well-informed answer. . . . I don't know what direction the country should go, let alone what direction it will go."

Looking toward the Future with Unbridled Optimism

Although college graduates in our sample portrayed a gloomy picture of national politics and the direction of the country, they were optimistic about their own futures. When thinking about their lives in general, only five percent thought their lives would be worse than those of their parents. Figure 4.12 reports the percentage of graduates who thought their lives would be equal or better than those of their parents. Those who thought their lives would be worse are omitted from the figure. This figure shows

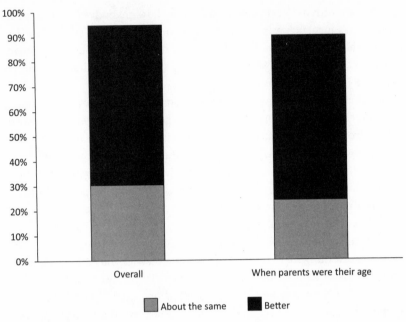

Figure 4.12 College graduates' comparisons of their own lives to those of their parents, overall and relative to when their parents were their age

that 30 percent of graduates thought their lives would be equal, which would still be a notable accomplishment, given that many graduates came from relatively advantaged families.[52] The vast majority of college graduates, almost two-thirds, thought that their lives would be better than those of their parents. Even when the question was more focused, asking not about life overall but about their life right now, two-thirds of college graduates still reported that their lives were better than those of their parents at a similar age.

These patterns may not be surprising in light of the psychological literature on positive illusions. Seminal work by Shelley Taylor and Jonathon Brown argued that individuals do not necessarily perceive themselves or their futures accurately; instead, their perceptions are considerably more positive than is objectively likely.[53] Thus, even though graduates in our sample faced difficult labor market conditions and a gloomy political context, they expected their own futures to be much more positive. This optimism fits well with the American belief in social mobility and the national culture that generally encourages a focus on the future and a belief in possibilities. Education, and college in particular, is still expected to bestow notable personal and economic rewards, even if they may be delayed.

Indeed, many of the graduates in our study remarked on the advantages they expected to gain as a result of their education. First-generation college students were particularly likely to explain their optimism in terms of education, noting how college degrees would help them to avoid the kinds of struggles their non–college-educated parents had endured. These first-generation graduates did not necessarily express specific ideas about how or why the college degree would matter, apart from noting that "I have a college degree" (Seth) and "I think it will be better because I have more education than my parents" (Cory). Underlying these comments was a faith in education in general, and in a college degree in particular. These graduates, like most of society, took the value and benefits of college education largely for granted; they believed their lives would be better because they had college degrees. And indeed, at least in the economic sense, college degrees bestow notable advantages over high school education. As the preceding chapter showed, however, a college education was far from being a guarantee of a bright economic situation in the short term.

When comparing their lives to those of their parents, graduates also noted the benefits of "emerging adulthood"—of having more time to make life-course transitions such as working full-time, getting married, having children, or having to live on their own. They associated this with good prospects down the road and better life situations than those their parents had enjoyed. Courtney noted the challenges of marrying young: "My parents . . . married really young and had children, and then they both went back to school. Both my parents are divorced. I think it's hard for them." Peter reflected on the difficulties of combining school and work: "I just had a better start. Both my parents worked full-time and went to school. It took them much longer to, I guess, get to a point where I am today because of that."

Even if their lives may not be better than those of their parents economically, the graduates believed that they would lead happy and fulfilling lives, either matching or surpassing those of their parents. Like the young adults portrayed in *Coming of Age in America*, whose optimism rested in part on an evolving conception of success that included self-growth and the personal quest for meaning and fulfillment, Rachel explained:[54]

Oh, boy. I guess it depends on the metric that we would use to measure it. In terms of income and money, my parents have done pretty well. I think that it will be difficult for me to achieve that level of success in a financial sense, partly because my chosen career path is different from theirs, and probably because the economy I am going into is different from the one they went into. . . . I'm not entirely convinced that income is the measure of success or happiness. . . . I think I can have an equally fulfilling and interesting and happy life as my parents, even if it looks different.

Regardless of the struggles these graduates were facing, they seemed to hold onto a strong sense of optimism that they would do as well or better than their parents. As Julie reminded us, "There's that human optimism, right?" Another graduate, Cory, noted, "If things work the way I expect, then I'll have a better life." Faith in the future remained strong even in the presence of current struggles, such as those experienced by Yvonne:

I have good ideas and I know what I want to do. I know my path will be positive, but things are moving at a lot slower pace than I expected. If nobody will give me a job, I'll just go start my own job to do what I want to do. . . . It will be different [from my parents' life]. It depends really on what you mean by "better." I know I won't be as rich as my parents, but I know that I will be doing something that I like.

The unwavering optimism of college graduates is also observable in national data. Figure 4.13 shows the percentages of twenty-two- to twenty-seven-year-olds who reported in the General Social Survey (GSS) that their own current standard of living was better than that of their parents when they were the same age. The percentages are shown separately for respondents who had attained college degrees and those who had not. While college graduates and their less educated peers had a similar starting point in 2000, their expectations diverged notably over time. In the early 2000s, college graduates experienced a particularly optimistic turn. This optimism was somewhat dampened during the recent recession, but began to pick back up in the 2012 survey. By contrast, the optimism of their less advantaged peers decreased steadily over time, creating an ever-growing gap between young adults with a college education and those without.

Noting the optimism of college students in *Generation on a Tightrope*, Levine and Dean theorized that part of it reflected their relatively sheltered lives, and the fact that they had yet to experience any large challenges. While in college, many four-year college students were supported by their parents and were somewhat protected from adult challenges that could dampen their perspectives. While this may be part of the story, we found in our research that even when reality hit after college and the graduates experienced significant challenges, they remained deeply optimistic.

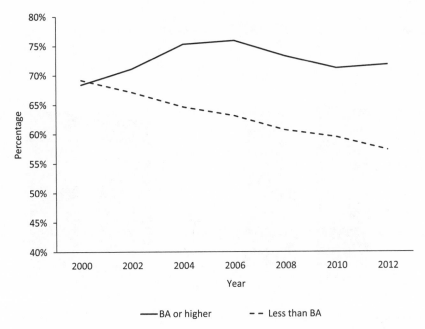

Figure 4.13 Percentages of young adults aged 22 to 27 who expect their standard of living to be better than that of their parents, by year and college degree (source: General Social Survey).

Granted, their parents continued to provide extensive support, perhaps lessening the blow—but even with parental support, some of the graduates were stuck in unskilled jobs or had no job at all. Despite these challenges, they remained optimistic.

Indeed, labor market conditions had little impact on the graduates' optimism. Figure 4.14 reports the percentages of graduates who believed that their lives would be better than those of their parents. The percentages are given separately for graduates who were employed versus those who were unemployed, and for those who found employment in skilled versus unskilled occupations. The similarity across the groups is remarkable. Graduates who were working in unskilled jobs, and even those who were currently unemployed, were as optimistic as their counterparts who were working or employed in better jobs.[55] It is thus likely that their optimism had less to do with the degree to which they may have been sheltered or had not experienced hardships, and more with an evolving conception of success. Young adults interviewed by Swartz and her colleagues in *Coming of Age in America* repeatedly talked about success not as "the destination,"

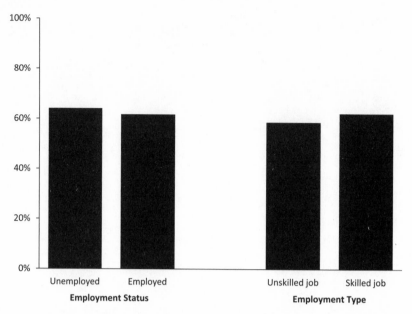

Figure 4.14 Percentages of graduates who believed that their lives overall will be better than those of their parents, by the graduates' employment conditions

but as "the road." And part of the young adult road today includes exploration, change, and uncertainty.[56]

While changing conceptions of success may help graduates maintain an
unshaken sense of optimism, the path to success, and especially to doing
as well as or better than their parents, is far from clear. Sociologists Barbara Schneider and David Stevenson astutely depicted American youth as
"motivated but directionless," with high ambitions but limited knowledge
about their chosen occupations. Like Schneider and Stevenson's "drifting
dreamers," whose "life plans are not realistic and are often ill informed,"
the graduates in our sample believed their lives would be better, but they
had few concrete ideas about how exactly that would become reality.[57] This
vagueness about how they might get to those greener pastures partly reflects the somewhat fluid and uncertain state of many of their lives: only
half of the graduates in our sample noted that their lives "rarely or never"
lacked clear goals and a sense of direction.

Some would argue that this uncertainty is an expected part of life in
one's twenties, a time of emerging adulthood when options are explored but
no firm commitments are made.[58] At the same time, there is a difference
between meandering and purposeful exploration—a difference between

drifting and sorting through one's choices. Social psychologist William Damon notes that a young adult's delay in making difficult choices and commitments "is characterized more by indecision than by motivated reflection, more by confusion than by the pursuit of clear goals, more by ambivalence than by determination."[59] Without a clear sense of purpose to give one's life direction and meaning, meandering and uncertainty can take a toll on one's vision of the future. Among our sample of college graduates, this sense of uncertainty put a dent into their expectations about how well they would do compared to their parents. Figure 4.15 shows that only 3 percent of graduates who reported that they "rarely or never" lacked direction expected to do worse than their parents, while five times as many—15 percent—of those who "fairly or very often" lacked direction anticipated that same outcome.[60] On the other end of the continuum, those who lacked direction fairly or very often were less confident in their chances of doing better than their parents: less than half thought they would do better than their parents, compared to more than two-thirds of the graduates who rarely or never lacked direction. Whether these dampened expectations were a result of a temporary state of meandering and uncertainty that will

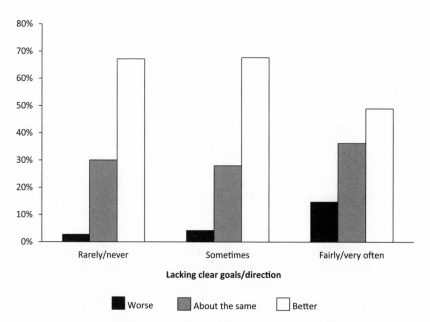

Figure 4.15 Percentages of graduates who expect their lives to be worse, the same, or better than those of their parents, by how often they feel they lack clear goals or direction

reverse in the future, or the more worrisome start of a long-term downward or flat trajectory, is unclear.

Young Adulthood: Emerging and Drifting

In the world of "emerging adulthood," the late teens and early twenties are an age of discovery and exploration. A four-year residential college experience is particularly conducive to fully experiencing this stage of life, as it affords students time and opportunity to learn about themselves and others. However, this period of exploration does not end with college; more than half of the graduates in our study reported that two years after college, their lives lacked clear goals and a sense of direction. This finding raises questions about the extent to which exploration during college may be characteristic more of meandering than of purposeful discovery. Indeed, prior studies have shown that as college students have increasingly come to define the objective of college in terms of economic rewards, the importance of college for formulating life values and goals has declined.[61]

Given the amount of uncertainty and instability at this stage of life, one might expect that young adults would worry about an uncertain future. However, the emerging adults in our study were optimistic. They saw endless possibilities, regardless of their current circumstances and the challenges they faced. They believed things would work out, even if they did not necessarily have plans for how that would happen. They were also convinced that their lives would be as good as those of their parents, if not better. This optimism in the face of challenges may be characteristic of the *Academically Adrift* cohort's generation.[62] It may also reflect new ways of understanding adulthood that are tied more closely to subjective sentiments than to objective accomplishments, and that focus on the journey rather than the final destination.[63]

Indeed, our graduates had a difficult time meeting a widely accepted objective marker of adulthood: financial independence. A substantial proportion of graduates lived with their parents two years after their on-time degree completion, and the vast majority, whether they lived with their parents or not, were financially dependent on them. Thus, despite the overwhelming emphasis on the economic value of college in both policy and academic discourse, college completion far from guaranteed financial independence early in these individuals' labor market careers. These patterns have implications not only for the changing conception of adulthood, but for the amplification of social inequality. As parents are expected to support their children longer, whether and how much that is possible varies across social classes, thus increasing the gap between young adults from more and less advantaged backgrounds during their twenties and beyond.[64]

If financial independence was elusive for this cohort of emerging adults, so too was civic engagement. College provided them with opportunities in the form of volunteering. However, a substantially lower proportion of graduates were still volunteering after they left college. Even more disconcerting is our finding that a large proportion of graduates were not well aware of the world around them or engaged with it, as was reflected in their reports of reading newspapers or discussing politics and public affairs. This may reflect the self-centered nature of emerging adulthood,[65] or the education system's decreasing emphasis on preparing individuals for participation in a democratic society.[66] Whatever the underlying causes of this tendency, colleges could adopt a more productive role in the development of values and dispositions for greater engagement with the world at large.

Although college may not instill values regarding long-term civic engagement, it does play a unique role in structuring opportunities for romantic partnership. Recent discussions about romantic relationships in college have focused on a "hook-up" culture, characterized by highly transient and non-committed relationships. While "hook-ups" are common, though perhaps less so than is commonly assumed,[67] college also provides a foundation for longer-term relationships. Among our cohort of graduates, approximately 50 percent had partners (i.e., were either married, cohabitating, or in serious romantic relationships) two years after college. Notably, for these college graduates in their early twenties, college was the primary source of partners. Indeed, many graduates partnered either with their college peers or with their counterparts from similar institutions. College thus plays a highly stratifying role in partner selection, which helps to increase social inequality over time, as similarly highly educated individuals combine economic, social, and cultural resources. The role of colleges, and particularly selective colleges, in contributing to inequality in partner choices is not fully appreciated when discussions of romantic relationships during college are singularly focused on the "hook-up" phenomenon.

Just as college is more consequential for finding partners than is often assumed, decisions individuals make in their early twenties may be more consequential than is frequently imagined. Conceiving of "emerging adulthood" as a time of exploration and discovery may perhaps inadvertently convey the message that the "twenty-something" decade is somewhat inconsequential. While this may be partially true for those from privileged origins who can be supported by familial resources, we are skeptical that this laissez-faire approach is uniformly applicable to all life-course trajectories. Meg Jay, clinical psychologist and author of *The Defining Decade*, argues that the consequences of exploration without an end in sight may lead "too many men and women to squander the most transformative years of their adult lives, only to pay the price in decades to come."[68] Whether adopting more or less optimistic perspectives about recent conceptions and manifestations of "emerging adulthood," social scientists agree that the twenties are crucial years for building the foundation for later life. Given the struggles experienced by the *Academically Adrift* cohort, it is imperative that higher-education institutions and society at large consider better ways of supporting transitions to adulthood.

5

A Way Forward

Large numbers of students pass through higher education experiencing few curricular demands, investing little in academic endeavors, and demonstrating only limited learning. But for every few students who have been adrift, others have been able to find paths in college to flourish, progress, and prosper. Consider Beth, born in a small town, whom we quoted in chapter 2. Her father ran a small business and her mother stayed at home. Neither her parents nor her older brother had made it to college. Beth, however, did. She took advantage of a low-cost public university in her home state that, although not a flagship university, had a reputation for excellence in several fields. Beth attributed her accomplishments to a solid upbringing that "taught discipline and [that] it's very important to work hard for where you want to go and what . . . you want to be in life."

Beth applied that lesson to how she approached college. "Honestly, I worked hard," she reported. "I always felt like I'm a genuinely hard worker and I studied a lot. I think it paid off." While her peers reported studying on average less than thirteen hours per week, a third of that with friends, Beth reported studying with friends fewer than five hours per week, in addition to studying alone more than twenty hours per week. Her study time in fact was double what her peers on average were investing, and roughly equivalent to what full-time college students in 1960 reported as their average engagement in academic preparation and study-ing time.[1] While college students today, on average, gain only 0.47 standard deviations on the CLA over four years of college, Beth's growth was close to double that amount: a gain of approximately one standard deviation from her freshman year to her senior year. Her level of improvement in gen-eral collegiate skills was again roughly equivalent to what college students several decades ago demonstrated on average in college. Today, however, gains of that magnitude are considerably less common.[2]

In college, Beth majored in a health-related field. When asked about her college program, Beth described it as rigorous and demanding:

> I think it was designed that way because it's a tough field and there's no room for errors. So, I feel almost as if some degrees—and I do not mean to belittle anybody, but you can't get away with just doing half-work. I mean you have to put yourself into it. If not, then you're not going to succeed in the field. . . . A lot of opportunities were offered. I was able to go to [a hospital] and be there for a couple of days to experience that. We were offered the opportunity to go to national and local professional meetings. Not all programs offered to do that. I think just our program director, and overall, she was tough. Even though I didn't like it sometimes, I think that it definitely made us better . . . [it] just forced us to be strong individuals and have a stronger knowledge base.

Although Beth chose an occupational field of study, it is clear from her overall comments that this curricular focus was complemented by aca-demic engagement in traditional liberal arts coursework. "I really had great relationships with a lot of my professors," she reported. When asked about her academic engagement, Beth volunteered information on an arts and science course, rather than on a specific class in her demanding health program: "I took the history of Islamic civilization class and I got really close with the professor."

While focusing primarily on her academic studies at college, Beth also found time to join a college athletic team that she credited with help-ing her develop social skills. She reported that upon entering college she realized:

> I needed to learn about other people. I come from a very small town. . . . It's not diverse. So I knew I needed to learn about other people, and who they are and where they come from. I think that being on the . . . team really

allowed me to see that. [It] is a very physically demanding sport. So, you also—that sort of opens your eyes to people's real personalities. So that was very interesting for me.

As we noted in chapter 2, Beth also developed ways of coping with peer behaviors she found troubling, and which colleges today often tolerate or ineffectively regulate. She reported that her freshman roommate did cocaine, her suitemate cut herself, and the young woman across the hall stole from her. Beth noted, "So many kids, they went out and partied. They skipped class."

While attempting to avoid undesirable peer behaviors as well as learning to negotiate them, Beth also was busy establishing meaningful and lasting social relationships. Two years after college, she noted that she was still in touch on e-mail and Facebook with about ten of her friends from college, and had "phone conversations at least once a week with not all of them, but several of them. We are all very close." In addition to this friendship network, Beth, during her junior year at college, met a young man. She was out with her friends; he was out with his. Beth reported: "Everyone was sort of socializing together and, I don't know, I guess it all took off from there." After they met, he also finished college. And in the summer two years after her graduation, they married—just a few weeks before we interviewed her. They then began living together and reported that they were economically independent and received no financial support from their parents.

Beth was also moving forward with her career goals. She had spent a year in graduate school pursuing additional training and gaining eligibility for board certification in her chosen field. Unlike some of her less fortunate peers, the difficulties she experienced in finding a position appropriate to her career aspirations were relatively short-lived:

I applied to probably fifty jobs—over fifty jobs. It had to be over fifty. The position that I hold is one that requires experience, and I did not have experience as a clinician. Coming into the field, I was only a student. I can tell them all the experience that I got as a student, but that didn't count. It was almost like catch-22. People, or I should say employers, wanted people with experience. How am I supposed to get experience if someone doesn't allow me to get experience? So I had several interviews. I interviewed in [multiple states]. Several interviews. I could continue on and on, and I think finally I got to a point where I just straight-out said, "You know, I just need someone to give me a chance to prove myself that I can be a valuable employee to your department." . . . Finally they offered me this position. I think I had about three interviews. I had a phone interview and two different on-site interviews. Just very fortunate. It was an answer to a prayer . . . even though it took me a long four months and I was living back at home. I don't think my parents really understood it. "Why aren't you getting the job? Why isn't anyone hiring you? You've gone through five years of school." I was working so hard and finally I got a job.

Although Beth ultimately found a desirable position, she still continues to strive to achieve her goals. She described her typical day in the following terms:

Well, right now I'm studying for my board examination, which is September sixteenth. So, on a daily basis I wake up at five a.m. I study until I start working, minus getting ready for work. I start work at seven-thirty a.m. and I work until four p.m. At four p.m. I leave work and I head straight to the gym. I work out from four-thirty p.m. to five-thirty p.m. Now, I'm coming home and learning how to make dinner. The rest of my night is devoted to studying.

Given Beth's demanding schedule, her civic engagement was more aspirational than realized. Nevertheless, she kept up with the news online and on television, was an "active voter," and had "high hopes of being a volunteer for some type of organization when I'm done with these boards." Beth was pessimistic about the direction of the country, noting, "I think we're in trouble"—but optimistic about her own future, commenting, "The direction of my life is going very well."

Beth's personal trajectory, however, has to be understood in context. Large numbers of students today do not apply themselves or develop academic skills in college. Thirty-six percent of full-time college students reported studying alone less than five hours per week. In a typical semester, 50 percent of students did not have a single class that required more than twenty pages of writing over the course of a semester, and 32 percent did not have a single class that required forty pages of reading per week. Over four years of college, if the CLA was scored on a one-hundred-point scale, 36 percent of students would not have demonstrated even a one-point gain. Students with low CLA scores at graduation were less likely to go on to full-time graduate programs or to avoid unemployment, job loss, and unskilled or marginal employment outcomes. But, like her peers, Beth was personally optimistic about the future. Although many college graduates had experienced difficult post-graduation transitions and were pessimistic about the future of the country, a remarkable 95 percent of them thought that their lives would be the same or better than those of their parents.

While many of her peers were wading into their early twenties—much as they had waded through college—aspiring but adrift, Beth at age twenty-four had already attained many traditional markers of adult status. She had completed her schooling, launched a career embracing a personally mean-ingful occupational calling, found a romantic partner, and left home to live independently with her spouse. Although social scientists are reluctant to make normative judgments about the increasing tendency for emerging adults not to make such transitions, it is clear that Beth's life trajectory stands in stark contrast to those of many of her peers. In fact, since college graduates today tend to marry at later ages, one might make normative judgments in quite the opposite direction: Has Beth settled too quickly, married too soon, and narrowed her career choices too early? If the cul-tural norm is for aspiring adults to spend prolonged periods adrift—and we believe that such is the case for recent college graduates—rather than applauding Beth's successful transitions, one might instead have trepida-tions about her "narrow set of accomplishments." Recall that 24 percent of college graduates two years out of college were living at home with their parents, 74 percent were still receiving parental financial assistance, and 51 percent were not in serious romantic relationships.

We believe, however, that Beth's story exemplifies many aspects of the constructive role that four-year colleges and universities can play in the lives of young adults. Individuals can acquire general and specific compe-tencies; forge meaningful and valuable social relationships; and develop positive attitudes and dispositions aligned more broadly with social mo-bility, civic engagement, and adult success. But it is not enough for college and university leaders to point to positive exemplars, such as Beth, and to be satisfied solely with producing a "talented tenth" from each college class destined for professional accomplishment and civic leadership. Colleges can and should be designed to promote success for all who attend them.

College Challenges

Why are contemporary colleges and universities not producing more suc-cess stories? Rather than defining undergraduate experiences in a manner conducive to the development of young adults, institutions today have let themselves be defined by the preferences of undergraduates.[3] Institutions make resource allocation decisions based on what will entice seventeen-year-old high school seniors to apply and enroll. State-of-the-art gymnasiums, student centers, dormitories, and athletic spectacles are often thought to suffice. Once students are enrolled, institutions give them broad latitude to choose their own course of study while failing to impose rigorous academic standards and leaving their social behavior largely unregulated. Rather than providing rigorous academic experiences to promote undergraduate learning and character formation, colleges and universities have embraced a model that focuses on encouraging social engagement and sociability, supporting students' psychological well-being, and catering to satisfying the consumer preferences of emerging adults.

American studies professor Andrew Delbanco astutely observes: "Over the past half-century or so, this expansion of freedom has been the most obvious change in college life—not just sexual freedom, but what might be called freedom of demeanor and deportment, freedom of choice as fields and courses have vastly multiplied, and, perhaps most important, freedom of judgment as the role of college as arbiter of values has all but disappeared. . . . Except in the hard sciences, academic failure, especially in the elite colleges, is rare; and cheating, except in the military academies, tends to be treated as a minor lapse."[4]

Rather than accommodating the preferences of emerging adults, colleges and universities have a responsibility to challenge some of their assumptions and offer them a compelling model of how education can be about more than simply the pursuit of "the college experience" and increased earnings. Our study shows that academic engagement in college can lead to broader development that helps individuals find purpose and meaning in work, relationships, and civic engagement. At the core of formal education is the role of educators in structuring educational experiences, not simply responding to student interests.

In part, that is what distinguishes formal schooling from the myriad self-directed learning opportunities available in our increasingly technology-enhanced society. Self-directed learning, sometimes referred to as "do-it-yourself" education and now often accessed online, provides lifelong opportunities for individual improvement, self-realization, and cognitive development. Anya Kamenetz, a "do-it-yourself" education advocate, argues, "Technology upsets the traditional hierarchies and categories of education. It can put the learner at the center of the educational process. Increasingly this means students will decide what they want to learn; when, where, and with whom; and they will learn by doing."[5] One would be hard pressed to find anyone opposed to the wider availability and use of self-directed learning platforms both within and outside of formal schooling.

Nevertheless, recognition of such learning opportunities does not excuse one from grappling with the question of how educators can work to better structure educational opportunities made possible by technological innovations. For example, educators in New York City and Chicago working through the Hive network have recently aimed to take advantage of digital technologies to better implement "connected learning" pedagogies. These programs seek to recognize a broad and inclusive set of youth interests and then to connect individuals, often with the use of digital technology, with adult mentors and peers who share their interests, and with opportunity structures aligned with adult success.[6] While this work has been focused primarily on adolescents, there are lessons for higher education as well. Specifically, a broad set of youth interests are potentially amenable to educators' efforts to channel and align individual orientations with adult opportunity structures. Educators should strive not just to make higher education more academically rigorous, but also to ensure that students understand the relevance of education for their lives. This is especially the case today, when many are beginning to question the value of college and wonder whether it is worth the cost.

Learning Outcomes: From Proposition to Practice

Colleges and universities have increased tuition at roughly twice the rate of inflation since 1980. From 1950 through 1980, college tuition at public universities was approximately 4 percent of the median family income and 20 percent at private universities; by 2005, college tuition at public universities had increased to more than 10 percent of the median family income and 45 percent at private universities.[7] If one considers tuition, fees, room, and board as a whole, the list price of many private and public universities today exceeds the US median household income of approximately $50,000.[8] These increases have put significant strains on college financing. State governments have not been able to find additional resources to allocate to public colleges and universities to support growth in expenditures. While the federal government, in part, has stepped in with the expansion of Pell Grants and other indirect forms of subsidy, students and families have also been required to meet increasing financial burdens through growing reliance on personal loans.

Given the high and increasing costs of college and the growing strains on federal, state, and private resources to support college-going, it is not surprising that public and policy discourse has increasingly shifted toward questioning the value of college. Although the pressures for higher-education institutions to demonstrate their value have been brewing for decades, they took center stage with the Spellings Commission report *A Test of Leadership: Charting the Future of Higher Education*. In the report, the commission noted "that students, parents, and policymakers are often left scratching their heads over the answers to basic questions" given the "lack of clear, reliable information about the cost and quality of postsecondary institutions, along with a remarkable absence of accountability mechanisms to ensure that colleges succeed in educating students."[9] Since the report, attention to accountability has increased, not only at the state but also at the federal level. However, any attempt to judge the value of college requires addressing at least two sets of issues, one normative and the other technical in nature. The outcomes of higher education have to be defined as well as measured. Neither of these components has a simple solution or has received adequate attention to date.

Normative Agreement

The first step to demonstrating value involves agreeing on what colleges and universities should accomplish. This is far from an easy task, as "the history of higher education has been a tale of ambivalent goals and muddled outcomes."[10] Higher-education institutions have always aimed to accomplish many ends, which are historically contingent and have changed from the time of original colonial colleges to the time of contemporary colleges and universities. Today, higher-education institutions can be conceived of as hubs "connecting multiple social processes that often are regarded as distinct," as well as "sieves for regulating the mobility processes underlying the allocation of privileged positions in the society, incubators for the development of competent social actors, and temples for the legitimation of official knowledge."[11]

An attempt to define outcomes for any of these purposes can be overwhelming, but in recent decades educators have attempted to address at least one of the goals of higher education: student learning. Working within and across disciplines, educators have aimed to develop working agreements and frameworks to define learning outcomes. For example, the Association of American Colleges and Universities (AAC&U), in the beginning of the twenty-first century, brought together stakeholders to advance "a set of educational outcomes that all students need from higher learning" with competencies "keyed to work, life, and citizenship." This effort, termed the Liberal Education and America's Promise (LEAP) Initiative, articulated the following four broad domains as "essential learning outcomes": knowledge of human capital and the physical and natural world, intellectual and practical skills, personal and social responsibility, and integrative and applied learning.[12] Although the LEAP framework implicitly built on normative assumptions closely aligned to liberal arts education, the AAC&U report also explicitly broadened its intended audience and goals by asserting that "the recommended learning outcomes can and should be achieved through many different programs of study and in all collegiate institutions, including colleges, community colleges, and technical institutes, and universities, both public and private."[13]

Following the LEAP initiative, the Lumina Degree Qualifications Profile articulated a framework that had a largely similar set of competencies but more explicitly recognized institutional distinctions across higher education. The Degree Qualifications Profile specified the following broad learning domains: specialized knowledge; broad, integrative knowledge; intellectual skills; applied learning; civic learning; and an undefined "institution-specific areas" component.[14] In addition to the LEAP initiative and the Lumina Degree Qualifications Profile, many individual disciplines have worked over the past decade to define internally what competencies and knowledge college graduates in their fields should attain. For example, the Lumina Foundation's Tuning USA Project was designed as "a faculty-driven process to articulate what a student knows and is able to do in a given discipline at the point of degree."[15] Educators in many of the STEM fields (i.e., science, technology, engineering, and mathematics) have been at the forefront of such efforts with the development of concept inventories of core ideas that are intended to guide both instruction and student assessment.[16] Historians have also come together to identify competencies that history majors should develop.[17]

These recent efforts to define the competencies, skills, and knowledge that college graduates should achieve share a few key features. First, there is acknowledgment that students should develop both general collegiate competencies and subject-specific skills. Second, in addition to general and subject-specific competencies, there are additional pedagogical objectives that once might have been referred to simply as the affective domain, including "civic learning" and "personal and social responsibility." Third, there should be systematic attempts to evaluate and assess student attainment of learning objectives, particularly those related to generic competencies and subject-specific domains.

This emerging normative consensus around student learning objectives is encouraging. However, state and federal policymakers have focused on a different set of goals—ones not necessarily aligned with an emphasis on a wide range of generic, subject-specific, and civic competencies. State accountability schemes, although they are of various magnitudes and scopes, have overwhelmingly focused on credentials.[18] While some of the metrics are more nuanced and either reflect steps in the process toward degree completion (such as the passing of remedial courses or persistence to the second year) or focus on specific credentials (such as those in the STEM fields), their end result is the counting of credentials. This focus inevitably raises questions about whether and to what extent credentials represent student learning. While one may hope that students who are learning a great deal are the ones who are persisting and graduating, recent studies on how students choose colleges,[19] ethnographies describing college climates and cultures,[20] and our own prior research on learning in higher education[21] raise doubts about this association. Indeed, sociologist David Labaree argued that an increasing focus on credentials can undercut learning "by promoting the acquisition of credentials with the minimum academic effort."[22] And at least one study that attempted to examine the relationship between graduation rates and the development of critical thinking skills directly at the institutional level found no association between the two outcomes. Schools that would be rewarded for facilitating the development of general collegiate competencies would not be the same schools that would be rewarded for high graduation rates.[23]

In addition to credentials, policy makers have recently focused on graduate wages. In early 2012, the Obama administration announced the release of the *College Scorecard*, which includes several metrics of student outcomes, among which are graduation rates as well as earnings.[24] The data for earnings are not yet available, but the administration has promised to collect and publish this information in the near future. Similarly, the National Governors Association released a report in 2011 entitled *Degrees for What Jobs?* The report narrowly defines the purpose of college in relation to labor market needs, and urges governors to demand that their higher-education institutions develop courses and programs to prepare students for "high-paying, high-demand" jobs and to require colleges and universities to collect and publicly report students' employability and wages.[25]

Using wages to evaluate institutions, however, is problematic in many respects. First is the normative disagreement about whether high earnings are the primary purpose of college, and whether students who choose to be teachers (or pursue other less well paid occupations) or work in the nonprofit sector ought to reflect poorly on their institutions. Second, colleges have relatively limited control over wages, which are influenced by many external factors, than they do over other outcomes such as learning or even persistence and graduation. Moreover, using wages to evaluate institutions is ineffective, as wages vary little across institutions. This may be a surprising claim, but it is backed by extensive social science research, which shows that college graduates' income differences across institutions are relatively small once students' prior individual characteristics are taken into account.[26] This is particularly the case for early earnings. Findings from a series of recent detailed studies in a number of states by Mark Schneider, who painstakingly documented early labor market outcomes of college graduates, illustrate this point well. Schneider found that recent graduates of flagship universities (more selective public universities, typically) actually earn slightly less than their non-flagship-attending counterparts. In Tennessee, first-year college graduates' earnings were slightly higher for individuals who had attended East Tennessee State University than for those who had attended the University of Tennessee or Tennessee State University. In Colorado, median first-year earnings were slightly higher for graduates from Metro State University of Denver than for graduates from the University of Colorado Boulder. In Virginia, graduates from Bluefield College and George Mason University had higher average first-year earnings that those from the University of Virginia. These studies show that attending a flagship college in these states clearly did not translate directly to higher early-career incomes relative to attending other colleges in the state.

It is not that attending college does not matter, but rather that differences between institutions—at least with respect to their selectivity—do not confer on graduates early labor market success in terms of earnings.[27] Therefore, one should be highly skeptical of efforts to base accountability frameworks for higher education around recent college graduates' earnings. Policy makers looking for levers to improve the accountability of colleges will need to look elsewhere.

Technical Obstacles

Part of policy makers' focus on outcomes such as graduation rates and wages rests on the fact that they can be relatively easily and uniformly measured across institutions. The US Department of Education requires all institutions to report graduation rates, which are publicly available through the Integrated Postsecondary Education Data System (IPEDS), and many states have or are developing systems that allow the tracking of students through state higher-education systems and the reporting of outcomes such as persistence and completion. The federal government also has the potential to use tax data to measure earnings, and some states, such as Florida and Texas, are adding wages to their educational data tracking systems. This is not to say that there are no measurement issues with graduation rates or wages, but the challenges associated with these criteria are smaller than those associated with measuring learning outcomes.[28]

Higher education has a dearth of validated instruments that can capture growth of a range of college-level skills and can be used effectively across institutions. The CLA instrument used in our study, for example, was made available to institutions only in the past decade and measures only generic competencies (i.e., critical thinking, complex reasoning, and writing). It does not capture subject-specific competencies that many educators focus on developing and that students aspire to master. Although students in some occupationally focused fields are assessed through professional licensing processes, common assessment instruments that allow for the longitudinal assessment of college students' subject-specific competencies are generally not available.

As a case in point, consider the experience of eighteen colleges and universities in the Voluntary Institutional Metrics Project. These institutions collectively came together, with support from the Bill and Melinda Gates Foundation, to develop a holistic framework for assessing college performance in five areas: "repayment and default rates on student loans, student progression and completion, institutional cost per degree, employment of graduates, and student learning."[29] The institutions were particularly frustrated, however, by difficulties in gaining access to college graduates' labor market data and by the absence of agreed-upon subject-specific learning outcomes. An initial report published by the project remarked, "There is a clear need for a focused effort to overcome the lack of comparative assessments of learning outcomes at the program (major/discipline) level. When joined with existing assessments of learning at the core skills level, such assessments would provide a basis for the use of learning outcomes to inform policy decision-making."[30]

Policy makers often interpret what they perceive as higher education's lukewarm response to demands for accountability as resistance. Apart from the normative disagreement about the purposes of college, however, higher education lacks the ability to demonstrate performance of the skills it aims to develop. Colleges and universities are thus left with limited options for responding to accountability demands in ways they believe are legitimate

and appropriate. Evaluation of faculty performance in teaching and learning, for example, often rests with course evaluations, without much evidence
that the evaluations track with learning outcomes, and indeed with evidence to the contrary.[31] Institutions would thus benefit from having access
to classroom observation protocols and student course evaluations that are
validated in reference to objectively measured learning outcomes. Contemporary colleges and universities lack the tools and instruments they need
to measure learning both systematically and effectively.

Although it is a substantial challenge, the development of these tools
only presents the beginning of the difficulties facing policy makers who
wish to hold higher-education institutions accountable. Even when the
tools are developed, how will the institutions be compared? One cannot
compare raw outcomes, whether those are graduation rates, wages, or performance on competency assessments. Instead, those measures have to be
adjusted for both student characteristics and, depending on the purposes
of the evaluation, available resources. In announcing the plan to develop a
new rating system for colleges and universities, the Obama administration
recognized this challenge by noting that "colleges with similar missions"
would be compared.[32] However, it is not clear what that means or how it
will be accomplished.

An extensive body of social science research has documented the challenges associated with making comparisons across institutions.[33] To date,
state systems have typically used very rudimentary adjustments, and some
have argued that this is necessary since the importance of transparency
makes developing "a highly sophisticated funding scheme based on econometric models" impractical.[34] Without the proper adjustments, however,
the accountability system can be neither effective nor legitimate. In pushing to hold higher-education institutions accountable, policy makers express an interest in changing behavior and rewarding schools that perform
well. However, if schools' contributions to student outcomes are not estimated with at least a reasonable amount of accuracy, the system could
be completely counterproductive, incentivizing undesirable behaviors and
falsely rewarding schools that do not produce desirable outcomes. The
current data capacity at both the state and the federal level is woefully inadequate for this purpose. For all of the foregoing reasons, as well as for
those documented in our earlier work in *Academically Adrift*, we believe
that accountability should operate at the institutional level, not at the state
or federal level. Federal and state governments have a role to play—elabo-
rated in the next section—but the responsibility for accountability rests
with higher-education institutions.

Measuring and Improving Learning Outcomes

The challenges involved in reaching a normative consensus regarding the outcomes of college, as well as for developing appropriate instruments and mechanisms for judging how much schools contribute to student outcomes, cannot be overstated. Recent technological advances, however, provide opportunities to make notable progress at least in the technical element of these challenges. Technology has dominated the higher education headlines in recent years. This is not surprising, given the dual concerns of wanting to produce more college graduates, especially as the United States has fallen behind a growing number of countries that are providing college education for a larger percentage of their youth,[35] and having to face increasingly resource-constrained environments. As in other industries, technology is hoped to improve productivity in higher education.

What is surprising, however, is not the interest in the use of technology but the narrow manner in which it has often been conceptualized and considered. In most contemporary policy discussions, technology is equated almost exclusively with online education or otherwise technology-enhanced classrooms. *The Chronicle of Higher Education*, for example, devoted a special issue to online learning and "MOOC Madness."[36] "Blended learning" (with classes that combine online and traditional instruction) has also been extensively discussed, as have "flipped classrooms" in which digital media is used as a substitute for formal lectures and instructors focus on facilitating discussion and problem-solving during class time.

While attention to technology has focused almost exclusively on the role of digital media in instruction, another fundamental technological change has gone largely unnoticed. In recent decades, technology has dramatically changed our ability to assess student performance and learning outcomes, both longitudinally and systematically, within and across institutions. For example, students are increasingly taking tests not with pencils and multiple-choice answer forms (a twentieth-century technological innovation), but with the assistance of computer interfaces. Computer-based assessments can use adaptive testing, which channels students to different questions based on their prior responses and thus allows for more precise estimates of students' skills and competencies. In addition, technology now exists to grade students' written responses automatically by computer algorithm, thus dramatically reducing the cost of assessing student learning.

Computers have also facilitated the move to performance-based assessment. That is, rather than asking students to recount specific facts, performance-based assessments require them to demonstrate their competence by carrying out applied tasks. The CLA performance task we relied on for this study has this character. The rise of performance-based assessments has coincided with growing pressure to move away from awarding degrees on the basis of course credit hours (i.e., student time in the classroom) and towards conferring them on the basis of demonstrated competencies. In 2013 the federal government began allowing colleges for the first time to have access to federal financing for degrees based on competency-based assessment rather than on traditional credit hours.[37]

While the federal government has been open to recognizing innovation, it has not helped to lead it. It has invested little in developing instruments that could assess different competencies in higher education, or in collecting data that could be used by social scientists to examine what types of activities and practices improve student learning outcomes. With close to five thousand degree-granting institutions in the country, it is terribly counterproductive for each institution to try to develop its own instruments for assessing learning. But that is indeed what is occurring and what is being implicitly promoted by federal policy. With accreditation agencies demanding that higher-education institutions assess learning outcomes, each institution—and, more to the point, each program at each institution—has in practice been asked to develop its own ways of measuring learning outcomes. Many institutions have no capacity to engage meaningfully in this endeavor, as their institutional assessment offices are typically understaffed and already burdened with existing reporting requirements. Academic programs similarly have limited institutional capacity or assessment knowledge to engage in this endeavor. The federal government, however, could provide resources to organizations, schools, or consortia of schools to leverage the potential of technology by developing instruments for measuring student learning in different domains. Once such instruments are developed and tested for reliability and validity, the federal government could also include at least a small number of them in its national longitudinal datasets.

This points to the second transformation facilitated by technology: an unprecedented improvement in the administrative capacity to collect, organize, and analyze individual student learning outcomes at institutional, state, and national levels. A few examples should suffice in conveying the scale and scope of this expanded capacity. At the college level, the National Student Clearinghouse systematically collects enrollment and graduation data for the entire US higher education system. Moreover, millions of freshmen and seniors in thousands of colleges and universities have been surveyed by the National Survey of Student Engagement and the Higher Education Research Institute at UCLA. Government data on employment outcomes is also increasingly being used to identify college graduates' labor market performance. At the elementary and secondary level, several states (including Florida, Texas, and North Carolina), as well as major cities (such as New York, Chicago, Los Angeles, and Houston), are collecting longitudinal data on student performance and enlisting the assistance of expert independent researchers to analyze the relationship between student learning outcomes and the malleable features of schools and classrooms.

This ability to collect and analyze longitudinal data systematically is nothing short of a revolutionary change occurring at the core of the administrative infrastructure responsible for the organization of education. In the beginning of the twentieth century, private foundations in the United States intervened to develop the administrative instruments necessary to organize schooling more effectively in areas where such capacity was lacking. For example, as educational historian Joan Malczewski documents, the Rockefeller Foundation and other philanthropies developed administrative systems—including taxation and administrative reporting requirements—that provided public schooling and indirectly expanded civic participation for African-Americans in the rural South.[38] Related work by historian Ellen Lagemann illustrates how the Carnegie Foundation for the Advancement of Teaching focused on another area requiring systematic attention: higher education. The Carnegie Foundation supported the development of two administrative devices used to organize the allocation and delivery of higher education for the rest of the twentieth century: the credit hour (used as a basis for faculty workload, student degree attainment, and college financing) and a standardized test used to promote meritocratic criteria for college admissions.[39] These foundations realized that the creation of improved administrative capacity was a relatively inexpensive lever to produce large-scale changes in education systems.

While there was considerable debate over whether standardized tests should be designed to measure human intelligence or mastery of academic knowledge, the twentieth century was nonetheless dominated by the use of standardized tests so that, as Nicholas Lemann notes, "the high scorers could be plucked out and given the best schooling and the average and low scorers consigned to a briefer, more limited education."[40] Tests in the twentieth century thus were primarily used to sort and allocate individuals. In the 1930s, however, there was an alternative initiative: the Eight-Year Study, organized by the Progressive Education Association and funded by the Carnegie and Rockefeller foundations—that tracked students longitudinally through college and used tests not for individual placement but to inform curricular design and institutional improvement.[41] Specifically, the goals of the Eight-Year Study were "(1) to fix attention primarily on the nature, the apparent needs, and the actual achievements of the individual student in his successive contacts with existing institutional forms; and (2) to consider the educational performance of school and college as a single cumulative process the parts of which, for any given student, should be complementary."[42] The study documented an average growth in college students' academic performance, from sophomore to senior year, of 0.50 standard deviations, with greater variation within than across institutions. Given the difficulties of collecting and analyzing data at that time, this early experiment, which advocated the use of testing for institutional analysis and improvement, was ahead of its time, and was largely ignored for the next several decades.

In recent decades, however, technology has increased the administrative capacity to use testing data, not just for the allocation of individuals to desirable positions in society, but also to guide policy reform, institutional improvement, and instruction. It is this potential of assessment that holds significant promise for the role of technology in improving learning outcomes. Longitudinal assessment of students can allow policy makers, institutions, and educators to make informed decisions about which educational innovations are desirable and cost-effective. Increased efficiency, productivity, and outcomes are dependent on improved administrative capacity to assess student performance and learning.

The growing use of educational assessment and evaluation to improve school performance and student outcomes in the United States has occurred regardless of whether the federal government has been dominated by the Republican or Democratic party.[43] The extent to which this is being driven by technology and not politics is clear in a recent OECD report on educational assessment and evaluation in twenty-eight countries. The report notes that "most OECD countries now see evaluation and assessment as playing a central strategic role, and are expanding their use."[44] In addition, the report describes in detail how "education systems are placing a stronger focus on measuring student outcomes, allowing comparisons of performance between schools and regions and over time."[45] The report places an emphasis on the importance of aligning measurement with pedagogical goals: "A critical aspect in the effectiveness of evaluation and assessment framework is its proper alignment with educational goals and student learning objectives."[46] While the focus of the OECD report was primarily on elementary and secondary education, its implications for higher education are clear, as is the importance for state governments to set aside adequate resources to collect and analyze such data, as well as to support institutions in their data collection and analysis.

While state and federal governments have a role to play—in providing resources and infrastructure to facilitate development of assessments as well as data collection—the potential to improve college and university performance through clearer articulation of student competencies, rigorous curricular design, and formative assessment cannot be fully realized without faculty and administrator commitment to embracing and adopting these changes internally. Educators have been deeply skeptical of the imposition of centralized accountability, and with good reason. In elementary and secondary education, federal efforts to mandate accountability have often been punitive or inappropriately focused on teacher performance rather than student learning. Higher education, where the role of individual instructors in student learning is recognized as more diffuse, provides a unique opportunity for successful school reform efforts.

Individuals within the system need the moral courage to act to improve our educational system, and to have confidence that in the long run colleges and universities that improve performance will be rewarded by both increased public support and greater student demand. As administrators work to develop assessment cultures and infrastructure, faculty have a professional responsibility to define appropriate standards and use available and emerging instruments to improve student learning. Schools as a whole also have a responsibility to provide clearer information to students on their individual performance. While some aspects of accomplishing this mandate may be daunting, others are fairly simple—such as, for example, reporting two grades on college transcripts: the grade received by the individual and the average grade received by the class as a whole. Students, parents, graduate schools, and employers would then have clearer information on whether a student excelled in his or her coursework or simply excelled in choosing classes with lenient grading standards.

Concerns about centralized accountability will not go away. If educators fail to devise creative solutions for existing problems and neglect to take up the challenge of demonstrating value on their own terms, institutions and programs will be judged on the basis of externally imposed outcomes, such as recent graduates' earnings, which are poorly suited for assessing undergraduate learning. Colleges and universities would thus do well to put in place internal assessment cultures that take advantage of the expanded technological capacity for assessment that is being developed and built around measures that educators can define themselves. The importance of doing this does not rest merely in avoiding less desirable accountability systems (which otherwise will be imposed on higher education), but in it being in the long-term interest of students, institutions, and the country.

Aspiring Adults Adrift

Our research documents that many emerging adults are adrift, but so too are the societal institutions designed to support and guide their development, including the colleges and universities they attend. The graduates we studied uniformly had developed confidence and optimism in their future. What was often missing, however, was a sense of what it took to realize their goals, as well as the skills necessary for such achievement. Rather than engaging in purposeful exploration, many students as undergraduates, and then later as graduates, were adrift. While prolonged periods of late adolescent meandering perhaps might have few long-term consequences for individuals from privileged origins, the costs for others are likely great.

In this book we have highlighted the many ways in which colleges structure life-course outcomes and are implicated in broader patterns of increasingly delayed individual transitions to adulthood. We have shown how the selectivity of the college attended is associated with a broad range of outcomes, including civic participation and relationship formation. College majors also matter for life-course outcomes. Perhaps most importantly, however, given our data and original motivation for the study, we have demonstrated that critical thinking, complex reasoning, and writing skills—a set of generic competencies that colleges aspire to cultivate, and which undergraduates are able to develop under the right conditions—have consequences for individuals. Better performance on the CLA assessment, an instrument designed to measure these generic competencies at the end of college, is associated with a lower likelihood of early-career unemployment, unskilled employment, and job loss. These labor market outcomes, in turn, are associated with other transitions, such as living arrangements and financial independence.

Colleges and universities that hope to improve their graduates' early labor market outcomes might embrace a set of different institutional strategies. One approach would be simply to increase the proportion of graduates who major in fields of study that have early-career payoffs, even though some of those curricular tracks have limited academic rigor associated with them, relatively low levels of student development of general collegiate skills (as measured by gains in CLA performance), and possibly inconsistent long-term career trajectories. We believe that such an approach would be cynical, and not in the general interest of students, schools, or society. A second institutional approach would be limited in character, but consistent with our findings. Specifically, colleges could expand career resources and opportunities for students to gain labor market experience through apprenticeships and internships. Cultivating relationships with a wider range of employers and offering more internships and job opportunities would likely serve to improve many graduates' early labor-market outcomes incrementally.[47] However, this focus on enhancing school-to-work institutional supports is not enough, nor is it consistent with our full set of empirical results.

Our findings, overall, suggest the importance of embracing a third institutional approach: enhancing academic rigor and improving student learning not only of subject-specific skills, but also of generic competencies (such as critical thinking, complex reasoning, and written communication). While those committed to traditional models of liberal arts education have long argued that the development of generic competencies is useful for citizenship and for graduates' capacity to live full and meaningful individual lives, we have shown that these skills also have labor market payoffs over and above the specific fields of study chosen. Colleges and universities thus have a responsibility to address the lack of academic rigor and limited learning we have reported. To prevent graduates from continuing to be adrift in the labor market following college, higher-education institutions could do more than simply shift the composition of graduates' fields of study or enhance career support services; they should ensure academic rigor and the engagement of all students, regardless of field of study, to promote positive outcomes in multiple and important domains in their lives. While a student's CLA performance at the point of graduation reflects not just his or her college curriculum, but twenty-plus years of human development, we have demonstrated that colleges indeed can contribute to a student's performance on these measures.

Colleges also could do more to help students develop the attitudes and dispositions they need to reach their aspirations. In chapter 1 we explicitly raised the issue of whether colleges should be concerned with students taking on extensive debt to socialize rather than study in college, only to find themselves underemployed after graduation, living at home with their parents while reporting high levels of individual satisfaction and well-being. As educators, we think they should be concerned. Consumer satisfaction is not a worthy aim for colleges and universities. A century ago, John Dewey wrote: "What the best and wisest parent wants for his own child, that must the community want for all of its children."[48] Colleges and universities need to attend to that vision—not to make schools narrower, but instead to align educational experiences more closely with adult success. Graduating large numbers of students who have attained high grades with little effort and achieved limited improvement in competencies such as critical thinking, complex reasoning, and writing is a disservice to the students who enroll in these schools, the families who put trust in these institutions, and the larger society that will be dependent on the productivity and citizenship of these graduates in the future.

Since the average four-year college student today studies alone a little more than an hour per day, and since a significant proportion of undergraduates do not have courses with either substantial reading or writing requirements, educators need to come together to agree on rigorous academic standards designed to promote both the development of generic competencies and subject-specific content mastery in occupationally related majors, disciplines, or interdisciplinary fields of study. Student exposure to rigorous coursework and high standards might also produce positive changes in the affective domain. College students today are often exposed to institutional settings that reward minimal effort with high grades (students who reported studying alone less than five hours per week had a 3.2 grade point average), and academic dishonesty is rampant and goes largely unpunished. For example, one recent study of students' self-reported cheating on exams at nine colleges and universities found that cheating increased from 26 percent in 1963 to 52 percent in 1993.[49] Given the lack of standards and rigor, it is hard to imagine that a student with limited academic engagement would greatly develop in affective areas such as civic engagement, moral development, leadership skills, and multicultural tolerance, regardless of whether his or her courses focused on Jacques Derrida or John Rawls.[50] Formal courses focused specifically on virtues, morality, and ethics are likely to be less effective at promoting desired dispositions, attitudes, and values than are the larger lessons learned and internalized through student experiences with school structure, relationships with educators, and interaction with adult authorities.[51]

Colleges and universities, not just students, have too often been academically adrift in recent decades. As we have attempted to highlight throughout this book, both students and the schools they attend exist in larger structural and cultural contexts that have created the conditions under which the observed learning outcomes occur. Widespread cultural commitment to consumer choice and individual rights, self-fulfillment and sociability, and well-being and a broader therapeutic ethic leave little room for students or schools to embrace programs that promote academic rigor. The serious promotion of student learning, let alone systematic use of assessments to improve academic outcomes, can be seen as a thankless task— especially when students as clients demand, and government resources subsidize and enable, a focus on a different and more easily delivered model of higher education which emphasizes the social aspects of college.

The hard work required to make these improvements will require courage and determination. Many stakeholders, however, have already begun the arduous task of collaborating to define desired competencies, align curricula, develop improved assessments, and commit their institutions to programs to improve student learning. They have taken this path not because it is easy, but because they believe the work will yield valuable individual, institutional, and societal dividends. Their efforts and investments serve as an example to students of how one embarks on purposeful paths of self-improvement.

Appendix A
Data, Methods, and Statistical Analyses

Analyses presented in this book build on the Determinants of College Learning (DCL) dataset, which was developed in partnership with the Council for Aid to Education (CAE). The CAE initiated the Collegiate Learning Assessment (CLA) Longitudinal Project in the fall of 2005, administering a short survey and the CLA instrument to a sample of freshmen at four-year institutions. The same students were contacted for the sophomore-year follow-up in the spring of 2007 and the senior-year follow-up in the spring of 2009. The Social Science Research Council (SSRC) joined the project during the sophomore-year follow-up, broadening the original CAE questionnaire to include additional survey questions regarding students' sociodemographic backgrounds, high school characteristics, and collegiate experiences. The SSRC collected course transcript data from participating institutions and obtained survey and test assessment data from the CAE for students who signed the SSRC consent form permitting the release of this information.

The senior-year sample included 1,666 respondents with valid CLA scores. Table A1.1 provides comparison of this sample to the national sample of college students attending four-year institutions from the Beginning Postsecondary Students (BPS) Longitudinal Study. To make the samples comparable, we restricted the BPS sample to traditional-age students (nineteen years old or younger as of December 31, 2003) who entered four-year institutions in the 2003–4 academic year. Given the spacing of BPS data collection, we used the second wave of data, capturing students in their junior year (as opposed to the senior year, as was the case for DCL). These comparisons indicate that our senior sample includes a slightly higher proportion of females and students from highly educated families (those whose parents completed graduate or professional degrees), as well as students with somewhat higher SAT scores. The high school GPA distribution and the proportion of students for whom English is not the primary language are virtually identical in both datasets, as is the average college GPA. Characteristics of the senior-year sample thus correspond reasonably well with the characteristics of students from a nationally representative sample.

Following the senior year, SSRC partnered with Harris Interactive to conduct annual surveys in the spring of 2010 and 2011, as well as interviews with a subsample of respondents in 2011. The CAE provided Harris Interactive with student contact information for the purpose of the follow-ups. For students who consented to participate, Harris Interactive conducted surveys and interviews and provided SSRC with the data containing student IDs that could be matched to the college data collected by the CAE. The 2011 survey included 967 respondents. Among those, 918 completed bachelor's degrees and had valid 2009 CLA scores, and represent the 2011 analytic sample. The interview sample was drawn from this 2011 graduate sample, stratified by gender and labor market outcomes, and included 80 respondents. Interview data was transcribed verbatim and analyzed in Dedoose. When using interview data to describe distribution of responses, two coders coded the data independently and a third coder resolved any inconsistencies. Codes included a combination of preexisting categories and new categories that emerged from the data analysis. Survey and interview protocols are included in appendix B.

While this appendix describes our primary quantitative analyses of the DCL sample, additional data sources were used throughout the chapters to complement patterns observed in the sample by presenting national trends for outcomes examined. Information regarding secondary data sources is included in the text, along with footnotes accompanying specific figures in each chapter. While secondary data sources provide a valuable portrayal of young adults' transitions, a unique aspect of our primary data is the Collegiate Learning Assessment (CLA), an objective measure of critical thinking, complex reasoning, and writing. Many analyses presented in the book thus highlight the relationship between CLA and post-college outcomes.

The Collegiate Learning Assessment (CLA) consists of three open-ended, as opposed to multiple-choice, assessment components: a performance task and two analytical writing tasks (make an argument and break an argument). According to the developers of this test, the CLA was designed to assess "core outcomes espoused by all of higher education—critical thinking, complex reasoning, problem solving and writing."[1] These *general skills* are "the broad competencies that are mentioned in college and university mission statements."[2] While the CLA as a whole is considered by some as state of the art, the performance task component of the test is the best developed and most sophisticated part of the assessment instrument; it is the component that the Organisation for Economic Cooperation and Development adopted for its cross-national assessment of higher education students' generic skill strand in the Assessment of Higher Education Learning Outcomes (AHELO) project.

We use students' scores on the performance task of the CLA as an indicator of their critical thinking, complex reasoning, and writing skills. In addition to being the most developed, this performance task was the most uniformly administered component across time and institutions. The CAE, the developer and administrator of the CLA, has published several examples of representative performance tasks and scoring rubrics online at http://www.collegiatelearning assessment.org/. For each performance task, students are provided with a "real world" scenario and a library of documents relevant to the scenario. Students have ninety minutes to read the scenario and accompanying materials, analyze and synthesize available information, and write a response to a question or a set of questions posed. All the materials are accessed by computer, and the responses are also written on computers.

Trained raters evaluate student responses based on rubrics developed by the CAE, the information on which is provided on the CAE website noted above. CAE began with a holistic approach to generic collegiate skills, which presumes that critical thinking, complex reasoning, and writing are intertwined and thus should be evaluated jointly. The CAE thus provided only one score for the CLA performance task, which means that we do not have separate component scores for the different types of skills assessed by the CLA.[3] A study organized by the Fund for the Improvement of Postsecondary Education (FIPSE) examined the instrumental construct validity of the CLA, ACT's Collegiate Assessment of Academic Proficiency (CAAP), and ETS's Measure of Academic Proficiency and Progress (MAPP) by administering all three tests in thirteen schools, with more than 1,100 students participating. While CAAP and MAPP rely on a multiple-choice format, score reliability with the CLA was high when considered at the aggregate school-level (correlations of .75 to .84).[4] All three instruments are accepted for reporting student gains in general collegiate skills by the Voluntary System of Accountability (VSA).

Statistical Analyses

Chapter 2

Statistical analyses in chapter 2 focus on two outcomes: senior-year CLA performance and graduate school attendance (for definitions of these outcomes, and all other variables, please see table A2.1). Analyses of CLA performance are based on the senior-year sample—that is, students who were in the sample in the spring of 2009 and had valid CLA scores at that time as well as at the beginning of college (fall 2005). The characteristics of the sample are described in table A1.2.

For regression analyses of CLA performance, we estimate senior-year CLA scores while controlling for freshman-year CLA scores (table A2.2). To consider how different dimensions of undergraduate education are related to CLA performance, we focus on two factors: college selectivity and field of study. We examine the relationship between these variables and CLA performance while controlling for a host of individual attributes, including sociodemographic characteristics (gender, race/ethnicity, parental education, and whether English was the home language) and academic preparation (SAT scores and high school GPA). Moreover, all models include a dummy variable indicating whether students attended high schools that were 70 percent or more non-white. While we considered other high school characteristics (such as public or private control, and percentage of students receiving free or reduced-price lunch), this is the only high-school–level characteristic that had a statistically significant relationship to earlier analyses reported in *Academically Adrift*. All models are adjusted for clustering of students within schools.

Models in table A2.2 serve as the basis for figure 2.4 (model 1) and figure 2.5 (model 2), which report predicted CLA scores by institutional selectivity and college major respectively. These predicted scores were estimated using the Stata "margins" command, with all but the variable of interest held at the mean. For college selectivity, predictions are made for schools of "high selectivity" representing one standard deviation above the mean, and "low selectivity" representing one standard deviation below the mean.

In addition, chapter 2 examines one post-college outcome: graduate school attendance. For this outcome, we analyze the sample of college graduates who completed the 2011 survey. The characteristics of the sample are described in the second column of table A1.2. The majority of respondents (86 percent) completed their bachelor's degrees in 2009, meaning within four-years of college entry. One percent of this sample completed college in 2011 and the remaining students completed college in 2010. For most of the respondents, 2011 thus represents two years since college graduation (or what we refer to as two years since on-time graduation).

At the time of the 2011 survey, students were asked whether they were enrolled in graduate school, whether they attended full-time or part-time, and in what type of programs they were enrolled. A few students who reported being enrolled in pre-baccalaureate programs (associate degrees or certificates) were excluded from analysis. Table A2.3 presents a multinomial logistic regression analysis predicting whether students were (a) enrolled in full-time master's, doctorate, or professional programs; (b) enrolled in part-time or other programs (i.e., students who chose "other" among program choices); or (c) not enrolled in graduate school. In this analysis we focus on the relationships between the students' senior-year CLA performance and institutional selectivity with their graduate school attendance. In order to examine the relationship between college major and graduate school attendance we had to conduct a binary logistic regression analysis, due to the small number of cases in specific college major categories across different graduate school outcomes. Logistic regression analysis examines whether graduates enrolled in full-time master's, doctoral, or professional programs as opposed to not having enrolled in any programs, or having enrolled in part-time and other programs. Similar results are obtained if only students who are not enrolled in graduate school are used as a reference. In addition to the key variables of interest, graduate school analyses control for students' sociodemographic characteristics (gender, race, and level of parents' education) and are adjusted for clustering of students within institutions.

Following models in table A2.3, we highlight the results for our key variables of interest by calculating predicted probabilities, which are estimated using the Stata "margins" command while keeping all other variables at their mean. Figure 2.7 reports predicted probabilities from model 2 for two outcomes: (1) enrolling in full-time master's, doctoral, or professional programs and (2) enrolling in part-time and other programs. The results are presented for students with "high" and "low" CLA scores, each category representing one standard deviation above and below the mean. Figure 2.8 shows the predicted probabilities of enrolling in full-time master's, doctoral, or professional programs across different fields of study (based on model 3).

Chapter 3

Chapter 3 focuses on labor market outcomes of our cohort of college graduates. We examined a range of outcomes, from income and unemployment to job search methods and job satisfaction. Definitions of labor market outcomes are provided in table A3.1, followed by their distributions in table A3.2. Analyses of current labor market outcomes are restricted to college graduates who were not enrolled in graduate school full-time and who had valid employment status information at the time of the 2011 survey ($N = 618$). Analyses of respondents losing a job in the prior year were conducted on a slightly larger sample of all individuals who held jobs, and were thus at risk of losing them, over the prior year ($N = 900$). Characteristics of the current labor market sample are presented in the final column of table A1.2. The actual number of cases varies across analyses due to additional restrictions (such as restricting to individuals who were employed) or missing cases on outcome measures.

After presenting descriptive statistics on graduates' labor market outcomes, we present results from a series of multivariate regression analyses, focusing in particular on the extent to which selectivity of the college attended, choice of college major, and performance on the CLA at the end of college were related to these outcomes. Table A3.6 also considers whether the job search method (and especially finding employment through college or an internship) was related to avoiding unskilled employment. All regression models control for sociodemographic characteristics (including gender, race/ethnicity, and parents' level of education) and are adjusted for clustering of students within institutions.

We begin by considering the most negative labor market outcome, unemployment (table A3.3), followed by whether an individual lost a job in the prior year (table A3.4). For graduates who were employed full-time, we examine their income, in both dollar and natural log forms (table A3.5).[5] Since income tends to be quite unstable during early labor market transitions, we also examine the characteristics of the jobs held by all respondents employed at the time of the survey. We distinguish marginal unskilled occupations from other jobs applying a coding scheme developed by sociologists Robert Hauser and John Robert Warren.[6] Hauser and Warren classified occupations in each of the 1990 census categories based on earnings and educational levels of incumbents. We rely on the educational dimension of their classification, which represents the started logit of the percentage of individuals in the employed civilian labor force who had completed at least some college as of 1990. The started logit transformation takes the following form: $ln\,[(p + 1)/(100 - p + 1)]$, where p is the percentage of respondents above a threshold level. We classify as unskilled occupations all jobs in which the majority of occupants have completed *less than even one year of college*. While, of course, a few jobs were difficult to classify (e.g., youth worker, swimming pool manager, pregnancy advocate, child welfare attendant), the vast majority of cases were quite easy to categorize, and our results were not significantly affected by the coding of ambiguous cases.[7] Some examples of unskilled occupations in our data include server, waitress, school bus driver, shipping dock loader, and nanny.

We use this unskilled occupation classification for a number of analyses. First, we consider whether someone is in an unskilled occupation if they were employed (table A3.6). Second, we consider whether someone is able to *avoid* both unemployment and unskilled employment, which we refer to as a positive employment outcome (table A3.7). Finally, we also include underemployment (working less than twenty hours per week) in our definition of successful employment, and model whether an individual is able to *avoid* negative employment—defined broadly as unemployment, unskilled employment, or underemployment, all three of which we refer to as positive full-time employment outcome (second half of table A3.7).

Throughout the chapter we highlight statistically significant results by reporting predicted probabilities for different outcomes in the figures. We calculated predicted probabilities for different majors, CLA scores, and college selectivity. For college major, we calculated predicted probabilities for each category. For continuous measures of CLA scores and college selectivity, we calculated predicted probabilities for "high" and "low" categories, in which "high" represents one standard deviation above the mean of the particular measure, and "low" represents one standard deviation below the mean. Predicted probabilities were calculated using the Stata "margins" command, with all but the variable of interest held at the mean.

Chapter 4

While chapter 3 focused on labor market outcomes, chapter 4 examined a range of social, cultural, and civic outcomes associated with transition to adulthood. Definitions of the outcomes examined in chapter 4 are provided in table A4.1, followed by the distribution of key measures in table A4.2. These analyses are based on a sample of college graduates who participated in the 2011 survey ($N = 918$). Characteristics of the sample are presented in table A1.2. Most of the measures in this chapter were examined primarily descriptively, as we aimed to present an overall portrayal of graduates' lives approximately two years after on-time degree completion. Some of the outcomes were also examined in a multivariate regression framework. All regression models control for sociodemographic characteristics (including gender, race/ethnicity, and parents' level of education) and are adjusted for clustering of students within institutions.

We begin by examining whether graduates lived with their parents or relatives (i.e., lived at home) during the 2011 survey (table A4.3), as well as whether they had received financial assistance from parents or adult relatives over the course of the past year (table A4.4). Since the preceding two chapters have described relationships between undergraduate experiences (including CLA performance and institutional selectivity) and labor-market and graduate-school outcomes, in this chapter we control for those undergraduate experiences but focus instead on the associations between different post-college outcomes. In particular, we explore whether challenging labor market circumstances—such as being unemployed or working in an unskilled job—are related to living at home or receiving financial assistance from parents. In those analyses we also control for full-time enrollment in graduate school.[8] Moreover, we consider whether other financial conditions—having college loan debt, especially high debt (i.e., over $30,000)—is related to the likelihood of a college graduate living at home or receiving financial assistance from parents. In the model predicting financial assistance, we also examine whether graduates who lived at home were more likely to report receiving financial assistance from parents than were those who did not live at home.

The third set of outcomes examined in chapter 4 focuses on romantic partners (table A4.5). The 2011 survey included questions about graduates' relationship status. Due to the age of the respondents, few were married, but some were cohabitating and others were in serious romantic relationships. We combine these three categories—married, cohabitating, and in a serious romantic relationship—to examine whether graduates had partners in 2011. For those who had partners, we estimate a logistic regression model predicting whether the partner was highly educated (i.e., had attended or completed a four-year college, as compared to not having attended or completed a four-year college). Finally, among graduates who were partnered with college-educated individuals (who had attended or completed a four-year college), we estimate the selectivity of their partners' institutions using OLS regression. For all partner outcomes, our primary variables of interests are two institutional-level characteristics: college selectivity and college female percentage (i.e., the percentage of students who were female at the institutions attended by the respondents, obtained from the Integrated Postsecondary Education Data System, or IPEDS).

The final series of outcomes examined in the multivariate regression context in chapter 4 are two measures referring to graduates' civic and political awareness (table A4.6). More specifically, we estimate the probability that graduates exhibit low levels of civic and political awareness by examining two outcomes: (1) reading newspapers online or in print monthly or never, and (2) discussing politics and public affairs monthly or never. The reference category includes individuals who read newspapers or discussed politics and public affairs more frequently.

To highlight statistically significant results, we report predicted probabilities for different outcomes throughout chapter 4. Predicted probabilities were calculated using the Stata "margins" command, with all but the variable of interest held at the mean. For all of the continuous measures, we calculated predicted probabilities for "high" and "low" categories, where "high" represents one standard deviation above the mean of the particular measure, and "low" represents one standard deviation below the mean.

Table A1.1. Student characteristics for DCL and BPS samples (proportions for categorical variables and means for continuous measures)

	DCL sample	BPS sample[a]
Sociodemographic characteristics		
Male	0.35	0.42
Race/ethnicity		
White	0.69	0.71
African-American	0.16	0.08
Hispanic	0.07	0.09
Asian	0.04	0.07
Other racial/ethnic groups	0.04	0.05
English not primary language	0.10	0.10
Parents' education		
High school or less	0.15	0.16
Some college	0.19	0.21
College degree	0.27	0.30
Graduate / professional degree	0.39	0.32
Academic characteristics		
High school GPA		
D or lower	0.00	0.00
C– / C	0.00	0.00
C / B–	0.03	0.04
B– / B	0.08	0.08
B / A–	0.37	0.32
A– / A	0.52	0.53
SAT	1157.04	1087.26
College GPA	3.27	3.16

[a] Beginning Postsecondary Students (BPS) Longitudinal Study, 2003–4 cohort.
The sample is restricted to students who entered four-year institutions and were 19 years of age or younger as of December 31, 2003. Students in the DCL sample are seniors, while students in the BPS sample are juniors.

Table A1.2. Characteristics of the samples used in the study

	Senior-year sample Chapter 2	2011 college graduate sample Chapters 2, 3, and 4	2011 labor market sample* Chapter 3
Sociodemographic characteristics			
Male	34.69	29.19	29.61
Race/ethnicity			
White	68.07	71.79	71.69
African American	16.09	12.85	11.97
Asian	7.38	7.95	7.93
Other racial/ ethnic groups	8.46	7.41	8.41
Parents' education			
High school or less	12.18	11.56	11.33
Some college	19.39	19.30	19.90
College degree	29.71	2.68	29.29
Graduate / professional degree	38.72	40.46	39.48
Institutional selectivity			
Continuous measure	1041.54	1052.24	1048.45
	(141.94)	(140.14)	(142.05)
Categorical (%)[2]			
Less selective	19.99	18.36	19.81
Selective	59.18	58.91	57.14
More selective	20.83	22.73	23.05
College major (%)			
Business	11.64	10.68	13.32
Education/social work	6.00		
Health	6.18		
Education / social work / health[1]		12.53	13.75
Social science / humanities	36.31	35.73	35.23
Math / natural science	18.73	18.63	13.59
Engineering / computer science	8.40	8.61	8.90

Table A1.2. *(continued)*

	Senior-year sample Chapter 2	2011 college graduate sample Chapters 2, 3, and 4	2011 labor market sample* Chapter 3
Communications	4.56		
Other	8.16		
Communications / other[1]		13.83	15.21
Senior CLA **performance**	**1223.06** (184.53)	**1252.34** (191.00)	**1247.67** (192.56)
Sample size	1666	918	618

[1] Categories combined for the 2011 sample, due to small number of cases.
[2] Classification based on the 2009 sample, with less selective institutions approximating the bottom quintile and more selective ones the top quintile.
* Sample of 2011 college graduates who were not enrolled full-time in graduate school and had valid employment status information.

Table A2.1. Description of variables considered in chapter 2

Variable name	Variable coding
Outcomes	
Senior CLA performance	Students' scores on the performance task component of the Collegiate Learning Assessment (CLA) in the spring of their senior year.
Graduate school attendance	Students' reports of enrollment in graduate school in 2011, aggregated into the following categories: not enrolled in graduate school; enrolled in full-time master's, doctorate, or professional programs; and enrolled part-time or in other types of programs.
College experiences	
College major	Dummy variables indicating students' self-reported undergraduate majors, aggregated into the following broad categories: business (reference), education/social work, engineering/computer science, communications, health, social science/humanities, science/math, and other. In the graduate school models, some of the categories are combined due to the small number of cases.

Table A2.1. *(continued)*

Variable name	Variable coding
College selectivity	Continuous variable equaling the 25th percentile of the SAT scores for the incoming freshman class at each institution. Data on SAT scores were obtained from the Integrated Postsecondary Education System (IPEDS) database. Predicted probabilities are calculated for "high" and "low" selectivity schools, categories indicating institutions one standard deviation above and below the mean, respectively. Some descriptive analyses use dummy variables indicating more selective, selective, and less selective institutions. More selective colleges are defined as schools with students scoring 1,180 or higher on their combined SAT at the 25th percentile; less selective colleges are defined as schools with students scoring 920 or lower on their combined SAT at the 25th percentile. These cutoffs approximate the top and bottom quintiles of the senior-year institutional selectivity distribution. Selective schools fall between these cutoffs.

Academic preparation and sociodemographic characteristics

SAT score	Continuous measure of students' combined math and verbal SAT scores (or ACT scores converted to an SAT scale, if SAT scores were not available) as reported by the institutions. The measure is standardized with a mean of 0 and a standard deviation of 1.
High school GPA	College reports of students' high school GPA on a 4.0 scale. High school GPAs reported to colleges on a 0–100 scale were converted to a 4.0 scale. If the college reported that a high school GPA was missing, this was replaced by the student's self-reported overall grades. The measure is standardized with a mean of 0 and a standard deviation of 1.
Parents' education	Dummy variables indicating the highest degree attained by either parent and categorized into: high school or less, some college (includes associate and technical degrees), college degree (reference), and graduate/professional degree.
Race/ethnicity	Dummy variables indicating students' self-reported racial/ethnic group, categorized as white (reference), African-American, Asian, or other racial/ethnic group.

Table A2.1. (*continued*)

Variable name	Variable coding
Academic preparation and sociodemographic characteristics	
Male	Dummy variable indicating that student's gender is male.
Non-English home language	Dummy variable indicating students who reported that English was not the primary language spoken in their home when they were growing up.
HS 70% or more nonwhite	Dummy variable indicating that students' high schools enrolled 70% or more nonwhite students (i.e., American Indians/Alaskan Natives, Asians/Pacific Islanders, Hispanic, and/or African-American students). Based on the Common Core of Data (CCD) and Private School Universe Survey (PSS).
Freshman CLA performance	Students' scores on the performance task component of the Collegiate Learning Assessment (CLA) in the fall of their freshman year.

Table A2.2. OLS regression models predicting senior CLA scores by college selectivity and field of study, controlling for sociodemographic and academic characteristics

	Baseline Coefficient (SE)	Model 1 Coefficient (SE)	Model 2 Coefficient (SE)	Model 3 Coefficient (SE)
College selectivity^		31.96 ** (8.55)		32.10 ** (9.14)
Field of study				
Education / social work			4.00 (26.15)	7.21 (26.72)
Engineering / computer science			18.02 (16.52)	23.95 (16.15)
Communications			5.90 (17.74)	0.78 (19.99)
Health			14.15 (15.19)	15.16 (15.48)
Social science / humanities			31.40 * (13.63)	14.03 (15.08)
Science / math			26.14 (16.86)	10.16 (16.72)

Table A2.2. *(continued)*

	Baseline Coefficient (SE)	Model 1 Coefficient (SE)	Model 2 Coefficient (SE)	Model 3 Coefficient (SE)
Other			11.45 (17.83)	–3.15 (18.75)
Academic characteristics				
SAT score^	66.35 ** (7.49)	49.31 ** (6.84)	62.98 ** (7.20)	48.60 ** (6.85)
High school GPA^	–5.27 (5.32)	–5.36 (5.49)	–5.03 (5.61)	–5.59 (5.62)
Freshman CLA performance^	35.65 ** (5.56)	34.15 ** (5.74)	34.60 ** (5.42)	33.63 ** (5.53)
Sociodemographic characteristics				
Male	–5.14 (9.50)	–3.12 (9.09)	–3.99 (10.18)	–4.51 (9.91)
Non-English home language	–5.90 (12.84)	–13.50 (11.91)	–6.25 (12.93)	–12.78 (12.04)
HS 70% or more nonwhite	–13.26 (10.86)	–10.13 (10.67)	–14.44 (11.21)	–11.13 (11.11)
Race/ethnicity (reference: white)				
African American	–80.20 ** (16.39)	–68.71 ** (18.75)	–84.42 ** (17.42)	–70.10 ** (18.42)
Asian	–8.01 (21.01)	–7.26 (19.12)	–10.74 (20.67)	–8.35 (18.97)
Hispanic or other racial/ ethnic groups	–19.68 (12.00)	–20.61 † (10.42)	–23.67 † (12.93)	–21.97 † (11.15)
Parents' education (reference: college degree)				
High school or less	5.95 (14.81)	9.89 (14.61)	5.26 (14.78)	10.24 (14.71)
Some college	–10.10 (11.88)	–3.71 (11.85)	–9.39 (11.58)	–2.99 (11.78)
Graduate / professional degree	15.99 * (7.31)	9.18 (7.12)	14.02 (7.44)	9.46 (7.03)
Intercept	1239.06 ** (11.27)	1238.57 ** (9.21)	1220.86 ** (15.18)	1229.16 ** (16.66)
R^2	0.35	0.36	0.35	0.37

†$p < .10$; *$p < .05$; **$p < .01$.

$N = 1,666$. Analyses are adjusted for clustering of students within schools.

^ Variables are standardized with a mean of 0 and a standard deviation of 1.

Table A2.3. Regression analyses predicting graduate school attendance by CLA performance, college selectivity, field of study, and sociodemographic characteristics

	Model 1		Model 2		Model 3
	Full-time master's, doctoral, or prof. program	Attend part-time or enrolled in other prog.	Full-time master's, doctoral, or prof. program	Attend part-time or enrolled in other prog.	Full-time master's, doctoral, or prof. program
	*Multinomial logistic regression^^*		*Multinomial logistic regression^^*		*Logistic regression^^^*
Senior CLA performance^	0.15 **	−0.02	0.12 †	−0.01	0.11 †
	(0.05)	(0.12)	(0.06)	(0.12)	(0.07)
College selectivity^			0.11	−0.03	−0.03
			(0.09)	(0.14)	(0.11)
Field of study (reference: business)					
Education / social work / health					0.50
					(0.37)
Engineering / computer science					0.80 **
					(0.29)
Social science / humanities					0.87 **
					(0.25)
Science / math					1.60 **
					(0.27)
Communications / other					0.52
					(0.33)
Sociodemographic characteristics					
Male	−0.03	−0.16	−0.01	−0.17	0.00
	(0.12)	(0.20)	(0.13)	(0.20)	(0.14)

Table A2.3. *(continued)*

	Model 1		Model 2		Model 3
	Full-time master's, doctoral, or prof. program	Attend part-time or enrolled in other prog.	Full-time master's, doctoral, or prof. program	Attend part-time or enrolled in other prog.	Full-time master's, doctoral, or prof. program
Race/ethnicity (reference: white)					
African-American	0.45 *	0.39	0.52 *	0.37	0.36
	(0.22)	(0.31)	(0.24)	(0.32)	(0.29)
Asian	0.04	-0.21	0.05	-0.21	-0.03
	(0.43)	(0.63)	(0.42)	(0.64)	(0.43)
Hispanic and other racial/ ethnic groups	-0.15	1.11 **	-0.15	1.11 **	-0.44
	(0.38)	(0.37)	(0.37)	(0.37)	(0.43)
Parents' education (reference: college degree)					
High school or less	0.29	-0.03	0.31	-0.04	0.39
	(0.28)	(0.50)	(0.28)	(0.51)	(0.28)
Some college	0.02	0.68 **	0.05	0.67 **	-0.06
	(0.20)	(0.24)	(0.21)	(0.25)	(0.23)
Graduate / professional degree	0.17	0.19	0.14	0.20	0.09
	(0.22)	(0.30)	(0.22)	(0.31)	(0.21)
Intercept	-0.87 **	-2.21 **	-0.89 **	-2.20 **	-1.80 **
	(0.17)	(0.27)	(0.17)	(0.27)	(0.30)
-2LL	1572.65		1570.96		1051.08
AIC	1608.65		1610.98		1081.08

† $p < .10$; *$p < .05$; **$p < .01$.

$N = 901$. Analyses are adjusted for clustering of students within schools.

^Variables are standardized with a mean of 0 and a standard deviation of 1.

^^ Reference category includes students not enrolled in graduate school.

^^^ Reference category includes students not enrolled in graduate school, enrolled part-time, or enrolled in other programs (i.e., other than master's, doctoral, or professional).

Table A3.1. Description of post-college outcomes examined in chapter 3

Variable name	Variable coding
Unemployed	Dummy variable indicating whether graduates were unemployed (i.e., not working and looking for work)
Underemployed	Dummy variable indicating whether graduates were working less than 20 hours per week
Part-time job	Dummy variable indicating whether graduates were working between 20 and 35 hours per week
Full-time job	Dummy variable indicating whether graduates were working more than 35 hours per week
Unskilled occupation	Dummy variable indicating whether graduates had a job in which the majority of incumbents had not completed even a year of college
Positive employment outcome	Dummy variable indicating that graduates had avoided unemployment and unskilled employment
Positive full-time employment outcome	Dummy variable indicating that graduates had avoided unemployment, underemployment, and unskilled employment
Job loss	Dummy variable indicating that graduates had lost a job in the preceding 12 months
Job search method*	Graduates' responses to the question "How did you find your job?" Responses were collapsed into four categories: formal means; college as an institution; internship, volunteer opportunity, or former employer; and family and friends.
Job satisfaction	Graduates' responses to the statement "Please rate your overall satisfaction with your primary job." Answers were recorded on a scale of 1 (very dissatisfied) to 7 (very satisfied).
Income	Graduates' responses to the question "What is your average annual salary in your primary job?" Response categories were in increments of $10,000 (i.e., $1–$9,999; $10,000–$19,999, . . . $50,000–$59,999, and $60,000 or more). A continuous variable was created from these categories, equaling the midpoint of each category (e.g., $1–$9,999 equals $5,000).

Note: Descriptions of college-related measures and sociodemographic characteristics are available in table A2.1.
*Categories were collapsed for analysis. Please see the survey instrument for original categories.

Table A3.2. Summary statistics for post-college outcomes examined in chapter 3

Variable	Percentage
Employment status	
Unemployed	7
Underemployed (< 20 hours)	4
Part-time job (20–35 hours)	12
Full-time job (< $20K)	15
Full-time job ($20–30K)	15
Full-time job ($30–40K)	21
Full-time job (> 40K)	26
Occupational status (selected categories)	
Underemployed (< 20 hours) skilled	3
Underemployed (< 20 hours) unskilled	1
Part-time or full-time (> 20 hours) unskilled	12
Job search method	
College as an institution	17
Internship, volunteering, or former employer	25
Family and friends	20
Formal means	38

Note: All analyses are restricted to graduates not enrolled full-time in graduate school.

Table A3.3. Logistic regression models predicting unemployment by CLA performance, college selectivity, field of study, and sociodemographic characteristics

	Model 1 Coefficient (SE)	Model 2 Coefficient (SE)
Senior CLA performance ˆ	−0.27 *	−0.21 †
	(0.13)	(0.12)
College selectivity ˆ		−0.19
		(0.22)
Field of study (reference: business)		
Education / social work / health		1.31 †
		(0.78)
Engineering / computer science		0.41
		(0.99)
Social science / humanities		1.18 †
		(0.63)
Science / math		0.63
		(0.68)
Communications / other		1.40 †
		(0.76)
Sociodemographic characteristics		
Male	0.21	0.45
	(0.28)	(0.31)
Race/ ethnicity (reference: white)		
African–American	0.14	0.24
	(0.35)	(0.47)
Asian	0.46	0.75
	(0.47)	(0.49)
Hispanic and other racial/ethnic	−0.20	−0.01
groups	(0.61)	(0.68)
Parents' education (reference: college degree)		
High school or less	0.18	0.17
	(0.58)	(0.57)
Some college	0.13	0.03
	(0.50)	(0.49)
Graduate / professional degree	−0.11	−0.06
	(0.39)	(0.43)
Intercept	−2.78 **	−3.91 **
	(0.31)	(0.67)
Pseudo R^2	0.02	0.04

†$p < .10$; *$p < .05$; **$p < .01$.

$N = 618$. Analyses are adjusted for clustering of students within schools.

ˆ Variables are standardized with a mean of 0 and standard deviation of 1.

Table A3.4. Logistic regression models predicting job loss by CLA performance, college selectivity, field of study, and sociodemographic characteristics

	Model 1 Coefficient (SE)	Model 2 Coefficient (SE)
Senior CLA performance ˆ	−0.34 * (0.14)	−0.28 * (0.14)
College selectivity ˆ		−0.17 (0.16)
Field of study (reference: business)		
Education / social work / health		0.48 (0.42)
Engineering/ computer science		−0.33 (0.57)
Social science / humanities		0.52 (0.58)
Science / math		−0.40 (0.34)
Communications / other		0.57 (0.52)
Sociodemographic characteristics *Male*	0.51 † (0.30)	0.68 * (0.33)
Race/ethnicity (reference: white)		
African American	−0.06 (0.38)	−0.07 (0.43)
Asian	−0.30 (0.63)	−0.12 (0.65)
Hispanic and other racial/ethnic groups	0.37 (0.51)	0.43 (0.54)
Parents' education (reference: college degree)		
High school or less	−0.36 (0.37)	−0.39 (0.36)
Some college	−0.31 (0.28)	−0.36 (0.29)
Graduate / professional degree	−0.47 (0.31)	−0.43 (0.33)
Intercept	−2.39 ** (0.16)	−2.75 ** (0.41)
Pseudo R^2	0.03	0.05

†$p < .10$; *$p < .05$; **$p < .01$.
$N = 900$. Analyses are adjusted for clustering of students within schools.
ˆ Variables are standardized with a mean of 0 and standard deviation of 1.

Table A3.5. OLS regression models predicting annual income by CLA performance, college selectivity, field of study, and sociodemographic characteristics

	Income in dollars		Logged income (*ln*)	
	Model 1 Coefficient (SE)	Model 2 Coefficient (SE)	Model 1 Coefficient (SE)	Model 2 Coefficient (SE)
Senior CLA performance^	323.35 (652.19)	102.54 (783.21)	−0.01 (0.03)	−0.02 (0.03)
College selectivity^		1820.12 (1245.56)		0.07 (0.04)
Field of study (reference: business)				
Education / social work / health		−3130.16 (3584.93)		−0.14 (0.14)
Engineering / computer science		11621.46 ** (2493.49)		0.32 ** (0.08)
Social science / humanities		−6404.94 * (2724.11)		−0.20 * (0.11)
Science / math		−6630.14 † (3455.84)		−0.19 (0.14)
Communications / other		−7516.80 * (2897.48)		−0.19 (0.12)
Sociodemographic characteristics				
Male	6024.82 ** (1727.26)	2300.54 (1620.22)	0.17 * (0.07)	0.06 (0.07)
Race/ ethnicity (reference: white)				
African American	1826.50 (2590.63)	1767.99 (2627.89)	−0.01 (0.10)	−0.01 (0.11)
Asian	−2513.29 (2145.63)	−2412.16 (1757.20)	−0.14 (0.10)	−0.14 (0.09)
Hispanic and other racial/ethnic groups	−3814.94 (2796.46)	−4202.75 (2731.66)	−0.17 (0.14)	−0.18 (0.13)

Table A3.5. *(continued)*

	Income in dollars		Logged income (*ln*)	
	Model 1 Coefficient (SE)	**Model 2** Coefficient (SE)	**Model 1** Coefficient (SE)	**Model 2** Coefficient (SE)
Parents' education (reference: college degree)				
High school or less	3920.27 (3778.18)	4309.73 (3561.08)	0.05 (0.16)	0.07 (0.15)
Some college	1767.13 (1511.73)	1770.32 (1937.97)	0.09 (0.06)	0.10 (0.07)
Graduate / professional degree	−1822.34 (1270.90)	−1303.27 (1316.68)	−0.09 (0.06)	−0.09 (0.06)
Intercept	32587.39 ** (1296.18)	36807.08 ** (2325.02)	10.27 ** (0.05)	10.40 ** (0.09)
R^2	0.05	0.14	0.03	0.08

Note: Analyses restricted to graduates not enrolled full-time in graduate school and working full-time.
†$p < .10$; *$p < .05$; **$p < .01$.
$N = 485$. Analyses are adjusted for clustering of students within schools.
^ Variables are standardized with a mean of 0 and standard deviation of 1.

Table A3.6. Logistic regression models predicting unskilled employment by CLA performance, college selectivity, field of study, job search method, and sociodemographic characteristics

	Model 1 Coefficient (SE)	**Model 2** Coefficient (SE)	**Model 3** Coefficient (SE)
Senior CLA performance^	−0.33 * (0.13)	−0.25 (0.15)	−0.29 † (0.15)
College selectivity^		−0.38 * (0.17)	−0.33 * (0.15)
Field of study (reference: business)			
Education / social work/ health		−0.12 (0.43)	−0.16 (0.49)
Engineering / computer science		−1.20 * (0.49)	−1.12 ** (0.44)
Social science / humanities		0.32 (0.42)	0.25 (0.41)
Science / math		0.38 (0.40)	0.42 (0.42)
Communications / other		0.13 (0.56)	0.06 (0.56)

Table A3.6. *(continued)*

	Model 1 Coefficient (SE)	Model 2 Coefficient (SE)	Model 3 Coefficient (SE)
Job search method			
Found job through college or internship			−1.81 ** (0.44)
Sociodemographic characteristics			
Male	0.16 (0.38)	0.31 (0.38)	0.50 (0.39)
Race/ethnicity (reference: white)			
African American	−0.10 (0.33)	−0.35 (0.39)	−0.29 (0.36)
Asian	0.33 (0.48)	0.25 (0.54)	0.21 (0.53)
Hispanic and other racial/ ethnic groups	−0.16 (0.45)	−0.30 (0.46)	−0.40 (0.45)
Parents' education (reference: college degree)			
High school or less	0.08 (0.47)	−0.04 (0.45)	−0.02 (0.43)
Some college	0.10 (0.38)	−0.01 (0.41)	0.04 (0.41)
Graduate / professional degree	−0.11 (0.32)	−0.04 (0.31)	−0.02 (0.30)
Intercept	−1.93 ** (0.35)	−2.03 ** (0.42)	−1.80 ** (0.43)
Pseudo R^2	0.02	0.04	0.09

†$p < .10$; *$p < .05$; **$p < .01$.

$N = 576$. Analyses are adjusted for clustering of students within schools.

^ Variables are standardized with a mean of 0 and standard deviation of 1.

Table A3.7. Logistic regression models predicting positive employment outcomes by CLA performance, college selectivity, field of study, and sociodemographic characteristics

	Positive employment outcome^^		Positive, full-time employment outcome^^	
	Model 1 Coefficient (SE)	Model 2 Coefficient (SE)	Model 1 Coefficient (SE)	Model 2 Coefficient (SE)
Senior CLA performance^	0.34 ** (0.11)	0.26 * (0.12)	0.25 ** (0.08)	0.18 † (0.09)
College selectivity^		0.32 * (0.14)		0.32 ** (0.12)
Field of study (reference: business)				
Education / social work / health		−0.31 (0.43)		−0.13 (0.39)
Engineering / computer science		0.73 (0.49)		0.59 (0.47)
Social science / humanities		−0.55 (0.42)		−0.46 (0.36)
Science / math		−0.44 (0.41)		−0.46 (0.37)
Communications / other		−0.51 (0.55)		−0.40 (0.46)
Sociodemographic characteristics				
Male	−0.20 (0.30)	−0.38 (0.32)	−0.11 (0.29)	−0.24 (0.30)
Race/ ethnicity (reference: white)				
African American	0.02 (0.31)	0.15 (0.37)	−0.04 (0.32)	0.14 (0.34)
Asian	−0.40 (0.32)	−0.44 (0.36)	−0.44 (0.34)	−0.43 (0.33)
Hispanic and other racial/ ethnic groups	0.20 (0.41)	0.19 (0.45)	−0.11 (0.32)	−0.09 (0.35)
Parents' education (reference: college degree)				
High school or less	−0.13 (0.29)	−0.06 (0.28)	−0.21 (0.29)	−0.15 (0.28)
Some college	−0.12 (0.34)	0.00 (0.34)	−0.23 (0.30)	−0.12 (0.29)
Graduate / professional degree	0.11 (0.26)	0.05 (0.25)	0.01 (0.25)	−0.04 (0.25)

Table A3.7. *(continued)*

| | Positive employment outcome^^ | | Positive, full-time employment outcome^^ | |
	Model 1 Coefficient (SE)	Model 2 Coefficient (SE)	Model 1 Coefficient (SE)	Model 2 Coefficient (SE)
Intercept	1.54 **	1.91 **	1.41 **	1.69 **
	(0.27)	(0.43)	(0.25)	(0.37)
Pseudo R²	0.02	0.04	0.02	0.03

†$p <.10$; *$p < .05$; **$p < .01$.
$N = 618$. Analyses are adjusted for clustering of students within schools.
^ Variables are standardized with a mean of 0 and a standard deviation of 1.
^^ Postive employment outcome is defined as avoiding unemployment and unskilled employment; positive full-time employment outcome is defined as avoidance of unemployment, underemployment, and unskilled emplyment.

Table A4.1. Description of post-college outcomes examined in chapter 4

Variable name	Variable coding*
Living arrangements	Graduates' responses to the question "Which category best describes your current living situation?" Responses were collapsed into the following categories: owning or renting on my own, renting with partner/spouse, renting with friends (met either in college or elsewhere), living with parents or relatives, and other.
Living at home	Dummy variable indicating that graduates reported living with parents or relatives.
Have college debt	Dummy variable indicating that graduates reported having student loan debt.
Amount of college debt	Graduates' reports of the amount of their student loan debt, conditional on having such debt. Response categories were in increments of $10,000 (i.e., $1–$9,999; $10,000–$19,999 . . . $50,000–$59,999, and $60,000 or more). The continuous variable was created from these categories, equaling the midpoint of each category (e.g., $1–$9,999 equals $5,000).
High college loan debt	Dummy variable indicating that graduates owed more than $30,000 in student loan debt.
Received financial assistance	Dummy variable indicating that graduates received financial assistance from parents during the preceding 12 months (see next variable).

Table A4.1. *(continued)*

Variable name	Variable coding*
Amount of financial assistance	Graduates' reports of the amount of financial assistance from parents, conditional on having received assistance. Variable generated using graduates' responses to the statement "Please indicate how much financial help you have received from your parent figures or other adult relatives during the past 12 months [e.g., Have your parents or relatives helped you with schooling expenses, buying a car, emergencies such as being out of work, sick or injured, given you money to make a down payment on a house, provided you with your own place to stay by covering the rent or given you other large financial or valuable gifts?]." Response categories were: less than $2,000, $2,000 to less than $5,000, $5,000 to less than $10,000, $10,000 to less than $20,000, $20,000 or more, and "I have not received any financial help from my parent figures or other adult relatives during the past 12 months." The continuous variable was created from these categories, equaling the midpoint of each category (e.g., $1–$1,999 equals $1,000).
Having a partner	Dummy variable indicating whether graduates reported being married, cohabitating, or being in a serious romantic relationship.
Meeting partner	Graduates' responses to the question "Where did you meet your partner/spouse?" Responses were collapsed into the following categories: high school, college, work, friends or family, online social networking site, and other.
Partner education	Graduates' responses to the question "What is the highest level of education completed by your spouse/partner to date?" Responses were collapsed into two categories: partner has attended or completed a four-year college, and partner has less than a college degree. Restricted to those who had partners (i.e., were not single).
Partner college selectivity	Selectivity of partner's college, restricted to those whose partner had attended or completed a four-year college. Selectivity is an institutional measure of the average of the 25th and 75th percentile of the combined math and verbal SAT scores for the incoming freshman class at each institution. Data on SAT scores were obtained from the Integrated Postsecondary Education Data System (IPEDS) database.
Reading newspapers	Graduates' responses to the question "How often do you read newspapers either online or in print?" Responses were collapsed into three categories: daily, weekly, and monthly or never.

Table A4.1. *(continued)*

Variable name	Variable coding*
Discussing politics/ public affairs	Graduates' responses to the question "How often do you discuss politics and public affairs with your family and friends (either in person, by phone or via the internet)?" Responses were collapsed into three categories: daily, weekly, and monthly or never.
Primary news source	Graduates' responses to the question "What is your primary source of news regarding recent events?" Analyses contrast two primary news sources: newspapers (online or print) versus social media (Twitter, Facebook, or other social network sites), e-mails from organizations, or websites other than those of newspapers.
Parent comparison now	Graduates' responses to the question "Compared to your parents when they were the age you are now, do you think your own standard of living now is much worse, somewhat worse, about the same, somewhat better, or much better?" Responses were collapsed into three categories: worse, about the same, and better.
Parent comparison overall	Graduates' responses to the question "Do you think your life overall is likely to be better or worse than your parents' lives have been?" Responses were collapsed into three categories: worse, about the same, and better.
Lack clear goals/ direction	Graduates' responses to the question "How often does your life seem to lack any clear goals or sense of direction?" Responses were collapsed into three categories: never or rarely, sometimes, and fairly or very often.

Note: Descriptions of college-related measures and sociodemographic characteristics are available in table A2.1.

* For most variables, categories were collapsed for analysis. Please see the survey instrument for original categories.

Table A4.2. Distribution of post-college outcomes examined in chapter 4 (all analyses are restricted to college graduates)

Variable	Percentage
Living arrangements	
Owning/renting on my own	28
Renting with partner/spouse	15
Renting with friends	30
Living with parents/relatives	24
Other	3
Received financial assistance from parents	74
Amount of financial assistance received from parents^	
Less than $2,000	47
$2,000 to less than $5,000	24
$5,000 to less than $10,000	14
$10,000 to less than $20,000	8
$20,000 or more	7
Romantic relationships	
Types of romantic relationships	
Married	8
Cohabitating	9
Serious romantic relationship	32
Single	51
Context in which graduates met their partners^^	
College	40
High school	14
Friends or family	19
Work	11
Online social networking sites	4
Other	12
Partner's education	
Partner attended or completed a four-year college^^	81
Partner attended the same college^^^	45
Partner attended a similarly selective college^^^	63
Civic engagement	
Frequency with which graduates read newspapers	
Monthly or never	32
Weekly	31
Daily	37

Table A4.2. *(continued)*

Variable	Percentage
Frequency with which graduates discuss politics/public affairs	
Monthly or never	39
Weekly	45
Daily	16
Graduates' life comparisons	
Overall comparison of their lives to those of their parents	
Worse	5
About the same	30
Better	64
Comparison of their lives now to when their parents were their age	
Worse	10
About the same	24
Better	66

^ Restricted to graduates who reported receiving some financial
assistance from their parents
^^ Restricted to graduates who did not report being single
^^^ Restricted to graduates who did not report being single.
Missing data on partners' institutions was imputed on the basis
of the proportions of partners attending same or similarly selective institutions in the available data.

Table A4.3. Logistic regression models predicting living at home by
employment and financial conditions, college selectivity, CLA
performance, and sociodemographic characteristics

	Model 1 Coefficient (SE)	Model 2 Coefficient (SE)	Model 3 Coefficient (SE)	Model 4 Coefficient (SE)
Employment and financial conditions				
Unemployed	1.51 ** (0.45)			
Unskilled employment		0.46 † (0.25)		
Enrolled in school full-time	−0.76 ** (0.20)	−0.82 ** (0.21)		
With college debt			0.08 (0.15)	
With high college debt (> $30,000)				−0.18 (0.22)

Table A4.3. *(continued)*

	Model 1 Coefficient (SE)	Model 2 Coefficient (SE)	Model 3 Coefficient (SE)	Model 4 Coefficient (SE)
College selectivity^	−0.15 (0.12)	−0.14 (0.12)	−0.17 (0.12)	−0.17 (0.12)
Senior CLA performance^	−0.11 (0.11)	−0.12 (0.11)	−0.13 (0.11)	−0.13 (0.11)
Sociodemographic characteristics				
Male	−0.41 † (0.22)	−0.37 † (0.20)	−0.35 † (0.20)	−0.37 † (0.20)
Race/ethnicity (reference: white)				
African American	0.43 (0.27)	0.44 (0.28)	0.35 (0.28)	0.37 (0.29)
Asian	0.64 * (0.27)	0.65 * (0.30)	0.65 * (0.31)	0.62 * (0.31)
Hispanic and other racial/ ethnic groups	0.78 * (0.34)	0.76 * (0.34)	0.81 * (0.32)	0.80 * (0.32)
Parents' education (reference: college degree)				
High school or less	−0.14 (0.33)	−0.12 (0.34)	−0.13 (0.31)	−0.12 (0.31)
Some college	0.42 * (0.21)	0.42 * (0.21)	0.40 * (0.20)	0.41 * (0.20)
Graduate / professional degree	−0.26 (0.27)	−0.26 (0.26)	−0.24 (0.27)	−0.27 (0.27)
Intercept	−1.13 ** (0.20)	−1.08 ** (0.20)	−1.30 ** (0.21)	−1.20 ** (0.18)
−2LL	912.64	929.79	954.3	953.77
AIC	936.64	953.79	976.3	975.77

†$p < .10$; *$p < .05$; **$p < .01$.

$N = 913$. Analyses are adjusted for clustering of students within schools.

^ Variables are standardized with a mean of 0 and a standard deviation of 1.

Table A4.4. Logistic regression models predicting students' receipt of financial assistance from parents, by financial and employment conditions, college selectivity, CLA performance, and sociodemographic characteristics

	Model 1 Coefficient (SE)	**Model 2** Coefficient (SE)	**Model 3** Coefficient (SE)	**Model 4** Coefficient (SE)
Financial and employment conditions				
Living at home	0.76 ** (0.17)			
With college debt		0.02 (0.21)		
Unemployed			0.55 (0.36)	
Unskilled employment				1.16 ** (0.32)
Enrolled in school full-time			0.27 † (0.15)	0.35 * (0.15)
College selectivity ˆ	−0.07 (0.12)	−0.08 (0.12)	−0.09 (0.12)	−0.07 (0.12)
Senior CLA performance ˆ	0.05 (0.08)	0.04 (0.08)	0.04 (0.08)	0.05 (0.08)
Sociodemographic characteristics				
Male	0.15 (0.19)	0.11 (0.18)	0.10 (0.19)	0.11 (0.18)
Race/ethnicity (reference: white)				
African American	−0.45 † (0.26)	−0.39 (0.25)	−0.41 † (0.25)	−0.40 † (0.24)
Asian	0.31 (0.24)	0.36 (0.22)	0.35 (0.22)	0.36 (0.22)
Hispanic and other racial/ethnic groups	−0.05 (0.30)	0.07 (0.28)	0.09 (0.28)	0.10 (0.29)
Parents' education (reference: college degree)				
High school or less	−0.72 ** (0.23)	−0.72 ** (0.22)	−0.74 ** (0.22)	−0.75 ** (0.21)
Some college	−0.27 (0.21)	−0.21 (0.21)	−0.21 (0.20)	−0.22 (0.21)
Graduate / professional degree	−0.01 (0.22)	−0.03 (0.21)	−0.04 (0.21)	−0.04 (0.22)

Table A4.4. *(continued)*

	Model 1 Coefficient (SE)	Model 2 Coefficient (SE)	Model 3 Coefficient (SE)	Model 4 Coefficient (SE)
Intercept	1.04 **	1.16 **	1.08 **	1.00 **
	(0.23)	(0.25)	(0.23)	(0.234)
−2LL	996.11	1010.19	1006.37	995.94
AIC	1018.11	1032.19	1030.37	1019.94

**p < 0.01; *p < 0.05; †p < 0.10

N = 891. Analyses are adjusted for clustering of students within schools.

^ Variables are standardized with a mean of 0 and a standard deviation of 1.

Table A4.5. Regression analyses examining different partnering outcomes, by institutional characteristics, CLA performance, and sociodemographic characteristics

	Having a partner	Partner attended or completed a four-year college ^^	Selectivity of partner's institution ^^^
	Logistic regression Coefficient (SE)	*Logistic regression* Coefficient (SE)	*OLS regression* Coefficient (SE)
Institutional characteristics			
College selectivity ^	−0.11	0.37 *	94.74 **
	(0.08)	(0.15)	(11.13)
College female percentage ^	−0.22 **	−0.08	1.34
	(0.07)	(0.17)	(14.27)
Senior CLA performance	0.06	0.03	0.36
	(0.09)	(0.13)	(7.23)
Sociodemographic characteristics			
Male	−0.63 **	0.66	8.78
	(0.15)	(0.42)	(13.28)
Race/ethnicity (reference: white)			
African American	−0.55 **	−0.04	30.18
	(0.21)	(0.46)	(61.36)
Asian	−0.66 *	−0.67	18.24
	(0.28)	(0.49)	(18.54)
Hispanic and other racial/ethnic groups	0.08	−0.87 †	−20.00
	(0.28)	(0.52)	(21.93)

Table A4.5. *(continued)*

	Having a partner	Partner attended or completed a four-year college^^	Selectivity of partner's institution^^^
	Logistic regression Coefficient (SE)	*Logistic regression* Coefficient (SE)	*OLS regression* Coefficient (SE)
Parents' education (reference: college degree)			
High school or less	0.30	0.43	1.06
	(0.26)	(0.56)	(19.89)
Some college	0.38	0.57	25.25
	(0.31)	(0.45)	(18.17)
Graduate / professional degree	0.22	0.68 †	23.98 †
	(0.18)	(0.37)	(13.73)
Intercept	0.06	1.94 **	1148.26
	(0.14)	(0.22)	(11.74)
N	734	358	218
–2LL	983.97	330.12	
AIC	1005.97	352.12	
R²			0.54

**p < 0.01; *p < 0.05; †p < 0.10.
Analyses are adjusted for clustering of students within schools.
^ Variables are standardized with a mean of 0 and a standard deviation of 1.
^^ Restricted to graduates who were partnered (i.e., married, cohabitating, or in serious romantic relationships)
^^^ Restricted to graduates whose partners had attended or completed a four-year college with valid IPEDS selectivity data

Table A4.6. Logistic regression models predicting low levels of civic and political awareness, by college selectivity, CLA performance, and sociodemographic characteristics

	Read newspapers monthly/never Coefficient (SE)	Discuss politics monthly/never Coefficient (SE)
College selectivity^	−0.43 **	−0.58 **
	(0.07)	(0.08)
Senior CLA performance^	−0.02	0.04
	(0.09)	(0.08)

Table A4.6. *(continued)*

	Read newspapers monthly/never Coefficient (SE)	Discuss politics monthly/never Coefficient (SE)
Sociodemographic characteristics		
Male	−0.82 **	−0.64 **
	(0.11)	(0.15)
Race/ethnicity (reference: white)		
African American	−0.18	−0.49 †
	(0.19)	(0.27)
Asian	−0.58 *	−0.18
	(0.23)	(0.24)
Hispanic and other racial/ethnic	−0.26	−0.11
groups	(0.24)	(0.25)
Parents' education (reference: college degree)		
High school or less	0.50 †	0.71 **
	(0.29)	(0.23)
Some college	−0.02	0.36
	(0.28)	(0.24)
Graduate / professional degree	−0.02	0.26 †
	(0.23)	(0.13)
Intercept	−0.54 **	−0.47 **
	(0.17)	(0.16)
−2LL	1083.69	1148.68
AIC	1103.69	1168.68
N	915	916

†$p < .10$; *$p < .05$; **$p < .01$. Analyses are adjusted for clustering of students within schools.
^ Variables are standardized with a mean of 0 and a standard deviation of 1.

Appendix B
Survey Instrument and Interview Protocol

CLA Spring 2011 Survey

Part I: Background Information

1. What institution did you attend when you participated in the Collegiate Learning Assessment (CLA) in 2009?
   A. [Institution that respondent attended]
   B. Boston College
   C. University of Colorado
   D. Notre Dame
   E. Michigan State
   F. None of these
   G. Decline to answer

2. In which country or region do you reside? _____

3. Are you . . . ?
   A. Male
   B. Female
   C. Decline to answer

4. In what year were you born? _____

Part II: Education and Expectations

Except where noted, the following questions were asked only if respondents did not complete their BA by the 2010 survey or did not participate in 2010:

5. Have you completed your bachelor's degree?

    A. Yes

    B. No

    C. Decline to answer

    If yes:

    5a. When did you complete your bachelor's degree?

    Month_____ Year _____   _____ Decline to answer

    5b. Which of these fields of study best describes your major(s)? Mark only one in each column. If you do not have a secondary major or minor field of study, mark "N/A (not applicable)."

        1. Agriculture
        2. Anthropology
        3. Architecture
        4. Biological/life sciences (biology, biochemistry, botany, zoology, etc.)
        5. Business (accounting, business administration, marketing, management, etc.)
        6. Communications (speech, journalism, television/radio, etc.)
        7. Computer and information sciences
        8. Economics
        9. Engineering and technology
        10. Education
        11. English and literature
        12. Ethnic, cultural studies, and area studies
        13. Foreign languages and literature (French, Spanish, Chinese etc.)
        14. Health-related fields (nursing, physical therapy, health technology, etc.)
        15. History
        16. Home economics and vocational home economics
        17. Criminal justice
        18. Liberal/general studies
        19. Mathematics
        20. Multi/interdisciplinary studies (international relations, ecology, environmental studies, etc.)
        21. Nursing and physical therapy
        22. Parks, recreation, leisure studies, sports management

23. Philosophy

24. Physical education

25. Physical sciences (physics, chemistry, astronomy, earth sciences, etc.)

26. Political science

27. Psychology

28. Religion

29. Public administration (city management, law enforcement, etc.)

30. Sociology

31. Visual and performing arts (art, music, theater, etc.)

33. Other

34. N/A

35. Decline to answer

If no (respondent has not completed BA):

5c. Do you still intend to complete your Bachelor's degree?

A. Yes

B. No

C. Decline to answer

If yes:

5c1. What field of study do you intend to major in?

1. Agriculture

2. Anthropology

3. Architecture

4. Biological/life sciences (biology, biochemistry, botany, zoology, etc.)

5. Business (accounting, business administration, marketing, management, etc.)

6. Communications (speech, journalism, television/radio, etc.)

7. Computer and information sciences

8. Economics

9. Engineering and technology

10. Education

11. English and literature

12. Ethnic, cultural studies, and area studies

13. Foreign languages and literature (French, Spanish, Chinese, etc.)

14. Health-related fields (nursing, physical therapy, health technology, etc.)

15. History

16. Home economics and vocational home economics

17. Criminal justice

18. Liberal/general studies

19. Mathematics

20. Multi/interdisciplinary studies (international relations, ecology, environmental studies, etc.)

21. Nursing and physical therapy

22. Parks, recreation, leisure studies, sports management

23. Philosophy

24. Physical education

25. Physical sciences (physics, chemistry, astronomy, earth sciences, etc.)

26. Political science

27. Psychology

28. Religion

29. Public administration (city management, law enforcement, etc.)

30. Sociology

31. Visual and performing arts (art, music, theater, etc.)

32. Undecided

33. Other

34. N/A

35. Decline to answer

If no (respondent does not intend to complete BA):

5c2. Please list the reason(s) why you have decided not to complete your Bachelor's degree. If you don't wish to respond to the question, please enter "DTA" for Decline to Answer. _____

6. Did you take out any student loans to help pay for your bachelor's degree?

A. Yes

B. No

C. Decline to answer

If yes:

6a. How much are you currently in debt—i.e., how much do you owe in the form of student loans?

A. $1–$9,999

B. $10,000–$19,999

C. $20,000–$29,999

D. $30,000–$39,999

E. $40,000–$49,999

F. $50,000–$59,999

G. $60,000 or more

H. I've repaid all of my student loans

I. Decline to answer

7. How much would you say your experiences during college have contributed to your development of skills in the following areas:

Not at all					A great deal		Decline to answer
1	2	3	4	5	6	7	8

Writing well

Solving complex problems

Thinking critically

Analyzing arguments

Using evidence to support arguments

Understanding data charts and graphs

Synthesizing information from different sources

8. If there is one thing you wished you had learned during college (academically or otherwise) but did not, what would it be? If you don't wish to respond to the question, please enter "DTA" for Decline to Answer.

_____

(This question was asked of all respondents)

9. During college, did you hold <u>a leadership position</u> in any of the following? Please select all that apply.

A. Student government

B. Volunteer/service organization

C. Student club/organization

D. Fraternity/sorority

E. Sports team

F. Campus newspapers

G. Other: (Please specify) _____

H. I did not hold a leadership position in college.

I. Decline to answer

The following questions were asked of all respondents:

10. What is the highest degree you expect to attain?

A. Bachelor's

B. Master's (e.g., MA, MS, MBA)

C. Doctorate

D. Professional (e.g., medical, law, architecture)

E. Other

F. Decline to answer

11. Are you currently pursuing an educational credential (certificate or degree)?
   A. Yes
   B. No
   C. Decline to answer

   If yes:
   11a. In regards to the educational credential (certificate or degree) that you're currently pursuing, are you attending full-time or part-time?
      A. Full-time
      B. Part-time
      C. Decline to answer

   11b. What credential (certificate or degree) are you working toward? If you don't wish to respond to the question, please enter "DTA" for Decline to Answer. _____

   11c. What is the concentration or field of study for your certificate/degree? If you don't wish to respond to the question, please enter "DTA" for Decline to Answer. _____

   11d. When do you expect to complete that certificate/degree?
      Month_____ Year _____   _____ Decline to answer

12. What job do you expect to have two years from now?
   1. Accountant
   2. Administrative assistant / secretary
   3. Advertising/marketing professional
   4. Architect
   5. Artist/designer
   6. Attorney
   7. Auto mechanic
   8. Business executive
   9. Computer specialist
   10. Construction worker
   11. Dentist
   12. Education administrator
   13. Engineer
   14. Engineering technician/support
   15. Entertainer/performer/sports prof.
   16. Farming/fishing/forestry worker
   17. Financial professional

18. Food preparation/service worker
19. Government professional
20. Health care administrator
21. Health care professional
22. Human resource professional
23. IT manager / network administrator
24. Journalist
25. Judge
26. Legal professional
27. Machine operator / production worker
28. Maintenance/mechanic/repair worker
29. Media/communications professional
30. Military
31. Personal care/service worker
32. Physician
33. Professor/instructor, higher ed.
34. Protective service worker
35. Religious professional
36. Sales agent/representative
37. Scientist, biological/physical/social
38. Social worker
39. Statistician
40. Teacher/instructor, K–12
41. Technician, science
42. Title agent
43. Tradesperson (e.g., plumber)
44. Transportation/equipment operator/worker
45. Travel agent
46. Other (please specify): _____
47. Decline to answer

13. What job do you expect to have ten years from now?
    1. Accountant
    2. Administrative assistant/secretary
    3. Advertising/marketing professional
    4. Architect
    5. Artist/designer
    6. Attorney
    7. Auto mechanic
    8. Business executive

9. Computer specialist

10. Construction worker

11. Dentist

12. Education administrator

13. Engineer

14. Engineering technician/support

15. Entertainer/performer/sports prof.

16. Farming/fishing/forestry worker

17. Financial professional

18. Food preparation/service worker

19. Government professional

20. Health care administrator

21. Health care professional

22. Human resource professional

23. IT manager/network administrator

24. Journalist

25. Judge

26. Legal professional

27. Machine operator/production worker

28. Maintenance/mechanic/repair worker

29. Media/communications professional

30. Military

31. Personal care/service worker

32. Physician

33. Professor/instructor, higher ed.

34. Protective service worker

35. Religious professional

36. Sales agent/representative

37. Scientist, biological/physical/social

38. Social worker

39. Statistician

40. Teacher/instructor, K–12

41. Technician, science

42. Title agent

43. Tradesperson (e.g., plumber)

44. Transportation/equipment operator/worker

45. Travel agent

46. Other (please specify): _____

47. Decline to answer

14. When choosing an occupation, how important are the following characteristics to you?

Not at all important				Very important			Decline to answer
1	2	3	4	5	6	7	8

Importance of your work

Challenge of your work

Pay

Benefits

Child care available at the workplace

Opportunities for promotion and advancement

Opportunities to use past training and education

Opportunities for further training and education

Job security

Job flexibility (e.g., flexible schedule, work from home)

Autonomy

Status/prestige

Helping others

Work being close to your family

15. Some people say that people get ahead by their own hard work; others say
that lucky breaks or help from other people are more important. Which do
you think is most important?
A. Hard work is most important
B. Hard work and luck are equally important
C. Luck or help from other people is most important
D. Decline to answer

16. Compared to your parents when they were the age you are now, do you
think your own standard of living now is . . .
A. Much worse
B. Somewhat worse
C. About the same
D. Somewhat better
E. Much better
F. Decline to answer

17. Do you think your life overall is likely to be better or worse than your par-
ents' lives have been?
A. Much worse
B. Somewhat worse
C. About the same

D. Somewhat better

E. Much better

F. Decline to answer

18. How often does your life seem to lack any clear goals or sense of direction?

A. Never

B. Rarely

C. Sometimes

D. Fairly often

E. Very often

F. Decline to answer

19. Are you currently . . . ? Please select all that apply.

A. Attending a teacher education credential program

B. Teaching

C. Aspiring to teach

D. None of these

E. Decline to answer

If yes to any of the above:

19a. How well do you think your <u>college education</u> has prepared you for teaching?

Not at all				Very well	Decline to answer
1	2	3	4	5	6

19b. What level/subject are you teaching or aspire to teach?

A. Elementary school

B. Middle school; indicate subject: _____

C. High school; indicate subject: _____

D. Decline to answer

19c. Have you taken a teaching licensing/credentialing exam?

A. Yes

B. No

C. Decline to answer

If yes:

19c1. Have you passed a teaching licensing/credentialing exam?

A. Yes

B. No

C. Decline to answer

19c2. What level/subject are you certified to teach?

A. Elementary school

    B. Middle school; indicate subject: _____

    C. High school; indicate subject: _____

    D. I am not certified yet to teach.

    E. I haven't received my results yet.

    F. Decline to answer

If you are currently teaching:

    19d. How extensive was your training in the following areas?

Did not have training in the area					Very extensive		Decline to answer
1	2	3	4	5	6	7	8

Classroom management/discipline

Subject matter

Curriculum development

Student assessment

Cultural sensitivity/diversity

Teaching students of varying levels of
interest/ability in the same classroom

    19e. Are you currently, or have you ever been, a part of a formal Teacher
        Induction Program? . . .

	Yes	No	Decline to answer
A. Organized by the college you attended?			
B. Organized by organizations other than the college you attended (e.g., TFA, school district)?			

    19f. Has your classroom ever been observed by any of the following? Please
        select all that apply.

    A. School administrator

    B. Mentor

    C. Another teacher

    D. Another member of your teacher training program

    E. My classroom has not been observed.

    F. Decline to answer

If yes:

    19f1. How useful was the feedback from the person(s) observing your
         classroom?

Not at all useful			Very useful		Decline to answer
1	2	3	4	5	6

19g. Has a formal mentor been assigned to you?

    A. Yes

    B. No

    C. Decline to answer

If yes:

19g1. How often do you meet?

    A. More than once a week

    B. Once a week

    C. Two to three times a month

    D. Once a month

    E. Less than once a month

    F. Other (Please specify:_____)

    G. Decline to answer

19g2. Overall, how useful is the mentoring experience?

Not at all useful			Very useful		Decline to answer
1	2	3	4	5	6

19h. What type of school are you teaching at?

    A. Public

    B. Charter

    C. Magnet

    D. Private

    E. Decline to answer

19i. In your estimate, what percentage of students at the school where you teach are non-white? _____%   _____ Decline to answer

20. Are you currently employed (including unpaid internships)?

    A. Yes

    B. No

    C. Decline to answer

If yes:

20a. Is your primary or most important job:

    A. A paid internship

    B. An unpaid internship

    C. Regular employment, part-time

    D. Regular employment, full-time

    E. Self-employed

    F. Other

    G. Decline to answer

Part III: Labor Market I

The questions in this section were asked only if the respondent was currently employed. If respondents had multiple jobs, they were instructed to answer the questions regarding their primary or most important job.

21. When did you start your current job? If you are not sure of the specific date, please provide your best estimate.
   Month (MM) _____   Year (YYYY) _____   _____ Decline to answer

22. Before starting your current job, how many months have you experienced the following? If these circumstances do not apply to you, please enter "0."

                                                               # of months

   A. Not working and looking for work   _____
   B. Not working but <u>not</u> actively looking for work   _____
   C. Decline to answer

23. What is your current job?
   1. Accountant
   2. Administrative assistant/secretary
   3. Advertising/marketing professional
   4. Architect
   5. Artist/designer
   6. Attorney
   7. Auto mechanic
   8. Business executive
   9. Computer specialist
   10. Construction worker
   11. Dentist
   12. Education administrator
   13. Engineer
   14. Engineering technician/support
   15. Entertainer/performer/sports prof.
   16. Farming/fishing/forestry worker
   17. Financial professional
   18. Food preparation/service worker
   19. Government professional
   20. Healthcare administrator
   21. Healthcare professional
   22. Human resource professional
   23. IT manager/network administrator

24. Journalist
25. Judge
26. Legal professional
27. Machine operator/production worker
28. Maintenance/mechanic/repair worker
29. Media/communications professional
30. Military
31. Personal care/service worker
32. Physician
33. Professor/instructor, higher ed.
34. Protective service worker
35. Religious professional
36. Sales agent/representative
37. Scientist, biological/physical/social
38. Social worker
39. Statistician
40. Teacher/instructor, K–12
41. Technician, science
42. Title agent
43. Tradesperson (e.g., plumber)
44. Transportation/equipment operator/worker
45. Travel agent
46. Other (please specify): _____
47. Decline to answer

25. What is your specific job title? If you don't wish to respond to the question, please enter "DTA" for Decline to Answer. _____

26. In a typical week, how many hours on average do you work in your primary job?
_____# of hours _____Decline to answer

27. What is your average annual salary in your primary job?
A. $1–$9,999
B. $10,000–$19,999
C. $20,000–$29,999
D. $30,000–$39,999
E. $40,000–$49,999
F. $50,000–$59,999
G. $60,000 or more
H. Decline to answer

28. In your primary job, are you working for yourself or for someone else?
   A. Myself (i.e., self-employed)
   B. Someone else
   C. Decline to answer

If you are currently working for yourself:

28a. What type of a business do you have? If you don't wish to respond to the question, please enter "DTA" for Decline to Answer. _____

28b. How much <u>financial support</u> did you receive from each of the following sources for starting your business?

	No support			A great deal of support			Decline to answer
	1	2	3	4	5	6	7	8
Family								
Friends								
Former employer								
Government small business office								
Bank loan								

28c. How much <u>technical/logistical support</u> did you receive from each of the following sources for starting your business?

	No support			A great deal of support			Decline to answer
	1	2	3	4	5	6	7	8
Family								
Friends								
Former employer								
Government small business office								
College personnel								

28d. Not including yourself, how many of the following types of employees/volunteers does your business have? If you don't have a specific type of employee/volunteer, please enter "0."

	# of employees
Part-time employees	_____
Full-time employees	_____
Friends/family who volunteer their time	_____
_____ Decline to answer	

If you are currently working for someone else in your primary job:

28e. What type of an employer are you working for?
   A. For profit
   B. Nonprofit
   C. Government (local, state, or federal)

    D. Military, including national guard

    E. Decline to answer

28f. How did you find your job?

    A. Friends from college, met through college activities (student clubs, fraternities/sororities, volunteering, etc.)

    B. Friends from college, met in contexts other than college activities

    C. Classified ads / job listings in the newspapers, on the web, etc.

    D. College personnel or career placement center

    E. Employment agency/office (e.g., labor dept., job fair)

    F. Former employer, company transfer, networking on a job

    G. Volunteering, internship, or community service

    H. On-campus recruiting

    I. Other (Please specify): _____

    J. Decline to answer

28g. Did your employer ask to see your college transcripts when you were being hired?

    A. Yes

    B. No

    C. Decline to answer

28h. To your knowledge, did the person(s) interviewing and/or hiring you attend your college/university?

    A. Yes

    B. No

    C. I don't know

    D. Decline to answer

28i. To your knowledge, have any of your coworkers attended your college/university?

    A. Yes

    B. No

    C. I don't know

    D. Decline to answer

28j. Do you aspire to have your own business in the future?

    A. Yes

    B. No

    C. Decline to answer

If yes:

28j1. What type of a business do you anticipate having? If you don't wish to respond to the question, please enter "DTA" for Decline to Answer. _____

28j2. How important do you think receiving <u>financial support</u> from each of the following sources will be for starting your business?

Not at all important   Very important   Decline to answer
1   2   3   4   5   6   7   8

Family
Friends
Former employer
Government small business office
Bank loan

28j3. How important do you think receiving <u>technical/logistical support</u> from each of the following sources will be for starting your business?

Not at all important   Very important   Decline to answer
1   2   3   4   5   6   7   8

Family
Friends
Former employer
Government small business office
College personnel

29. Using a scale of 1 to 7, where 1 means "very dissatisfied" and 7 means "very satisfied," please rate your overall satisfaction with your primary job.

Very dissatisfied   Very dissatisfied   Decline to answer
1   2   3   4   5   6   7   8

30. Again, using a scale of 1 to 7, where 1 means "very dissatisfied" and 7 means "very satisfied," how satisfied are you with these aspects of your primary job?

Very dissatisfied   Very dissatisfied   Decline to answer
1   2   3   4   5   6   7   8

Importance of your work
Challenge of your work
Pay
Benefits
Child care available at the workplace
Opportunities for promotion and advancement
Opportunities to use past training and education

Opportunities for further training and education
Job security
Job flexibility (e.g., flexible schedule, work from home)
Autonomy
Status/prestige
Helping others
Work is close to your family

31. How often do you use the following skills and knowledge in your primary job?

Never					All the time		Decline to answer
1	2	3	4	5	6	7	8

Writing
Solving complex problems
Thinking critically
Analyzing arguments
Using evidence to support arguments
Understanding data charts and graphs
Synthesizing information from different sources
Knowledge from your major
Teamwork/collaboration

32. Have you held any jobs other than your current primary job since May 2009 (either prior to or at the same time)?
   A. Yes
   B. No
   C. Decline to answer

   If yes:

   32a. For any jobs you have held since May 2009, either prior to or at the same time as your current primary job, please list the job title, start/end dates, and average number of hours worked per week. Please include all part-time and full-time employment, as well as self-employment. If you are not sure of specific dates or hours worked, please provide your best estimate.

Job title	Start date	End date	Average number of hours worked per week
1.			
2.			
3.			
4.			

5.

_____Decline to answer

Part IV: Labor Market II

The questions in this section were only asked if the respondent was not currently employed.

33. Are you seeking a full-time or a part-time job for pay at this time?

    A. Yes

    B. No

    C. Decline to answer

    If yes:

    33a. Over the past twelve months, how many months were you unem-
        ployed? _____ months

    _____ Decline to answer

    33b. Which of the following have you done to find work during the last
        month? Please select all that apply.

    A. Applied and/or searched for positions posted in newspaper classified ads

    B. Applied and/or searched for positions posted in trade publications

    C. Applied and/or searched for positions using online employment search
        engines—e.g., CareerBuilder.com, Monster.com

    D. Attended networking events

    E. Made individual networking efforts

    F. Applied for positions through employment/staffing firms

    G. Applied and/or searched for positions on specific company websites

    H. Used the services of career placement centers

    I. Used on-campus recruiting services

    J. I haven't done anything to find work during the last month.

    K. Other (please specify): _____

    L. Decline to answer

34. Have you worked for pay, either part-time or full-time, in the last 12
    months?

    A. Yes

    B. No

    C. Decline to answer

    If yes, please answer the following questions about your <u>most recent</u> job for
    pay. If you have held multiple jobs at the time, answer the questions regard-
    ing your primary or most important job.

34a. Please provide the start and end dates for your most recent job. If you are not sure of specific dates, please provide your best estimate.

Start of your most recent job:Month _____   Year _____
End of your most recent job: Month _____   Year _____
_____ Decline to answer

34b. What was the reason for leaving your most recent job?
   A. I was terminated.
   B. I was laid off due to downsizing.
   C. The job wasn't the right fit for me.
   D. I was experiencing personal difficulties that prevented me from working.
   E. I moved out of the area.
   F. I am taking care of my children.
   G. I am taking care of family members.
   H. Other (please specify): _____
   I.   Decline to answer

35. What was your most recent job?
   1. Accountant
   2. Administrative assistant/secretary
   3. Advertising/marketing professional
   4. Architect
   5. Artist/designer
   6. Attorney
   7. Auto mechanic
   8. Business executive
   9. Computer specialist
   10. Construction worker
   11. Dentist
   12. Education administrator
   13. Engineer
   14. Engineering technician/support
   15. Entertainer/performer/sports Prof.
   16. Farming/fishing/forestry worker
   17. Financial professional
   18. Food preparation/service worker
   19. Government professional
   20. Healthcare administrator
   21. Healthcare professional
   22. Human resource professional

23. IT manager/network administrator

24. Journalist

25. Judge

26. Legal professional

27. Machine operator/production worker

28. Maintenance/mechanic/repair worker

29. Media/communications professional

30. Military

31. Personal care/service worker

32. Physician

33. Professor/instructor, higher ed.

34. Protective service worker

35. Religious professional

36. Sales agent/representative

37. Scientist, biological/physical/social

38. Social worker

39. Statistician

40. Teacher/instructor, K–12

41. Technician, science

42. Title agent

43. Tradesperson (e.g., plumber)

44. Transportation/equipment operator/worker

45. Travel agent

46. Other (please specify): _____

47. Decline to answer

35a. What was your specific job title at your most recent job? If you don't wish to respond to the question, please enter "DTA" for Decline to Answer. _____

36. In a typical week, how many hours on average did you work in your most recent job?

_____ # of hours   _____ Decline to answer

37. What was your average annual salary in your most recent job?
   A. $1–$9,999
   B. $10,000–$19,999
   C. $20,000–$29,999
   D. $30,000–$39,999
   E. $40,000–$49,999
   F. $50,000–$59,999

G. $60,000 or more

H. Decline to answer

38. In your most recent job, were you working for yourself or for someone else?

A. Myself (i.e., self-employed)

B. Someone else

C. Decline to answer

If you were working for yourself:

38a. What type of a business did you have? If you don't wish to respond to the question, please enter "DTA" for Decline to Answer. _____

38b. How much <u>financial support</u> did you receive from each of the following sources for starting your business?

	No support			A great deal of support			Decline to answer
1	2	3	4	5	6	7	8

Family

Friends

Former employer

Government small business office

Bank loan

38c. How much <u>technical/logistical support</u> did you receive from each of the following sources for starting your business?

	No support			A great deal of support			Decline to answer
1	2	3	4	5	6	7	8

Family

Friends

Former employer

Government small business office

College personnel

38d. Not including yourself, how many of the following types of employees/volunteers did your business have? If you didn't have a specific type of employee/volunteer, please enter "0."

	# of employees
Part-time employees	_____
Full-time employees	_____
Friends/family who volunteer their time	_____
_____ Decline to answer	

If you were working for someone else:

38e. What type of an employer were you working for in your most recent job?

    A. For profit

    B. Nonprofit

    C. Government (local, state, or federal)

    D. Military, including national guard

    E. Decline to answer

38f. How did you find your most recent job?

    A. Friends from college, met through college activities (student clubs, fraternities/sororities, volunteering, etc.)

    B. Friends from college, met in contexts other than college activities

    C. Classified ads / job listings in the newspapers, on the web, etc.

    D. College personnel or career placement center

    E. Employment agency/office (e.g., labor dept, job fair)

    F. Former employer, company transfer, networking on a job

    G. Volunteering, internship or community service

    H. On-campus recruiting

    I. Other (Please specify) _____

    J. Decline to answer

38g. Did your most recent employer ask to see your college transcripts when you were being hired?

    A. Yes

    B. No

    C. Decline to answer

38h. To your knowledge, did the person(s) interviewing and/or hiring for your most recent job attend your college/university?

    A. Yes

    B. No

    C. I don't know

    D. Decline to answer

38i. To your knowledge, did any of your coworkers at your most recent job attend your college/university?

    A. Yes

    B. No

    C. I don't know

    D. Decline to answer

38j. Do you aspire to have your own business in the future?

    A. Yes

    B. No

    C. Decline to answer

If yes:

38j1. What type of a business do you anticipate having? If you don't wish to respond to the question, please enter "DTA" for Decline to Answer. _____

38j2. How important do you think receiving <u>financial support</u> from each of the following sources will be for starting your business?

Not at all important						Very important	Decline to answer
1	2	3	4	5	6	7	8

Family

Friends

Former employer

Government small business office

Bank loan

38j3. How important do you think receiving <u>technical/logistical support</u> from each of the following sources will be for starting your business?

Not at all important						Very important	Decline to answer
1	2	3	4	5	6	7	8

Family

Friends

Former employer

Government small business office

College personnel

39. Using a scale where of 1 to 7, where 1 means "very dissatisfied" and 7 means "very satisfied," please rate your overall satisfaction with your most recent job.

Very dissatisfied					Very dissatisfied	Decline to answer
1	2	3	4	5	6	7	8

40. Again, using a scale of 1 to 7, where 1 means "very dissatisfied" and 7 means "very satisfied," how satisfied are you with these aspects of your most recent job?

Very dissatisfied					Very dissatisfied	Decline to answer
1	2	3	4	5	6	7	8

Importance of your work
Challenge of your work
Pay
Benefits
Child care available at the workplace
Opportunities for promotion and advancement
Opportunities to use past training and education
Opportunities for further training and education
Job security
Job flexibility (e.g., flexible schedule, work from home)
Autonomy
Status/prestige
Helping others
Work is close to your family

41. How often do you use the following skills and knowledge in your most recent job?

Never   All the time   Decline to answer
   1   2   3   4   5   6   7   8

Writing
Solving complex problems
Thinking critically
Analyzing arguments
Using evidence to support arguments
Understanding data charts and graphs
Synthesizing information from different sources
Knowledge from your major
Teamwork/collaboration

42. Have you held any jobs other than your most recent job referenced in the preceding questions since May 2009 (either prior to or at the same time)?
A. Yes
B. No
C. Decline to answer

If yes:

42a. For any jobs you have held since May 2009, either prior to or at the same time as your most recent job, please list the job title, start/end dates and average number of hours worked per week. Please include all part-time and full-time employment as well as self-employment. If you are not sure of specific dates or hours worked, please provide your best estimate.

Job title	Start date	End date	Average number of hours worked per week
1.			
2.			
3.			
4.			
5.			

_____Decline to answer

Part V: Family and Social Context

43. How often do you read newspapers either online or in print?
    A. Daily
    B. Weekly
    C. Monthly
    D. I don't read newspapers.
    E. Decline to answer

44. How often do you discuss politics and public affairs with your family and friends (either in person, by phone, or via the internet)?
    A. Every day
    B. At least once a week
    C. At least once a month
    D. Less than once a month
    E. Never
    F. Decline to answer

45. What is your primary source of news regarding recent events?
    A. Newspapers (online or in print)
    B. Radio
    C. TV
    D. Blogs
    E. Twitter, Facebook, or other online social network sites
    F. E-mails from organizations/websites other than newspapers
    G. Family, friends, and colleagues
    H. Other
    I. Decline to answer

46. We are going to ask you about a set of book titles. For each of the titles, we will ask you about your level of knowledge about the book and any impressions you might have about it.

46a. Amy Chua, *Battle Hymn of the Tiger Mother* (Penguin Press, 2011)
   A. I have read the book.
   B. I have not read the book, but have viewed media coverage of it.
   C. I am not aware of this book.
   D. Decline to answer

46b. Richard Arum and Josipa Roksa, *Academically Adrift* (University of Chicago Press, 2011)
   A. I have read the book.
   B. I have not read the book, but have viewed media coverage of it.
   C. I am not aware of this book.
   D. Decline to answer

46c. Rebecca Cox, *The College Fear Factor* (Harvard University Press, 2011)
   A. I have read the book.
   B. I have not read the book, but have viewed media coverage of it.
   C. I am not aware of this book.
   D. Decline to answer

47. How many hours in an average month do you currently participate as a volunteer in the following organizations/activities (i.e., you are not an employee of these organizations and are not getting paid for your services)? If you don't participate in an activity, please enter "0."

	# hours per month
Youth organizations	_____
(such as coaching sports, scouting, etc.)	
Political organizations or local government activities	_____
Religious organizations (not including worship)	_____
Social service agencies	_____
Educational organizations and activities	_____
(such as PTA, tutoring, recruiting/interviewing for your college, etc.)	
Community centers	_____
Environmental and conservation organizations	_____
Other (specify) : _____	_____
_____Decline to answer	

48. If you think about your close friends, ones you communicate with regularly, how many of them did you meet at . . .

None of them	A few of them	Many of them	Most of them	All of them	Decline to answer
0	1	2	3	4	5

High school
College
Work (including internship)
Volunteer/service activities
Church or other religious organizations
Other

49. Which category best describes your current living situation?
    A. Owning
    B. Renting on my own
    C. Renting with my partner/spouse
    D. Renting with college friends/roommates
    E. Renting with friends/roommates other than those met in college
    F. Living with parents or relatives
    G. Other
    H. Decline to answer

50. Please indicate how much financial help you have received from your parent figures or other adult relatives during the past 12 months. (E.g., have your parents or relatives helped you with schooling expenses, buying a car, emergencies such as being out of work, sick or injured, given you money to make a down payment on a house, provided you your own place to stay by covering the rent or given you other large financial or valuable gifts?)
    A. Less than $2,000
    B. $2,000 to less than $5,000
    C. $5,000 to less than $10,000
    D. $10,000 to less than $20,000
    E. $20,000 or more
    F. I have not received any financial help from my parent figures or other adult relatives during the past 12 months
    G. Decline to answer

51. In the past 12 months, was there ever a time when you were not able to pay a bill, such as the full amount of rent or mortgage, a gas, electric, or other utility bill, or any other bill, because you did not have enough money?
    A. Yes
    B. No
    C. I do not have any bills to pay
    D. Decline to answer

52. Currently, about how much in total do you owe on credit cards?
    A. $1–$999
    B. $1,000–$1,999

    C. $2,000–$2,999
    D. $3,000–$3,999
    E. $4,000–$4,999
    F. $5,000–$7,499
    G. $7,500–$9,999
    H. $10,000 or more
    I.   I do not have any credit card debt
    J.   Decline to answer

53. Is anybody in your immediate family self-employed?
    A. Yes
    B. No
    C. Decline to answer

54. What city/town, state and country do you live in?
    City_____   State_____   Zip Code _____
    _____ Decline to answer

55. Have you experienced any of the following since May 2010? Please select all that apply.
    A. Parent(s) getting divorced
    B. Parent(s) losing a job
    C. Losing a job yourself
    C. Losing a member of the family (parents, siblings or children)
    D. Difficulties paying college loans
    E. Difficulties finding a job
    F. Serious illness
    G. Other major life challenges; specify _____
    H. None of these
    I.   Decline to answer

56. Are you currently:
    A. Married
    B. Cohabitating
    C. In a serious romantic relationship
    D. Single
    E. Decline to answer

If you are married, cohabitating, or in a serious romantic relationship:
56a. How long have you been in this relationship?
        _____ months _____years
        _____ Decline to answer

56b. What is your spouse/partner's gender?

A. Male

B. Female

C. Decline to answer

56c. What is your spouse/partner's race/ethnicity?

A. African American

B. Asian

C. Hispanic

D. Non-Hispanic white

E. Other

F. Decline to answer

56d. What is the highest level of education completed by your spouse/partner to date?

A. Less than high school

B. High school diploma or a GED

C. Vocational certificate

D. Associate degree

E. Bachelor's degree

F. Master's (e.g., MA, MS, MBA)

G. Doctorate or professional degree (e.g., medical, law, architecture)

H. Still enrolled in school

I. Decline to answer

If partner is still enrolled in school:

56d1. What type of a degree is your spouse/partner working toward?

A. High school diploma or a GED

B. Vocational certificate

C. Associate degree

D. Bachelor's degree

E. Master's (e.g., MA, MS, MBA)

F. Doctorate or professional (e.g., medical, law, architecture)

G. Decline to answer

If your partner has ever attended or is currently attending college:

56d2. What college/s did s/he attend? If your spouse/partner attended multiple colleges, please list them in order of importance.

_____

_____

_____

56e. Where did you meet your spouse/partner?
   A. High school
   B. College
   C. Work (including internship)
   D. Church or other religious organizations
   E. Through friends or family
   F. Online social networking site
   G. Dating service
   H. Other
   I. Decline to answer

56f. What is the highest level of education completed by your spouse/partner's parents?
   A. Less than high school
   B. High school diploma or a GED
   C. Some college, less than a Bachelor's degree
            (including associate and technical degrees)
   D. Bachelor's degree
   E. Graduate or professional degree
   F. Decline to answer

   If you are currently not married:
   56g. Do you plan to get married someday?
      A. Yes
      B. No
      C. Decline to answer

   If yes:
   56g1. Around what age are you planning to be married at?
      A. 20–25
      B. 26–30
      C. 31–35
      D. 36–40
      F. After 40
      G. Decline to answer

57. Do you have any biological children?
   A. Yes
   B. No
   C. Decline to answer

If no:
57a. Do you plan to have children?
    A. Yes
    B. No
    C. Decline to answer

      If yes:
      57a1. Around what age do you plan on having children?
          A. 20–25
          B. 26–30
          C. 31–35
          D. 36–40
          F. After 40
          G. Decline to answer

58. How many children under the age of 18 live in your household?
    A. 0
    B. 1
    C. 2
    D. 4
    E. More than 4
    F. Decline to answer

CLA Summer 2011 Interview Protocol

Part I: Social Networks and Current Living Arrangements

1. Do you stay in touch with any friends you met in college? If so, how often and in what way do you stay in touch with them? How exactly did you meet them in college? Would you say they are an important part of your life now? If yes, in what ways?

2. Please tell us about your current living situation. Who are you living with? How long have you lived in this situation?
    A. How do you share financial household costs?
    B. Do you anticipate that those living arrangements will change in the next year or so? If yes, in what ways will they change?

The following question was asked if respondents said they were in a relationship in the spring 2011 survey:
3A. Last spring in your survey you noted that you were in a serious romantic relationship. Please describe exactly how you met the person with whom you are in a romantic relationship.

The following question was asked if respondents said they were not in a relationship *in the spring 2011 survey:*

3B. Last spring in your survey you noted that you were single. Have you been in a romantic relationship in the last year or two? If so, how did you meet that person, how long were you together, and what do you think led to the break up?

Part II: Employment and Graduate School

The following questions were asked if respondents said they were enrolled in graduate school *in the spring 2011 survey:*

4a. Last spring you told us you were enrolled in school. How did you decide to enroll in that particular program?

4b. Was the undergraduate college you attended involved in this choice? If so, please provide details.

4c. What did your parents think of your decision to continue your education? What did your friends think about this decision?

4d. How would you compare your academic experiences in graduate school to your academic experiences as an undergraduate? For example, has the work been easier or harder? In what ways has it been similar or different?

4e. Is your graduate program related to your field of study during college? [Note: probe to explore inconsistencies, if the fields are not the same, ask how they decided to change their educational/labor market trajectory.]

4f. What skills/knowledge/abilities did you acquire during college that were most beneficial for graduate school?

The following questions were asked if respondents said they were unemployed *in the spring 2011 survey:*

5a. Last spring you told us you were unemployed. How many hours per week were you actively looking for work?

5b. What was your strategy for finding work? Please describe specific methods you used to find work.

5c. Did you consider moving to find work in a different city or state? If so, what supported or prevented such a move?

5d. Have you found a job since? If yes, what is your current job? How did you find it? If no, are you continuing to seek employment? Have you done anything specific in the last 7 days to find work?

The following questions were asked of all respondents:

6a. Please tell us about your most recent job. What exactly do [or did] you do on a typical day?

6b. Was this job related to your field of study during college? What skills/ knowledge/abilities did you acquire during college that were most beneficial for this job?

6c. [*optional probe*] Is there anything in particular that you wish you had learned in college, anything that would have been particularly beneficial for this job? If yes, please explain.

6d. How did you find that job? Can you describe the process from the time you heard about the job to the time you began working?

6e. [*optional probe*] Did you get any direct assistance from your college in your job search (e.g., career services or faculty letters of recommendation)? If so, please provide us with specific details about help you received.

6f. [*optional probe*] Do you think the college you attended was at all helpful indirectly? For example, through alumni networks or institutional reputation? Can you tell us any incidents in your job search that might illuminate how your college was in any way indirectly helpful?

6g. [*optional probe*] Did you receive help from your family in your job search? If so, again please provide us details.

6h. How about your friends from college? Were those relationships helpful in locating a job?

7. In terms of work, what sort of job do you personally expect to have four years from now? Please describe how college has assisted you or not in attaining these goals. Have you done anything since college that supports achieving your expectations? If yes, can you give us some specific examples?

Part III: College Experiences

The following questions were asked of all respondents:

8. Thinking back to your college years, what were some of the experiences, events, or occasions when you learned the most academically? Please provide details of those experiences, what they were, how they led to learning, and what specifically you learned.

9. How academically engaged would you say you were in college? Please describe what type of a student you were academically in terms of your academic activities, commitment and effort?

10. What about socially, what were some of the experiences, events, or occasions when you learned the most socially? Please provide details of those experiences, what they were, how they led to learning, and what specifically you learned.

11. [*optional probe*] How socially engaged would you say you were in college? Please describe what type of a student you were socially, in terms of social activities.

12. Is there anything you wished you would have done differently in college?

13. Did you leave college with student loans? If you did, how have you managed and experienced your student loans since college? Has it been difficult or easy meeting these financial obligations? If you have struggled, please provide details to illustrate these difficulties.

Part IV: Civic Involvement and Expectations for the Future

The following questions were asked of all respondents:

14. How do you keep up with current affairs? What are your primary sources of news? Please provide specifics about these sources and how regularly you consult them.

15. [*optional probe*] How active are you politically? Do you volunteer or actively participate in political organizations? When was the last time you voted in an election?

16. [*optional probe*] How do you feel about the direction the country is currently heading in?

17. How do you feel about the direction your life is currently heading in?
    Do you think your life will be better or worse than your parents? Please
    explain why.

18. Is there anything else you would like to share about your college experi-
    ences, employment or other matters to help us better understand your life
    trajectory?

Notes

Chapter 1

1. Names of students reported throughout this book are pseudonyms used to protect individual confidentiality.

2. C. Wright Mills, *The Sociological Imagination* (New York: Oxford University Press, 1959).

3. Eighty-six percent of our sample graduated on time in 2009. For a full description of our methodology, sample, and data, see appendix A in this volume.

4. Jeffrey J. Arnett, *Emerging Adulthood: The Winding Road from the Late Teens through the Twenties* (New York: Oxford University Press, 2004).

5. David L. Kirp, *Shakespeare, Einstein, and the Bottom Line: The Marketing of Higher Education* (Cambridge, MA: Harvard University Press, 2003), 7.

6. Sheila Slaughter and Gary Rhoades, *Academic Capitalism and the New Economy* (Baltimore: John Hopkins University Press, 2004), 1.

7. Richard Matasar, "A Commercialist Manifesto: Entrepreneurs, Academics and Purity of Heart and Soul," *Florida Law Review* 48 (1996): 783, as cited in Kirp, *Shakespeare, Einstein, and the Bottom Line*, 98.

8. Julia Edwards, "Stephen Trachtenberg is Not Sorry," *National Journal*, October 1, 2012, http://www.nationaljournal.com/features/restoration-calls/stephen-trachtenberg -is-not-sorry-20120927?page=1.

9. Benjamin Ginsberg, *The Fall of the Faculty: The Rise of the All-Administrative University and Why It Matters* (Oxford: Oxford University Press, 2009), 2.

10. US Department of Education, National Center for Educational Statistics (NCES), *Digest of Educational Statistics, 2006*, by Thomas D Synder, Sally A. Dillow, and Charlene M. Hoffman, NCES 2007–017 (Washington: US Department of Education), table 227, as cited in Ginsberg, *The Fall of the Faculty*, 26.

11. For a discussion of how different actors within the higher education system have responded to measuring student learning outcomes, see Richard Arum, "Stakeholder and Public Responses to Measuring Student Learning," *Society* 50 (2013): 230–35.

12. Christopher P. Loss, *Between Citizens and the State: The Politics of American Higher Education in the 20th Century* (Princeton, NJ: Princeton University Press, 2012), 38.

13. Louis B. Hopkins, "Personnel Procedure in Education: Observations and Conclusions Resulting from Visits to Fourteen Institutions of Higher Learning," in *Educational Record* 7 (Washington: American Council on Education, 1926), 3–5, as cited in Loss, *Between Citizens and the State*, 34.

14. Loss makes the point that the admission forms used were adopted from similar ones that had been developed by personnel management specialists for the US Army. Personal information was also used to screen individual candidates to exclude applications based on ethnic origins. See Loss, *Between Citizens and the State*, 39–41.

15. Loss, *Between Citizens and the State*, 47–49.

16. Loss, *Between Citizens and the State*, 21.

17. Loss, *Between Citizens and the State*, 51.

18. Richard Arum, *Judging School Discipline: The Crisis of Moral Authority* (Cambridge, MA: Harvard University Press, 2009), 13.

19. Lauren Edelman, "Legal Ambiguity and Symbolic Structures: Organizational Mediation of Civil Rights Law," *American Journal of Sociology* 97 (1992): 1531–76; Lauren Edelman, "Legal Environments and Organizational Governance: The Expansion of Due Process in the Workplace," *American Journal of Sociology* 95 (1990): 1401–40.

20. Lawrence White, "Judicial Threats to Academe's 'Four Freedoms,'" *Chronicle of Higher Education*, December 1, 2006, as cited in Amy Gadja, *The Trials of Academe: The New Era of Campus Litigation* (Cambridge, MA: Harvard University Press, 2009), 15.

21. Howard Becker, Blanche Geer, and Everett Hughes, *Making the Grade: The Academic Side of College Life* (New Brunswick, NJ: Transaction Publishers, [1968] 1995), 7.

22. Sophomores in our data who reported studying alone less than five hours per week had grade point averages of 3.2 in their official transcripts.

23. David Riesman, *On Higher Education: The Academic Enterprise in an Era of Rising Student Consumerism* (New Brunswick, NJ: Transaction Publishers, 1980), 6.

24. Brian Jacob, Brian McCall, and Kevin M. Stange, "College as a Country Club: Do Colleges Cater to Students' Preferences for Consumption?" NBER working paper no. 18745 (Cambridge, MA: National Bureau of Economic Research, 2013).

25. Riesman, *On Higher Education*, 379.

26. Christian Smith with Melinda Lundquist Denton, *Soul Searching: The Religious and Spiritual Lives of American Teenagers* (New York: Oxford University Press, 2005), 162.

27. Smith, *Soul Searching*, 163.

28. Jennifer M. Silva, *Coming Up Short: Working Class Adulthood in an Age of Uncertainty* (New York: Oxford University Press, 2013), 21. See also Jonathan Imber, ed., *Therapeutic Culture: Triumph and Defeat* (Piscataway, NJ: Transaction Press, 2004).

29. Steven Brint and Allison M. Cantwell, "Undergraduate Time Use and Academic Outcomes: Results from University of California Undergraduate Experience Survey 2006," *Teachers College Record* 112 (2010): 2441–70.

30. Émile Durkheim, "On Education and Society," in *Power and Ideology in Education*, eds. Jerome Karabel and A. H. Halsey (Oxford: Oxford University Press, 1977), 92.

31. David Riesman, *The Lonely Crowd* (New Haven: Yale University Press, 2001 [1950]), 21.

32. Riesman, *Lonely Crowd*, 63.

33. Riesman, *Lonely Crowd*, 65.

34. Riesman, *Lonely Crowd*, 63.

35. Riesman, *Lonely Crowd*, 65.

36. Todd Gitlin, foreword to *The Lonely Crowd*, by David Riesman (New Haven: Yale University Press, 2001 [2000]), *xvi*.

37. Mitchell Stevens, *Creating a Class* (Cambridge, MA: Harvard University Press, 2007), 244.

38. Elizabeth A. Armstrong and Laura T. Hamilton, *Paying for the Party: How College Maintains Inequality* (Cambridge, MA: Harvard University Press, 2013), 21.

39. According to Armstrong and Hamilton, *Paying for the Party*, this may be particularly the case for middle- and upper-middle-class students. See also Jenny M. Stuber, *Inside the College Gates: How Class and Culture Matter in Higher Education* (Lanham, MD: Lexington Books, 2011); Mary Grigsby, *College Life Through the Eyes of Students* (Albany: State University Press of New York, 2009); Kathleen Bogle, *Hooking Up: Sex, Dating, and Relationships on Campus* (New York: New York University Press, 2008); and Rebekah Nathan, *My Freshman Year: What a Professor Learned by Becoming a Student* (Ithaca, NY: Cornell University Press, 2005).

40. Mary C. Waters, Patrick J. Carr, and Maria J. Kefalas, introduction to *Coming of Age in America: The Transition to Adulthood*, eds. Mary C. Waters, Patrick J. Carr, Maria J. Kefalas, and Jennifer Holdaway (Berkeley: University of California Press, 2011), 9.

41. Frank F. Furstenberg, Rubén G. Rumbaut, and Richard A. Settersten, "On the Frontier of Adulthood: Emerging Themes and New Directions," in *On the Frontier of Adulthood: Theory, Research, and Public Policy*, ed. Richard A. Settersten, Frank F. Furstenberg, and Rubén G. Rumbaut (Chicago: University of Chicago Press, 2008), 18.

42. Waters et al., introduction to *Coming of Age*, 1.

43. Richard Settersten and Barbara E. Ray, *Not Quite Adults: Why 20-Somethings Are Choosing a Slower Path to Adulthood, and Why It's Good for Everyone* (New York: Bantam Books, 2010), 83.

44. Katherine S. Newman, *The Accordion Family: Boomerang Kids, Anxious Parents, and the Private Toll of Global Competition* (Boston: Beacon, 2012), xix–xx.

45. Smith, *Lost in Transition*, 238.

46. Furstenberg, Rumbaut, and Settersten, "On the Frontier," 17.

47. John H. Pryor et al., *The American Freshman: Forty Year Trends, 1966–2006*, report of the Cooperative Institutional Research Program at the UCLA Higher Education Research Institute (Los Angeles: UCLA Higher Education Research Institute, 2007), 70–71.

48. Eurostudent IV 2008–11 data series "Form of Housing by Gender and Study Programme," in Dominic Orr, Christoph Gwosc, and Nicolai Netz, *Social and Economic Conditions of Student Life in Europe: Synopsis of Indicators, Final Report, Eurostudent IV 2008–2011*, report of Eurostudent (Hannover, Germany: Eurostudent, 2011).

49. See James S. Coleman, *The Adolescent Society: The Social Life of the Teenager and Its Impact on Education* (Westport, CT: Greenwood Publishing Group, 1981).

50. Michael J. Rosenfeld, *The Age of Independence: Interracial Unions, Same-Sex Unions, and the Changing American Family* (Cambridge, MA: Harvard University Press, 2007), 59.

51. Furstenberg, Rumbaut, and Settersten, "On the Frontier," 17.

52. Furstenberg, Rumbaut, and Settersten, "On The Frontier," 20.

53. See, for example, Geraldine Baum, "Student Loans Add to Angst at Occupy Wall Street," *Los Angeles Times*, October 25, 2011, http://articles.latimes.com/2011/oct/25 /nation/la-na-occupy-student-loans-20111026; Tamar Lewin, "Official Calls for Urgency on College Costs," *New York Times*, November 11, 2011, http://www.nytimes.com/2011 /11/30/education/duncan-calls-for-urgency-in-lowering-college-costs.html?smid =pl-share; and Samantha Stainburn, "Promises, Promises," *New York Times*, October 26, 2009, http://www.nytimes.com/2009/11/01/education/edlife/01forprofit-t.html.

54. See Arum, "Stakeholder and Public Responses," 234: "Since the release of *Academically Adrift* in January 2011, coverage of our work has increasingly come to focus on the issue of college costs and value. A search of news references of *Academically Adrift* in Lexis-Nexis Academic Universe clearly demonstrates this trend. In the first three months following publication, the book received 115 references in indexed sources with 43 percent of these references also including the search terms 'cost!' or 'value.' Over the next six months, the book received 93 news references with 55 percent utilizing these terms; the next six months had 61 references with 64 percent mentioning these terms; and the last six months ending on October 15, 2012, included 54 news references with 74 percent invoking these items."

55. David B. Grusky et al., *How Much Protection Does a College Degree Afford? The Impact of the Recession on Recent College Graduates*, report of Pew Charitable Trusts, Economic Mobility Project (Washington: Pew Charitable Trusts, 2013).

56. Yujia Liu and David B. Grusky, "The Payoff to Skill in the Third Industrial Revolution," *American Journal of Sociology* 118 (2013): 1330–74.

57. Liu and Grusky, "The Payoff to Skill in the Third Industrial Revolution," 1359.

58. Liu and Grusky, "The Payoff to Skill in the Third Industrial Revolution," 1357.

59. Liu and Grusky, "The Payoff to Skill in the Third Industrial Revolution," 1332.

60. David H. Autor, Frank Levy, and Richard J. Murnane, "The Skill Content of Recent Technological Change: An Empirical Investigation," *Quarterly Journal of Economics* 118 (2003): 1279–1333; W. Norton Grubb and Marvin Lazerson, "Vocationalism in Higher Education: The Triumph of the Education Gospel," *Journal of Higher Education* 76 (2005):1–25.

61. Derek Bok, *Our Underachieving Colleges: A Candid Look at How Much Students Learn and Why They Should Be Learning More* (Princeton, NJ: Princeton University Press, 2006); Association of American Colleges and Universities (AAC&U), *How Should Colleges Assess and Improve Student Learning? Employers' Views on the Accountability Challenge* (Washington: AAC&U, 2008); National Research Council, *Education for Life and Work: Developing Transferable Knowledge and Skills in the 21st Century*, (Washington: National Academies Press, 2012).

62. Jill Casner-Lotto, Linda Barrington, and Mary Wright, *Are They Really Ready to Work? Employers' Perspectives on the Basic Knowledge and Applied Skills of New Entrants to the 21st Century U.S. Workplace*, report of the Conference Board (Washington: Conference Board, 2006).

63. Karin Fischer, "A College Degree Sorts Job Applicants, but Employers Wish It Meant More," *Chronicle of Higher Education*, March 12, 2013, http://chronicle.com /article/The-Employment-Mismatch/137625/#id=overview.

64. The Organisation of Economic Co-operation and Development, *OECD Skills*

Outlook 2013: First Results from the Survey of Adult Skills (Paris: OECD Publishing, 2013), see figures 3.9, 3.10, 5.5.

65. Organisation of Economic Co-operation and Development, *Time for the U.S. to Reskill? What the Survey of Adult Skills Says* (Paris: OECD Publishing, 2013), 11.

66. See Stephen Klein, Ou Lydia Liu, and James Sconing, *Test Validity Study Report* (Washington: Fund for the Improvement of Postsecondary Education, 2009), http://cae .org/images/uploads/pdf/13_Test_Validity_Study_Report.pdf; and Ernest T. Pascarella et al., "How Robust are the Findings of Academically Adrift?" *Change: The Magazine of Higher Learning*, May/June 2011, 20–24.

67. Ernerst Pascarella et al., "How Robust are the Findings of *Academically Adrift?*"

Chapter 2

1. For an apt discussion of college as a time of exploration and personal development, see Jeffrey J. Arnett, *Emerging Adulthood: The Winding Road from Late Teens Through the Twenties* (New York: Oxford University Press, 2004).

2. Christopher P. Loss, *Between Citizens and the State: The Politics of American Higher Education in the 20th Century* (Princeton, NJ: Princeton University Press, 2012).

3. Alexandra Robbins, *Pledged: The Secret Life of Sororities* (New York: Hyperion, 2004); Murray Sperber, *Beer and Circus: How Big-Time College Sports is Crippling Undergraduate Education* (New York: Henry Holt, 2001).

4. Émile Durkheim, *The Rules of Sociological Method* (New York: Free Press, [1895] 1950), 6; see also, Émile Durkheim, *Moral Education: A Study in the Theory and Application of the Sociology of Education* (New York: Free Press, [1925] 1950).

5. David Riesman, *The Lonely Crowd: A Study of the Changing American Character* (New Haven: Yale University Press, [1950] 2001).

6. Riesman, *Lonely Crowd*, 64.

7. Riesman, *Lonely Crowd*, 143.

8. Riesman, *Lonely Crowd*, 46.

9. Riesman, *Lonely Crowd*, 23.

10. James S. Coleman, *The Adolescent Society: The Social Life of the Teenager and its Impact on Education* (New York: Free Press of Glencoe, 1961); see also Murray Milner, *Freaks, Geeks, and Cool Kids: American Teenagers, Schools, and the Culture of Consumption* (New York: Routledge, 2004).

11. Elizabeth A. Armstrong and Laura T. Hamilton, *Paying for the Party: How College Maintains Inequality* (Cambridge, MA: Harvard University Press, 2013); Mary Grigsby, *College Life Through the Eyes of Students* (Albany: State University Press of New York, 2009).

12. Mitchell Stevens, Elizabeth Armstrong, and Richard Arum, "Sieve, Incubator, Temple, Hub: Empirical and Theoretical Advances in the Sociology of Higher Education," *Annual Review of Sociology* 34 (2008): 123.

13. However, as Grigsby (*College Life through the Eyes of Students*) and others have pointed out, the perception of diversity is amplified among white students.

14. George D. Kuh, "The Other Curriculum: Out-of-Class Experiences Associated with Student Learning and Personal Development," *Journal of Higher Education* 66 (1995): 123–55.

15. Armstrong and Hamilton, *Paying for the Party*.

16. Annette Lareau, *Unequal Childhoods: Class, Race, and Family Life* (Berkeley: University of California Press, 2003).

17. Riesman, *Lonely Crowd*, 143.

18. Gary R. Pike and George D. Kuh, "Relationships among Structural Diversity, Informal Peer Interactions and Perceptions of the Campus Environment," *Review of Higher Education* 29 (2006): 425–50.

19. Charles Blaich, *How do Students Change over Four Years of College?*, report of the Center of Inquiry in the Liberal Arts at Wabash College (Crawfordsville, IN: Center of Inquiry in the Liberal Arts at Wabash College, 2011), http://www.liberalarts.wabash.edu/storage/4-year-change-summary-website.pdf.

20. Josipa Roksa et al., "Racial Gaps in Critical Thinking: The Role of Institutional Context," paper presented at the 2014 AERA meeting, Philadelphia, April 3–7, 2014.

21. Riesman, *Lonely Crowd*.

22. Grigsby, *College Life through the Eyes of Students*, 64.

23. Alexander W. Astin, *What Matters in College? Four Critical Years Revisited* (San Francisco: Jossey-Bass, 1993); Vincent Tinto, *Leaving College: Rethinking the Causes and Cures of Student Attrition* (Chicago: University of Chicago Press, 1994).

24. See, for example, Sylvia Hurtado and Deborah Faye Carter, "Effects of College Transition and Perceptions of the Campus Racial Climate on Latino College Students' Sense of Belonging," *Sociology of Education* 70 (1997): 324–45; and William G. Tierney, "An Anthropological Analysis of Student Participation in College," *Journal of Higher Education* 63 (1992): 603–18.

25. Elizabeth Aries and Maynard Seider, "The Interactive Relationship Between Class Identity and the College Experience: The Case of Lower Income Students," *Qualitative Sociology* 28 (2005): 419–43; Jenny M. Stuber, *Inside the College Gates: How Class and Culture Matter in Higher Education* (Lanham, MD: Lexington Books, 2011).

26. Lareau, *Unequal Childhoods*.

27. Stuber, *Inside the College Gates*.

28. Armstrong and Hamilton, *Paying for the Party*.

29. The distribution of hours in a typical week is as follows: attending class, 13.9; studying (alone and with peers), 12; working, volunteering, fraternities/sororities, and student clubs, 19.3; sleeping (estimated), 46.2; socializing, recreating, and other, 76.6. Hours sleeping are estimated based on the detailed time-use data reported in *Taming the River* by Charles et al. (2009). Since students' reports exceeded the 168 hours available in a week, we adjusted the estimates to reflect a 168-hour week. In *Academically Adrift*, due to a calculation error, we slightly underestimated the amount of time students spend sleeping. See Camille Z. Charles et al., *Taming the River: Negotiating the Academic, Financial, and Social Currents in Selective Colleges and Universities* (Princeton, NJ: Princeton University Press, 2009).

30. Steven Brint and Allison M. Cantwell, "Undergraduate Time Use and Academic Outcomes: Results from the University of California Undergraduate Experience Survey 2006," *Teachers College Record* 112 (2010): 2441–70.

31. Richard Arum and Josipa Roksa, *Academically Adrift: Limited Learning on College Campuses* (Chicago: University of Chicago Press, 2011), 97.

32. National Survey of Student Engagement, *Assessment for Improvement: Tracking Student Engagement over Time: Annual Results from 2009* (Bloomington: Indiana University Center for Postsecondary Research, 2009).

33. Ray Franke et al., *Findings from the 2009 Administration of the College Senior Survey (CSS): National Aggregates*, report of the Cooperative Institutional Research Program at

the UCLA Higher Education Research Institute (Los Angeles: University of California, Los Angeles Higher Education Research Institute, 2010).

34. Southern Association of Colleges and Schools Commission on Colleges (SACSCOC), *Credit Hours Policy Statement* (Decatur, GA: SACSCOC, 2012), http://www .sacscoc.org/subchg/policy/CreditHours.pdf.

35. Philip S. Babcock and Mindy Marks, "The Falling Time Cost of College: Evidence from Half a Century of Time Use Data," *Review of Economics and Statistics* 93 (2011): 468–78.

36. Authors' calculations comparing high school cohorts from High School and Beyond (class of 1982), the National Education Longitudinal Study (class of 1992), and the Educational Longitudinal Study (class of 2004).

37. Dominic Orr, Christoph Gwosc, and Nicolai Netz, *Social and Economic Conditions of Student Life in Europe: Synopsis of Indicators, Final Report, Eurostudent IV 2008–2011*, report of Eurostudent (Hannover, Germany: Eurostudent, 2011).

38. For descriptive purposes, schools were divided into quintiles based on the 2009 sample, with those in the bottom quintile regarded as less selective, those in the top quintile as more selective, and those in the middle three quintiles as selective. See further description in table A2.1 in appendix A.

39. Steven Brint, Allison M. Cantwell, and Robert A. Hanneman, "The Two Cultures of Undergraduate Academic Engagement," *Research in Higher Education* 49 (2008): 383–402; Steven Brint, Allison M. Cantwell, and Preeta Saxena, "Disciplinary Categories, Majors, and Undergraduate Academic Experiences: Rethinking Bok's 'Underachieving Colleges' Thesis," *Research in Higher Education* 53 (2012): 1–25.

40. Derek Bok, *Our Underachieving Colleges: A Candid Look at How Much Students Learn and Why They Should Be Learning More* (Princeton, NJ: Princeton University Press, 2006); Association of American Colleges and Universities (AAC&U), *How Should Colleges Assess and Improve Student Learning? Employers' Views on the Accountability Challenge* (Washington: AAC&U, 2008); National Research Council, *Education for Life and Work: Developing Transferable Knowledge and Skills in the 21st Century* (Washington: National Academies Press, 2012).

41. A recent replication using data from the Wabash National Study of Liberal Arts Education, relying on a different sample and a multiple-choice measure of critical thinking (the Collegiate Assessment of Academic Proficiency, or CAAP), produced a virtually identical estimate; students in the Wabash Study gained 0.44 standard deviations on the CAAP measure of critical thinking over four years of college. See Ernest T. Pascarella et al., "How Robust Are the Findings of *Academically Adrift*?" *Change: The Magazine of Higher Learning*, May/June 2011: 20–24.

42. In earlier work, we have referred to this finding as indicating that 36 percent of students demonstrated no statistically significant gains on the CLA over four years of college (and 45 percent over the first two years of college). Detailed descriptive information provided in the appendixes of *Academically Adrift* provides readers with the opportunity to recalculate these numbers based on different assumptions of underlying distributions and amounts of measurement error. Regardless of whether the proportion of students showing no statistically significant gain would be somewhat smaller or larger under these different assumptions, the data reveal that many students show very little evidence of gains on the CLA. We thus prefer the descriptive approach to presenting the data. The CLA scores in our samples vary by approximately 1,000 points. For descriptive purposes, if we were

to convert it to a 100-point scale, 36 percent of seniors (and 45 percent of sophomores) would not have improved more than one point on the test since their freshman year.

43. This comparison is based on two different samples: the sophomore sample in *Academically Adrift* and the senior sample used in this study. The senior sample, of course, is more selective (the students have higher SAT scores, higher initial CLA scores, etc.). If we considered only students who were in the sample at all three time points (i.e., those who made it not only to the sophomore but also to the senior year), the gain over the first two years would be 0.086 standard deviations per semester. If anything, students gained more on the CLA in their first two years of college than in their last two.

44. Ola Svenson, "Are We All Less Risky and More Skillful Than Our Fellow Drivers?" *Acta Psychologica* 47 (1981): 143–48.

45. Jill Casner-Lotto, Linda Barrington, and Mary Wright, *Are They Really Ready to Work? Employers' Perspectives on the Basic Knowledge and Applied Skills of New Entrants to the 21st Century U.S. Workplace*, report of the Conference Board (Washington: Conference Board, 2006).

46. For descriptive purposes, schools were divided into quintiles based on the 2009 sample, with those in the bottom quintile regarded as less selective, those in the top quintile as more selective, and those in the middle three quintiles as selective. See further description in table A2.1 in appendix A. This categorization is different from that used for model-based results of predicted CLA scores.

47. Karl L. Alexander and Aaron M. Pallas, "School Sector and Cognitive Performance: When Is a Little a Little?" *Sociology of Education* 58 (1985), 120.

48. For a statistical explanation of why this formulation can be considered to estimate growth between two time points, see Thomas Hoffer, Andrew M. Greeley, and James S. Coleman, "Achievement Growth in Public and Catholic Schools," *Sociology of Education* 58 (1985): 82.

49. Other research has shown this pattern of substantially more variation existing within than across institutions with respect to several other outcomes. For recent examples, see Kevin Carey, *A Matter of Degrees: Improving Graduation Rates in Four-Year Colleges and Universities*, report of the Education Trust (Washington: Education Trust, 2004); Charles Blaich, "How do Students Change?"; National Survey of Student Engagement, *Promoting Engagement for All Students: The Imperative to Look Within* (Bloomington: Indiana University Center for Postsecondary Research, 2008).

50. Supplemental fixed effects models (which include indicators for each institution except one) show that once all stable institutional-level characteristics are controlled, the coefficients for race/ethnicity and SAT scores decrease even further, although they remain statistically significant.

51. This is likely an underestimate of the extent to which students change majors for two reasons: (a) we are working within a set number of categories (thirty-three), which means that fine-grained changes within those categories are not captured; and (b) students sometimes start with a particular major, change the major, and then revert back to the original. We are not capturing this type of change, but only the similarity of the students' majors at the points of entry and completion.

52. See endnote 46 and table A2.1 in appendix A for definitions.

53. Franke et al., *Findings from the 2009 Administration of the College Senior Survey* (Los Angeles: UCLA Higher Education Research Institute, 2010).

54. Eliot Aronson and Judson Mills, "The Effect of Severity of Initiation on Liking for a Group," *The Journal of Abnormal and Social Psychology* 59 (1959): 177.

55. Reported percentages are based on the first follow-up of the respective B&B cohorts—i.e., the 1994 follow-up of the 1992–93 cohort, the 2001 follow-up of the 1999–2000 cohort, and the 2009 follow-up of the 2007–8 cohort.

56. Interestingly, while there is an association between institutional selectivity and graduate school attendance in a bivariate model, the selectivity of the undergraduate institution does not predict the likelihood of graduate school attendance, net of other factors (see table A2.3 in appendix A).

57. The high category represents one standard deviation above the mean, and the low category one standard deviation below the mean.

58. Supplemental analyses similarly reveal that a student's college GPA is related to the probability of his or her attending full-time master's, professional, or doctoral programs, but is not related to the probability of his or her attending other and part-time programs.

59. Due to the small numbers of cases, we had to collapse the multinomial logit into a logistic regression, comparing full-time master's, professional, and doctoral programs with nonenrollment or enrollment in part-time and other programs. Similar patterns are obtained if the reference group is restricted to students who are not enrolled in graduate school.

60. Eric Eide and Geetha Waehrer, "The Role of the Option Value of College Attendance in College Major Choice," *Economics of Education Review* 17 (1998): 73–82.

61. Loss, *Between Citizens and the State*, 22.

62. George D. Kuh et al., *What Matters to Student Success: A Review of the Literature* (Washington: National Postsecondary Education Cooperative, 2006).

63. Riesman, *Lonely Crowd*.

64. Kuh, "The Other Curriculum," 123.

65. Gary S. Becker, *Human Capital: A Theoretical and Empirical Analysis, with Special Reference to Education* (Chicago: University of Chicago Press, [1964] 2009).

66. AAC&U, *How Should Colleges Assess and Improve Student Learning?*

67. Casner-Lotto et al., *Are They Really Ready to Work?*

68. Bok, *Our Underachieving Colleges*.

Chapter 3

1. Megan McArdle, "Is College a Lousy Investment?" *Newsweek*, September 9, 2012, http://www.thedailybeast.com/newsweek/2012/09/09/megan-mcardle-on-the-coming -burst-of-the-college-bubble.html; Adam Davidson, "The Dwindling Power of a College Degree," *New York Times*, November 23, 2011, http://www.nytimes.com/2011/11/27 /magazine/changing-rules-for-success.html; Alex Williams, "Saying No to College," *New York Times*, November 30, 2012, http://www.nytimes.com/2012/12/02/fashion/saying-no -to-college.html?smid=pl-share. It is worth noting, however, that there has also been media coverage focusing on the continued positive economic value of college degrees (see, for example, Tamar Lewin, "Value of College Degree is Growing, Study Says," *New York Times*, September 21, 2010, http://www.nytimes.com/2010/09/21/education/21college .html; Andrew J. Rotherham, "Actually, College Is Very Much Worth It," *Time*, May 19, 2011, http://www.time.com/time/nation/article/0,8599,2072432,00.html), as well as coverage bringing attention to the general debate on the topic (see e.g., Derek Thompson, "The Value of College Is: (a) Growing (b) Flat (c) Falling (d) All of the Above," *Atlantic*, September 27, 2011, http://www.theatlantic.com/business/archive/2011/09/the-value -of-college-is-a-growing-b-flat-c-falling-d-all-of-the-above/245746/).

2. While many college graduates' lifetime earnings will not catch up to those of high school graduates (who have foregone college) until their early thirties, over their careers these initial investments in education will yield very high rates of return. Since Gary Becker's seminal work in the 1960s, it has been well established and widely accepted by almost all social scientists that college is a good investment for most students. Becker argued that the typical high school graduate at the time of his analysis would receive approximately a 10- to 11-percent private rate of return attending college, as compared to a 7 percent return investing in corporate manufacturing—another investment characterized by high liquidity and large risks. Although the point estimates of returns to college have fluctuated since the 1960s, given changes in cost and earnings, the central tenet of Becker's work is not seriously contested. Sociologists Yu Xie and Jennie Brand recently demonstrated that this is particularly true for disadvantaged youth. See Yu Xie and Jennie Brand, "Who Benefits Most from College? Evidence from Negative Selection in Heterogeneous Economic Returns to Higher Education," *American Sociological Review* 75 (2010): 273–302. See also Gary Becker, *Human Capital: A Theoretical and Empirical Analysis, with Special Reference to Education* (Chicago: University of Chicago Press, [1964] 2009).

3. Prior research has established that even after controlling for years of education, test scores have a modest positive association with labor market success. See, for example, Claude S. Fischer et al., *Inequality by Design: Cracking the Bell Curve Myth* (Princeton, NJ: Princeton University Press, 1996).

4. It is virtually impossible to disentangle the relative contributions of these different mechanisms whereby college has effects on labor market success, as individuals with varying levels and types of education tend to differ along all three dimensions that are argued to lead to improved labor market outcomes. For example, consider the selectivity of the college attended. Both the credentialist and the social network approaches would expect that going to a more selective college would confer advantages on students attending it, either through signaling or through improved access to valuable social networks. An approach that focused on student learning and the development of cognitive skills would expect that student labor market outcomes would mainly vary to the extent that the development of those skills differed across colleges of varying selectivity levels.

5. Underlying the common belief in the importance of social networks is the reality that one often finds jobs through network relationships. However, there is actually only mixed evidence in existing empirical research that employment positions found by these means are significantly better than other jobs. While research on the extent to which individual social relationships are associated with positive employment outcomes is inconclusive, research on school-employer linkages suggest that these mechanisms can be significant—although the individuals who take advantage of these mechanisms are selected on other underlying factors that might themselves be responsible for the positive employment outcomes.

6. This is a big assumption. There has been a rise in rates of college matriculation over the past few decades. However, less than 60 percent of college students are earning degrees. Bowen et al. find that minority and poor students have lower graduation rates, even when controlling for other factors. Their findings suggest that institutional resources and policies (such as financial aid) affect rates of graduation. See William G. Bowen, Matthew M. Chingos, and Michael S. McPherson, *Crossing the Finish Line: Completing College at America's Public Universities* (Princeton, NJ: Princeton University Press, 2009).

7. If one compared the ratios of logged percentages of unemployment, those without college degrees were 1.7 times more likely to be unemployed.

8. We distinguish between part-time employment of fewer than twenty hours per week and part-time employment of twenty or more hours per week, as the former category is considerably more marginal in terms of both income and labor force attachment. The distribution of reported income for respondents working fewer than twenty hours per week was as follows: 72%, less than $10,000; 21%, between $10,000 and $19,999; and 7%, greater than $20,000. For graduates working twenty or more hours per week, the distribution was: 34 %, less than $10,000; 51%, between $10,000 and $19,999; 9%, between $20,000 and $30,000; and 5%, greater than $30,000 (percentages do not sum to 100 due to rounding).

9. The status attainment tradition that developed from Blau and Duncan's (1967) seminal work rests on the repeated demonstration of this relationship. See Peter M. Blau and Otis Dudley Duncan, *American Occupational Structure* (New York: Free Press, 1967).

10. Specifically, our cutoff is zero on the Hauser and Warren education dimension of their started logit of the proportion of individuals in the employed civilian labor force who had completed at least some college as of 1990, based on 1990 census occupational codes. The started logit transformation takes the following form: $ln\,[(p + 1)/(100 - p + 1)]$. See Robert M. Hauser and John Robert Warren, "Socioeconomic Indexes for Occupations: A Review, Update and Critique," *Sociological Methodology* 27 (1997): 177–298.

11. In our analysis we have applied a very conservative cutoff that potentially biases our findings in the direction of underreporting the prevalence of recent college graduates holding employment in unskilled occupations. For a methodological approach that utilizes a less conservative cutoff, see Jaison R. Abel, Richard Deitz, and Yaqin Su's 2014 Federal Reserve Bank of New York report "Are Recent College Graduates Finding Good Jobs?" The report distinguishes among occupations based on reports of the level of education required for the job (as opposed to the actual educational level of individuals in occupational positions) and defines underemployment as any occupation that fewer than 50 percent of respondents reported required a college degree. The authors claim that 44 percent of recent college graduates (and 33 percent of college graduates who have reached their thirties) are underemployed—that is, are in occupations that do not require college degrees.

12. Throughout this chapter, we highlight respondents' major and institutional selectivity, as those represent important dimensions of variation examined in statistical analyses.

13. For descriptive purposes, institutions were divided into three selectivity categories, approximating the top quintile (more selective), three middle quintiles (selective), and the bottom quintile (less selective) of the senior year distribution (see table A2.1). This categorization is different from that used for predicted probabilities.

14. We also ran supplementary analyses separately by gender, to explore possible variation in male and female school-to-work processes. We found few statistically significant differences in coefficients by gender, and the few differences we did find were likely artifacts of our small sample size. For example, African-American male college graduates were less likely to be unemployed than were African-American female college graduates, Asian male college graduates were less likely to have lost a job over the prior year than were Asian female college graduates, and female college graduates who had majored in engineering and computer science or had attended selective colleges were less likely to be working in unskilled jobs than were similar male graduates. Given that

the differences in coefficients by gender are not consistent across outcomes, we refrain from reporting and discussing them in the text.

15. We have repeatedly made this suggestion in a *New York Times* editorial, in government hearings, and elsewhere, but to no avail. Social scientists who are frustrated by the limitations of our data should join us in pressuring the federal government to add objective performance measures to the data they make publicly available for research purposes.

16. See Anthony Carnevale, Ban Cheah, and Jeff Strohl, *Hard Times: College Majors, Unemployment and Earnings,* report of the Georgetown Public Policy Institute, Center on Education and the Workforce (Washington: Georgetown Public Policy Institute, 2013), http://www9.georgetown.edu/grad/gppi/hpi/cew/pdfs/HardTimes.2013.2.pdf. The larger sample sizes in their analyses allow for more fine-grained distinctions across majors as well as across programs within majors. They find that graduates who had majored in humanities, social sciences, communication, psychology, and social work had higher rates of recent college graduate unemployment than did business majors. Given that they find lower rates of unemployment for education and health professions, we refrain from identifying those fields of study in the text, regardless of the fact that in our analysis they fall into broad field-of-study categories with higher rates of unemployment.

17. Michael Hout, "More Universalism and Less Structural Mobility: The American Occupational Structure in the 1980s," *American Journal of Sociology* 93 (1988): 1358–1400.

18. Other possibilities exist, of course, such as firm or plant closings, as well as personal moves and other reasons for job loss. However, in supplementary analysis we found evidence that approximately half of the graduates who reported job loss had been terminated or laid off, or had temporary jobs that had not been extended by employers. In our 2011 survey, we asked unemployed respondents why they were unemployed. Of the nineteen respondents who reported both having lost a job in the prior year and being unemployed at the time of the survey (spring 2011), twelve reported having been terminated or laid off, or having had a temporary job not extended by an employer.

19. In addition to CLA performance, gender is related to job loss, with males being more likely to experience job loss than females.

20. Low and high CLA categories are defined as one standard deviation above or below the mean of the senior CLA scores.

21. Table A3.5 also includes regressions for logged income (ln), and the explained variance in these models is slightly lower, so we reference the regressions for income in dollars in the text. Student reports of income are constrained by the closed-ended survey structure that does not generate specific details on outliers at the top of the distribution. Given the categorical nature of self-reported income, we also ran ordered logit models with the pattern of significant effects similar to those discussed in the text.

22. For a review of this literature, see Theodore P. Gerber and Sin Yi Cheung, "Horizontal Stratification in Postsecondary Education: Forms, Explanations, and Implications," *Annual Review of Sociology* 34 (2008): 299–318.

23. High categories refer to one standard deviation above the mean, and low to one standard deviation below the mean, of college selectivity and senior CLA scores.

24. In table A3.7 we also present an alternative operationalization of this outcome. In addition to unemployment and working in unskilled occupations, 4 percent of graduates in the labor force were working fewer than twenty hours per week. One can include consideration of this additional negative labor market outcome, under-

employment, by conducting an analysis that defines labor market success as avoiding unemployment, underemployment, and unskilled occupations. Twenty-three percent of college graduates who were not enrolled full-time in graduate school were experiencing one of these negative labor market outcomes two years after on-time graduation. Graduates who had attended highly selective colleges had an 83 percent likelihood of avoiding such a negative outcome two years after on-time graduation, compared to a 73 percent likelihood if they had attended low selectivity colleges. Students who performed well on the CLA had an 81 percent likelihood of avoiding this broadly defined negative outcome, compared to a 75 percent likelihood if they had performed less well on the assessment as seniors.

25. High categories refer to one standard deviation above the mean, and low to one standard deviation below the mean, of college selectivity and senior CLA scores.

26. Mark Granovetter, *Getting a Job: A Study of Contacts and Careers* (Chicago: University of Chicago Press, [1974] 1995), 11. Italics in original.

27. The range of estimates for the occurrence of this job search strategy vary widely from 20 percent to 60 percent, given differences in sampling and research methods. See Granovetter, *Getting a Job*, 139–41.

28. Of course, some alumni continue to use college career resources long after they graduate, but current students and recent alumni are the main beneficiaries of these resources.

29. Sarah Damaske, "Brown Suits Need Not Apply: The Intersection of Race, Gender and Class in Institutional Network Building," *Sociological Forum* 24 (2009): 404.

30. Damaske, "Brown Suits Need Not Apply," suggests that some college career centers' mission to promote social mobility is in tension with their need to maintain good relationships with potential employers. In an attempt to show employers that their colleges are viable sources for high-quality employees, career center staff may restrict students' access to potential employers in a way that reproduces class and racial inequality. For instance, if a career center staff perceives that potential employers are not interested in hiring minority workers, they may unintentionally or intentionally limit minority students' access to these employers.

31. James E. Rosenbaum, *Beyond College for All: Career Paths for the Forgotten Half* (New York: Russell Sage Foundation, 2001), 209.

32. As discussed above, forcing respondents to describe such a complex process in a closed-ended way is somewhat limiting. We compensate for this limitation by supplementing our survey data with in-depth interview data from eighty recent graduates.

33. Qualitative research suggests that the job search process is actually quite complex, making it difficult for survey instruments to accurately capture how common it is for people to find jobs through personal contacts. For instance, most surveys do not capture the fact that many people employ multiple job search strategies at the same time, often supplementing formal applications with informal "back channel" strategies such as having a personal contact put in a good word for them with hiring managers. Furthermore, with a few exceptions (see Granovetter, *Getting a Job*), most studies restrict their samples to people who have actively searched for work, despite the fact that research has shown that a significant portion of people (29 percent, in Granovetter's 1974 study) find jobs without actively searching for them. Thus, it can be difficult to obtain a clear understanding of how common it is to find a job through personal contacts.

34. When confronted with a closed-ended survey asking them to select one job search method, these respondents could have chosen either one. Given the generally

meritocratic philosophical leanings of the American population, it is likely that such a respondent would opt for the "employment agency or advertisement" response.

35. For reasons discussed in the following subsection, "Internships, Volunteer Opportunities, and Former Employers," this figure is likely higher than our survey data suggests.

36. See tables A3.5 and A3.6 in appendix A.

37. Elizabeth A. Armstrong and Laura T. Hamilton, *Paying for the Party: How College Maintains Inequality* (Cambridge, MA: Harvard University Press, 2013), 199.

38. Armstrong and Hamilton, *Paying for the Party*, 200.

39. Nan Lin, "Social Networks and Status Attainment," *Annual Review of Sociology* 25 (1999): 481. However, personal contacts may also play quite a large role in hiring at the *top* of the occupational status hierarchy (See Lin, "Social Networks and Status Attainment," 482, and Granovetter, *Getting a Job*).

40. Due to the limited number of cases in our sample, we combined college resources and internship categories in our analysis.

41. Damaske, "Brown Suits Need Not Apply," suggests that low-status institutions may allow employers with "bad" job openings to participate in their career fairs, as they often have difficulty recruiting participation from "good" employers. This is unlikely to be the case at most of the institutions included in our sample.

42. These positive associations are most certainly also related to selection, and thus one cannot assume that they are causal in character.

43. In bivariate descriptive analyses, we found that only 2 percent of graduates who reported having located jobs through their colleges experienced negative labor market outcomes (defined here as working in an unskilled occupation). By contrast, 18 and 21 percent of those who found work through formal means or personal ties, respectively, were working in unskilled jobs.

44. There is a dearth of rigorous survey data on the prevalence of skills testing in hiring processes, but recent accounts in the HR professional press and mainstream media suggest that it is becoming increasingly common. Historically, skills testing has been more common for positions that do not require a bachelor's degree, but anecdotal evidence suggests that it is becoming increasingly common across the education spectrum. See Thomas Friedman, "How to Get a Job," *New York Times*, May 28, 2013, http://www.nytimes.com/2013/05/29/opinion/friedman-how-to-get-a-job.html?src=ISMR_AP_LO_MST_FB. See also Dave Zielinski, "Effective Assessments," *HR Magazine* 56 (2011), http://www.shrm.org/publications/hrmagazine/editorialcontent/2011/0111/pages/0111zielinski.aspx.

45. Arne L. Kalleberg, "Work Values and Job Rewards: A Theory of Job Satisfaction," *American Sociological Review* 42 (1977): 124–43.

46. Kalleberg, "Work Values and Job Rewards," 125.

47. The means between the groups were statistically different at the $p < .05$ level (standard errors adjusted for school-level clustering). While CLA performance was statistically associated with overall job satisfaction in a bivariate analysis, these results were not statistically significant when controlled for a range of other factors in the multivariate framework employed elsewhere in this chapter.

48. Stephen Vaisey, "Education and Its Discontents: Overqualification in America, 1972–2002," *Social Forces* 85 (2006): 835–64.

49. The means between the groups were statistically different at the $p < .01$ level (standard errors adjusted for school-level clustering).

50. Correlations with overall job satisfaction and use on the job of the following competencies were as follows: writing, 0.322; solving complex problems, 0.412; thinking critically, 0.456; analyzing arguments, 0.301; using evidence to support arguments, 0.322; understanding data charts and graphs, 0.303; synthesizing information from different sources, 0.395; knowledge from major, 0.401; teamwork/collaboration, 0.383 (all correlations significant at the $p < .01$ level).

51. Students that reported studying alone more than five hours per week had even higher self-assessments of learning: for critical thinking, 87 percent had positive reports of self-reported learning (i.e., the top three categories of a seven category scale) and 32 percent reported the highest category; for written communication, 72 percent had positive reports in the top three categories and 21 percent reported the highest category.

Chapter 4

1. Jeffery J. Arnett, *Emerging Adulthood: The Winding Road from Late Teens through the Twenties* (New York: Oxford University Press, 2004). Arnett defines emerging adulthood as spanning from the ages of eighteen to twenty-five, with flexibility at the upper boundary. Respondents in our sample were approximately twenty-three years of age in 2011.

2. Arnett, *Emerging Adulthood*, 210.

3. Arnett, *Emerging Adulthood*, 210.

4. Richard Settersten and Barbara Ray, "What's Going on with Young People Today? The Long and Twisting Path to Adulthood," *The Future of Children* 20 (2010): 19–41.

5. Jeffrey J. Arnett, "Learning to Stand Alone: The Contemporary American Transition to Adulthood." *Human Development* 41 (1998): 5–6.

6. Robert Bellah et al., *Habits of the Heart: Individualism and Commitment in American Life* (Berkeley: University of California Press, 1985).

7. Carl Desportes Bowman, "Holding them Closer," *Hedgehog Review* 15.3 (2013): 8–23.

8. Richard A. Settersten and Barbara E. Ray, *Not Quite Adults: Why 20-Somethings Are Choosing a Slower Path to Adulthood and Why It's Good for Everyone* (New York: Bantam Books, 2010).

9. Katherine S. Newman, *The Accordion Family: Boomerang Kids, Anxious Parents, and the Private Toll of Globalization* (Boston: Beacon, 2012).

10. CLA performance and college selectivity are not related to whether graduates live at home in the full model presented in table A4.3. Those variables are statistically significant in reduced models, especially before employment and schooling variables are included. Relationships between CLA and college selectivity with educational and labor market outcomes were explored in preceding chapters. In this discussion, we are thus highlighting the more proximal influences of post-college outcomes.

11. A continuous measure of the amount of debt is also not statistically significant.

12. Richard Settersten and Barbara Ray, "What's Going On with Young People Today?" For a recent review of the literature on the implications of the demographic trends for increasing inequality, see Judith A. Seltzer and Suzanne M. Bianchi, "Demographic Change and Parent-Child Relationships in Adulthood," *Annual Review of Sociology*, 39 (2013): 275–90.

13. Supplemental multinomial logistic regression models indicate that men are more likely to live with friends than are women, compared to either living with parents or living alone or with spouses or partners ($p < 0.05$).

14. Michael Kimmel, *Guyland: The Perilous World Where Boys Become Men* (New York: Harper, 2008).

15. Eric Klinenberg, *Going Solo: The Extraordinary Rise and Surprising Appeal of Living Alone* (New York: Penguin, 2012).

16. The original question asked whether respondents received assistance from "parents or relatives." However, given the description of assistance provided in the interviews, as well as prior research on family assistance for young adults (see references in the following paragraph), it is safe to assume that the majority of assistance came from parents. For simplicity, therefore, we describe the findings in terms of "assistance from parents."

17. Anna Manzoni, "An Intersectional Approach to Measuring Youth Pathways to Independence" (paper presented at the spring 2013 meeting of RC28, Trento, Italy, May 16–18, 2013).

18. Robert Schoeni and Karen Ross, "Material Assistance from Families during the Transition to Adulthood," in *On the Frontier to Adulthood: Theory, Research, and Public Policy*, ed. Richard Settersten, Frank Furstenberg, and Rubén Rumbaut (Chicago: University of Chicago Press, 2005), 396.

19. Patrick Wightman et al., "Historical Trends in Parental Financial Support of Young Adults," PSC report no. 13-801 (Ann Arbor: University of Michigan Population Studies Center, 2013).

20. Settersten and Ray, "What's Going on With Young People Today?" 20.

21. Wightman et al., "Historical Trends in Parental Financial Support."

22. Frank Furstenberg, "On a New Schedule: Transitions to Adulthood and Family Change," *The Future of Children* 20 (2010): 67.

23. Schoeni and Ross, "Material Assistance from Families," 396.

24. Settersten and Ray, *Not Quite Adults*.

25. Settersten and Ray, "What's Going on With Young People Today?"

26. Kathleen Bogle, *Hooking Up: Sex, Dating, and Relationships on Campus* (New York: New York University Press, 2008).

27. Arthur Levine and Diane Dean, *Generation on a Tightrope: A Portrait of Today's College Student* (San Francisco: Wiley, 2012).

28. Elizabeth A. Armstrong and Laura T. Hamilton, *Paying for the Party: How College Maintains Inequality* (Cambridge, MA: Harvard University Press, 2013).

29. Thomas DiPrete and Claudia Buchmann, *The Rise of Women: The Growing Gender Gap in Education and What It Means for American Schools* (New York: Russell Sage Foundation, 2013).

30. Ben Gose, "Liberal-Arts Colleges Ask: Where Have the Men Gone?," *Chronicle of Higher Education*, June 6, 1997; Susan Thomson, "Male Students' College Achievement Gap Brings Concern," *Washington Post*, August 31, 2003.

31. Low and high presence of women refers to one standard deviation below and above the mean.

32. Notably, this pattern held for both women and men. The interaction between gender and the percentage of females at the college was not statistically significant.

33. For differences in relationship patterns between African American and white teenagers and young adults, see US Department of Health and Human Services, Office of the Assistant Secretary for Planning and Evaluation, *Pathways to Adulthood and Marriage: Teenagers' Attitudes, Expectations, and Relationship Patterns*, by Robert G. Wood, Sarah Avellar, and Brian Goesling, PP08-66 (Washington: US Department of Health and Human Services, 2008), 12. For differences in relationship patterns among Asian

American adolescents, see Karen Carver, Kara Joyner, and J. Richard Udry, "National Estimates of Adolescent Romantic Relationships," in *Adolescent Romantic Relations and Sexual Behavior: Theory, Research, and Practical Implications*, ed. Paul Florscheim (Mahwah, NJ: Lawrence Erlbaum Associates Publishers, 2003), 23–56.

34. Richard Breen and Leire Salazar, "Educational Assortative Mating and Earnings Inequality in the United States," *American Journal of Sociology* 117 (2011): 808–43.

35. High selectivity represents one standard deviation above the mean, and low selectivity represents one standard deviation below the mean.

36. $r = 0.737, p < 0.01$.

37. Institutions were divided into three selectivity categories approximating the top quintile, three middle quintiles, and the bottom quintile of the senior-year distribution (see table A2.1). We calculated the percentage of respondents whose partners attended institutions in the same selectivity category.

38. Miller McPherson, Lynn Smith-Lovin, and James M. Cook, "Birds of a Feather: Homophily in Social Networks," *Annual Review of Sociology* 27 (2001): 415–44.

39. Karly Sarita Ford and Richard Arum, "Same-College Partnering: Educational Homogamy 1975–2005," working paper (New York: New York University, 2013).

40. Richard Arum, Josipa Roksa, and Michelle Budig, "The Romance of College Attendance: Higher Education Stratification and Mate Selection," *Research in Social Stratification and Mobility* 26 (2008): 107–21.

41. Arnett, *Emerging Adulthood*.

42. Constance A. Flanagan and Peter Levine, "Civic Engagement and the Changing Transition to Adulthood," *The Future of Children* 20 (2010): 159–79.

43. See Flanagan and Levine, "Civic Engagement," for the importance of "being there" in institutional settings for civic engagement of young adults.

44. Levine and Dean, *Generation on a Tightrope*.

45. See discussion of the political life-cycle model in Flanagan and Levine, "Civic Engagement."

46. David Labaree, "Public Goods, Private Goods: The American Struggle over Educational Goals," *American Educational Research Journal* 34 (1997): 39–81.

47. High selectivity refers to one standard deviation above the mean, and low selectivity to one standard deviation below the mean.

48. CLA performance is statistically significant and of large magnitude in a bivariate model; once individual characteristics are included, it declines and drops to $p < 0.10$. Including institutional selectivity has a notable effect, decreasing the CLA coefficient by 80 to 90 percent and dropping it to zero.

49. Levine and Dean, *Generation on a Tightrope*, 139.

50. The original survey question included more categories for primary news sources. We have collapsed categories and highlighted key comparisons.

51. The number of interviewees who have answered this question is 78, which translates into 17 percent of the sample having a positive outlook.

52. Forty percent of graduates had at least one parent who had a graduate or professional degree, and two-thirds had at least one parent who had completed at least a college degree.

53. Shelley E. Taylor and Jonathon D. Brown, "Illusion and Well-Being: A Social Psychological Perspective on Mental Health," *Psychological Bulletin* 103 (1988): 193–210.

54. Teresa Toguchi Swartz, Douglas Hartmann, and Jeylan T. Mortimer, "Transitions

to Adulthood in the Land of Lake Wobegon," in *Coming of Age in America: The Transition to Adulthood in the Twenty-First Century*, ed. Mary C. Waters, Patrick J. Carr, Maria J. Kefalas, and Jennifer Holdaway (Berkeley: University of California Press, 2011), 59–105.

55. Percentages of graduates who believe that their lives overall will be better than those of their parents: unemployed, 64 percent; employed, 62 percent; employed in unskilled occupations, 59 percent; employed in skilled occupations, 62 percent. See figure 4.14.

56. Swartz et al., "Transitions to Adulthood."

57. Barbara Schneider and David Stevenson, *The Ambitious Generation: America's Teenagers Motivated but Directionless* (New Haven: Yale University Press, 1999), 7.

58. Arnett, *Emerging Adulthood*.

59. William Damon, *The Path to Purpose: Helping Our Children Find Their Calling in Life* (New York: Simon and Schuster, 2008).

60. Percentages of graduates who expect their lives to be better, the same, or worse than those of their parents, depending on how often they feel they lack goals or direction: rarely or never (2.8 percent worse, 30 percent same, 67.1 percent better); sometimes (4.3 percent worse, 28 percent same, 67.1 percent better); fairly or very often (14.8 percent worse, 36.2 percent same, 49 percent better). See figure 4.15.

61. Levine and Dean, *Generation on a Tightrope*; Waters et al., ed., *Coming of Age in America: The Transition to Adulthood in the Twenty-First Century* (Berkeley: University of California Press, 2011).

62. Levine and Dean, *Generation on a Tightrope*.

63. Waters et al., *Coming of Age in America*.

64. Settersten and Ray, *Not Quite Adults*.

65. Arnett, *Emerging Adulthood*.

66. Labaree, "Public Goods, Private Goods."

67. Elizabeth A. Armstrong, Paula England, and Alison C. K. Fogarty, "Orgasm in College Hookups and Relationships," in *Families as They Really Are*, ed. Barbara Risman (New York: Norton, 2009), 362–77.

68. Meg Jay, *The Defining Decade: Your Twenties Matter—and How to Make the Most of Them Now* (New York: Hachette, 2012), xxiii.

Chapter 5

1. Philip Babcock and Mindy Marks, "The Falling Time Cost of College: Evidence from Half a Century of Time Use Data," *Review of Economics and Statistics* 93 (2011): 468–78.

2. Ernest T. Pascarella and Patrick Terenzini, *How College Affects Students: A Third Decade of Research* (San Francisco: Jossey-Bass, 2005).

3. Brian Jacob, Brian McCall, and Kevin M. Stange, "College as a Country Club: Do Colleges Cater to Students' Preferences for Consumption?" NBER Working Paper no. 18745 (Cambridge, MA: National Bureau of Economic Research, 2013).

4. Andrew Delbanco, *College: What it Was, Is, and Should Be* (Princeton, NJ: Princeton University Press, 2012), 19–20.

5. Anya Kamenetz, *DIY U: Edupunks, Edupreneurs, and the Coming Transformation of Higher Education* (White River Junction, VT: Chelsea Green Publishing, 2010).

6. With the support of the John D. and Catherine T. MacArthur Foundation, research on these programs—which includes the Quest secondary schools, the Hive

learning networks, and the YOUmedia drop-in sites—is soon to be completed (see http://steinhardt.nyu.edu/ihdsc/connecting_youth).

7. Claudia Dale Goldin and Lawrence F. Katz, *The Race between Education and Technology* (Cambridge, MA: Harvard University Press, 2009), 278.

8. US Census Bureau, *Statistical Abstracts 2012,* Table 691 (Washington: US Census Bureau).

9. US Department of Education, *A Test of Leadership: Charting the Future of US Higher Education*, report of the Secretary of Education's Commission on the Future of Higher Education (Washington: US Department of Education, 2006).

10. David F. Labaree, "Public Goods, Private Goods: The American Struggle over Educational Goals," *American Educational Research Journal* 34 (1997): 41.

11. Mitchell Stevens, Elizabeth Armstrong, and Richard Arum, "Sieve, Incubator, Temple, Hub: Empirical and Theoretical Advances in the Sociology of Higher Education," *Annual Review of Sociology* 34 (2008): 128.

12. American Association of Colleges & Universities (AAC&U), "The LEAP Vision for Learning: Outcomes, Practices, Impact, and Employers' Views" (Washington: AAC&U, 2011), 8.

13. AAC&U, "The Leap Vision," 8.

14. Lumina Foundation, "The Degree Qualifications Profile" (Indianapolis: Lumina Foundation, 2011).

15. Lumina Foundation, "Tuning USA," Lumina Foundation, http://tuningusa.org /About/What_is_Tuning.aspx.

16. Wendy K. Adams and Carl E. Wieman, "Development and Validation of Instruments to Measure Learning of Expert-Like Thinking," *International Journal of Science Education* 33 (2011): 1289–1312.

17. Stanley N. Katz, James Grossman, and Tracy Steffes, *The History Major and Undergraduate Liberal Education*, report of the National History Center Working Group to the Teagle Foundation (New York: Teagle Foundation, 2008).

18. Dennis Jones, *Outcomes-Based Funding: The Wave of Implementation*, report of the National Center for Higher Education Management Systems and Complete College America (Boulder, CO: National Center for Higher Education Management Systems, 2013), http://www.completecollege.org/pdfs/Outcomes-Based-Funding-Report-Final.pdf.

19. Brian Jacob, Brian McCall, and Kevin M. Stange, "College as a Country Club: Do Colleges Cater to Students' Preferences for Consumption?" NBER working paper no. 18745 (Cambridge, MA: National Bureau of Economic Research, 2013).

20. Elizabeth A. Armstrong and Laura T. Hamilton, *Paying for the Party: How College Maintains Inequality* (Cambridge, MA: Harvard University Press, 2013); Mary Grigsby, *College Life through the Eyes of Students* (Albany: State University Press of New York, 2009).

21. Richard Arum and Josipa Roksa, *Academically Adrift: Limited Learning on College Campuses* (Chicago: University of Chicago Press, 2011).

22. David F. Labaree, "Public Goods, Private Goods," 65.

23. Josipa Roksa, "Estimating Value of Higher Education: The State of Knowledge and Future Directions," working paper (Charlottesville: University of Virginia, 2013).

24. US Department of Education, College Affordability and Transparency Center, "College Scorecard" (Washington: US Department of Education, 2013), http://www .whitehouse.gov/issues/education/higher-education/college-score-card.

25. National Governors Association, *Degrees for What Jobs? Raising Expectations for*

Universities and Colleges in a Global Economy, report of the NGA Center for Best Practices (Washington: National Governors Association, 2011), http://www.nga.org/files/live /sites/NGA/files/pdf/1103DEGREESJOBS.PDF.

26. For a review of this literature, see Theodore P. Gerber and Sin Yi Cheung, "Horizontal Stratification in Postsecondary Education: Forms, Explanations, and Implications," *Annual Review of Sociology* 34 (2008): 299–318.

27. Colleges differ in the composition of fields of study they offer to students. Because college majors track with early labor-market earnings, to the extent that colleges have varying proportions of students majoring in different subjects, earning differences occur in relation to the vocational character of the composition of majors across colleges.

28. One of the principal challenges in calculating graduation rates is deciding who is included in the denominator. Graduation rates reported in IPEDS, for example, refer to first-time full-time students, who represent an ever-decreasing proportion of the undergraduate student body and thus lack relevance for many schools and students. Similarly, wages need to be adjusted for students who are in graduate school, as well as for those who are not in the labor force for other reasons.

29. Paul Fain, "New Yardstick of Quality," *InsideHigherEd,* July 10, 2013, http://www .insidehighered.com/news/2013/07/10/voluntary-performance-measures-gates-backed -group.

30. Voluntary Institutional Metrics Project, *A Better Higher Education Data and Information Framework for Informing Policy* (Washington: HCM Strategists, 2013), 22.

31. Valen E. Johnson, *Grade Inflation: A Crisis in College Education* (New York: Springer-Verlag, 2003).

32. The White House, "Fact Sheet on the President's Plan to Make College More Affordable: A Better Bargain for the Middle Class" (Washington: The White House, 2013), http://www.whitehouse.gov/the-press-office/2013/08/22/fact-sheet-president-s-plan -make-college-more-affordable-better-bargain.

33. For a recent review, see Thomas Bailey and Di Xu, *Input-Adjusted Graduation Rates and College Accountability: What is Known from Twenty Years of Research?*, report of HCM Strategists' Context for Success Project and Columbia University's Community College Research Center (Washington: HCM Strategists, 2012), http://www.hcmstrategists.com /contextforsuccess/papers.html.

34. David L. Wright et al., *College Participation, Persistence, Graduation, and Labor Market Outcomes: An Input-Adjusted Framework for Assessing the Effectiveness of Tennessee's Higher Education Institutions,* report of HCM Strategists' Context for Success Project (Washington: HCM Strategists, 2012), http://www.hcmstrategists.com/contextforsuccess /papers.html.

35. Organisation for Economic Co-operation and Development (OECD), *Education at a Glance 2012: OECD Indicators* (OECD Publishing, 2012).

36. Chronicle of Higher Education, "MOOC Madness," October 1, 2012, http:// chronicle.com/section/Online-Learning/623/.

37. Kelly Field, "Student Aid Can Be Awarded for 'Competencies,' Not Just Credit Hours, U.S. Says," *Chronicle of Higher Education,* March 19, 2013.

38. Joan Malczewski, "Weak State, Stronger Schools: Northern Philanthropy and Organizational Change in the Jim Crow South," *Journal of Southern History* 75 (2009): 963.

39. Ellen Lagemann, *Private Power for the Public Good: A History of the Carnegie Foundation for the Advancement of Teaching* (Middletown, CT: Wesleyan University Press).

40. Nicholas Lemann, *The Big Test: The Secret History of the American Meritocracy* (New York: Farrar, Straus and Giroux, 1999), 23.

41. A cohort of students was also tracked longitudinally from seventh grade through high school.

42. William Learned and Ben Wood, *The Student and His Knowledge: A Report to the Carnegie Foundation on the Results of the High School and College Examinations of 1928, 1930, and 1932* (New York: Carnegie Foundation for the Advancement of Teaching; 1938), xvi.

43. Susan H. Fuhrman and Richard F. Elmore, *Redesigning Accountability Systems for Education* (New York: Teachers College Press, 2004).

44. Organisation for Economic Co-operation and Development (OECD), "Synergies for Better Learning: An International Perspective on Evaluation and Assessment" (OECD Publishing, 2013), 13.

45. OECD, "Synergies for Better Learning," 14.

46. OECD, "Synergies for Better Learning."

47. In light of the fact that funding for colleges' career services offices was cut by an average of 16 percent in 2012, this may be a challenging task. See Andy Chan and Tommy Derry, eds., "A Roadmap for Transforming the College-to-Career Experience" (Winston-Salem, NC: Wake Forest University, 2013), http://rethinkingsuccess.wfu.edu /files/2013/05/A-Roadmap-for-Transforming-The-College-to-Career-Experience.pdf.

48. John Dewey, *The School and Society* (Chicago: University of Chicago Press, 1915), 3.

49. Donald L. McCabe, Linda Klebe Treviño, and Kenneth D. Butterfield, "Cheating in Academic Institutions: A Decade of Research," *Ethics & Behavior* 11 (2001): 219–32.

50. Indeed, when researchers in the Wabash National Study of Liberal Arts Education attempted to document longitudinal growth on a number of indicators reflecting components of affective growth and personal development, little evidence of gains over four years of college were evident. The Wabash Study included well-known measures of moral reasoning (the Defining Issues Test, DIT-2), leadership (the Socially Responsible Leadership Scale, SRLS-R2), and attitudes, cognitions, and behaviors regarding diversity (Miville-Guzman Universality-Diversity Scale, M-GUDS-S). By collecting longitudinal data on students from entry into college through their senior year, researchers using the Wabash data have been able to report value-added measures of these different indicators. The Wabash Study found that most of the affective and personal development indicators showed smaller gains over time than did measures of generic higher-order skills, such as critical thinking. See Charles Blaich and Kathleen Wise, *From Gathering to Using Assessment Results: Lessons from the Wabash National Study*, report of the National Institute for Learning Outcomes Assessment (NILOA) (Urbana: University of Illinois and Indiana University, NILOA, 2011), http://www.learningoutcomeassessment .org/documents/Wabash_001.pdf.

51. James Davison Hunter, *The Death of Character: Moral Education in an Age without Good or Evil* (New York: Basic Books, 2008).

Appendix A

1. Richard Hersch, "Going Naked," *AAC&U Peer Review* 9 (2007): 6.

2. Stephen Klein, Richard Shavelson, and Roger Benjamin, "Setting the Record Straight," *Inside Higher Ed*, February 8, 2007, http://www.insidehighered.com /views/2007/02/08/benjamin.

3. CAE has since started to provide distinct scores for different components of general collegiate skills. However, those component scores were not available for our sample.

4. Stephen Klein, Ou Lydia Liu, James Sconing, *Test Validity Study Report* (Washington: Fund for the Improvement of Postsecondary Education, 2009), http://cae.org /images/uploads/pdf/13_Test_Validity_Study_Report.pdf.

5. For income as well as occupational characteristics, we consider respondents' employment at the time of the 2011 survey. If the respondents were unemployed at that time, we consider their most recent employment.

6. Robert M. Hauser and John Robert Warren, "Socioeconomic Indexes for Occupations: A Review, Update and Critique," *Sociological Methodology* 27 (1997):177–298.

7. In addition, for respondents in 2011 who declined to specify job titles, we used 2010 job titles when available. Thirteen individuals who were employed declined to identify their job titles in both 2010 and 2011. We coded these individuals based on their response to a question about whether they were satisfied that their occupation used their prior education and training; if they indicated that they were very dissatisfied (i.e., one or two on a seven-point scale of "very dissatisfied" to "very satisfied"), they were coded as being in unskilled occupations.

8. Those labor market outcomes are coded only for respondents not enrolled full-time in graduate school. Therefore, to include both measures in analyses (labor market and graduate school enrollment), all students enrolled full-time in graduate school are coded as zero for the labor market measures.

Bibliography

Abel, Jaison R., Richard Deitz, and Yaqin Su. "Are Recent College Graduates Finding Good Jobs?" *Current Issues in Economics and Finance* 20/1 (2014):1–8.

Adams, Wendy K., and Carl E. Wieman. "Development and Validation of Instruments to Measure Learning of Expert-Like Thinking." *International Journal of Science Education* 33 (2011): 1289–1312.

Alexander, Karl L., and Aaron M. Pallas. "School Sector and Cognitive Performance: When Is a Little a Little?" *Sociology of Education* 58 (1985): 115–28.

Aries, Elizabeth, and Maynard Seider. "The Interactive Relationship between Class Identity and the College Experience: The Case of Lower Income Students." *Qualitative Sociology* 28 (2005): 419–43.

Armstrong, Elizabeth A., Paula England, and Alison C. K. Fogarty. "Orgasm in College Hookups and Relationships." In *Families as They Really Are,* edited by Barbara Risman, 362–77. New York: Norton, 2009.

Armstrong, Elizabeth A., and Laura T. Hamilton. *Paying for the Party: How College Maintains Inequality.* Cambridge, MA: Harvard University Press, 2013.

Arnett, Jeffrey J. *Emerging Adulthood: The Winding Road from the Late Teens through the Twenties.* New York: Oxford University Press, 2004.

———. "Learning to Stand Alone: The Contemporary American Transition to Adulthood." *Human Development* 41 (1998): 295–315.

Aronson, Eliot, and Judson Mills. "The Effect of Severity of Initiation on Liking for a Group." *The Journal of Abnormal and Social Psychology* 59 (1959): 177–181.

Arum, Richard. *Judging School Discipline: The Crisis of Moral Authority.* Cambridge, MA: Harvard University Press, 2009.

———. "Stakeholder and Public Responses to Measuring Student Learning." *Society* 50 (2013): 230–35.

Arum, Richard, and Josipa Roksa. *Academically Adrift: Limited Learning on College Campuses.* Chicago: University of Chicago Press, 2011.

Arum, Richard, Josipa Roksa, and Michelle Budig. "The Romance of College Atten-
    dance: Higher Education Stratification and Mate Selection." *Research in Social
    Stratification and Mobility* 26 (2008):107–21.
Association of American Colleges & Universities (AAC&U). *The LEAP Vision for Learn-
    ing: Outcomes, Practices, Impact, and Employers' Views.* Washington: AAC&U, 2011.
    ———. *How Should Colleges Assess and Improve Student Learning? Employers' Views on
    the Accountability Challenge.* Washington: AAC&U, 2008. http://www.aacu.org/leap
    /documents/2008_Business_Leader_Poll.pdf.
Astin, Alexander W. *What Matters in College? Four Critical Years Revisited.* San Francisco:
    Jossey-Bass, 1993.
Autor, David H., Frank Levy, and Richard J. Murnane. "The Skill Content of Recent
    Technological Change: An Empirical Investigation." *Quarterly Journal of Economics*
    118 (2003): 1279–1333.
Babcock, Philip S., and Mindy Marks. "The Falling Time Cost of College: Evidence
    from Half a Century of Time Use Data." *Review of Economics and Statistics* 93 (2011):
    468–78.
Bailey, Thomas, and Di Xu. *Input-Adjusted Graduation Rates and College Accountability:
    What Is Known from Twenty Years of Research?* Report of HCM Strategists' Context
    for Success Project and Columbia University's Community College Research Center.
    Washington: HCM Strategists, 2012. http://www.hcmstrategists.com/contextfor
    success/papers.html.
Baum, Geraldine. "Student Loans Add to Angst at Occupy Wall Street." *Los Angeles
    Times,* October 25, 2011. http://articles.latimes.com/2011/oct/25/nation/la-na
    -occupy-student-loans-20111026.
Becker, Gary S. *Human Capital: A Theoretical and Empirical Analysis, with Special Refer-
    ence to Education.* Chicago: University of Chicago Press, [1964] 2009.
Becker, Howard, Blanche Geer, and Everett Hughes. *Making the Grade: The Academic
    Side of College Life.* New Brunswick, NJ: Transaction Publishers, [1968] 1995.
Bellah, Robert N., Richard Madsen, William M. Sullivan, Ann Swidler, and Steven M.
    Tipton. *Habits of the Heart: Individualism and Commitment in American Life.* Berkeley:
    University of California Press, 1985.
Blaich, Charles. *How do Students Change over Four Years of College?* Report of the Center
    of Inquiry in the Liberal Arts at Wabash College. Crawfordsville, IN: Center of
    Inquiry in the Liberal Arts at Wabash College, 2011. http://www.liberalarts.wabash
    .edu/storage/4-year-change-summary-website.pdf.
Blaich, Charles, and Kathleen Wise. *From Gathering to Using Assessment Results:
    Lessons from the Wabash National Study.* Report of the National Institute for Learning
    Outcomes Assessment (NILOA). Urbana, IL: University of Illinois and Indiana
    University, NILOA, 2011. http://www.learningoutcomeassessment.org/documents
    /Wabash_001.pdf.
Blau, Peter M., and Otis Dudley Duncan. *American Occupational Structure.* New York:
    Free Press, 1967.
Bogle, Kathleen. *Hooking Up: Sex, Dating, and Relationships on Campus.* New York: New
    York University Press, 2008.
Bok, Derek. *Our Underachieving Colleges: A Candid Look at How Much Students Learn and
    Why They Should Be Learning More.* Princeton, NJ: Princeton University Press, 2006.
Bowen, William G., Matthew M. Chingos, and Michael S. McPherson. *Crossing the Fin-*

ish Line: Completing College at America's Public Universities. Princeton, NJ: Princeton University Press, 2009.

Bowman, Carl Desportes. "Holding Them Closer." *Hedgehog Review* 15.3 (2013): 8–23.

Breen, Richard, and Leire Salazar. "Educational Assortative Mating and Earnings Inequality in the United States." *American Journal of Sociology* 117 (2011): 808–43.

Brint, Steven, and Allison M. Cantwell. "Undergraduate Time Use and Academic Outcomes: Results from University of California Undergraduate Experience Survey 2006." *Teachers College Record* 112 (2010): 2441–70.

Brint, Steven, Allison M. Cantwell, and Robert A. Hanneman. "The Two Cultures of Undergraduate Academic Engagement." *Research in Higher Education* 49 (2008): 383–402.

Brint, Steven, Allison M. Cantwell, and Preeta Saxena. "Disciplinary Categories, Majors, and Undergraduate Academic Experiences: Rethinking Bok's 'Underachieving Colleges' Thesis." *Research in Higher Education* 53 (2012): 1–25.

Carey, Kevin. *A Matter of Degrees: Improving Graduation Rates in Four-Year Colleges and Universities*. Report of the Education Trust. Washington: The Education Trust, 2004.

Carnevale, Anthony, Ban Cheah, and Jeff Strohl. *Hard Times: College Majors, Unemployment and Earnings*. Report of the Georgetown Public Policy Institute, Center on Education and the Workforce. Washington: Georgetown Public Policy Institute, 2013. http://www9.georgetown.edu/grad/gppi/hpi/cew/pdfs/HardTimes.2013.2.pdf.

Carver, Karen, Kara Joyner, and J. Richard Udry. "National Estimates of Adolescent Romantic Relationships," in *Adolescent Romantic Relations and Sexual Behavior: Theory, Research, and Practical Implications*, edited by Paul Florscheim, 23–56. Mahwah, NJ: Lawrence Erlbaum Associates Publishers, 2003.

Casner-Lotto, Jill, Linda Barrington, and Mary Wright. *Are They Really Ready to Work? Employers' Perspectives on the Basic Knowledge and Applied Skills of New Entrants to the 21st Century U.S. Workplace*. Report of the Conference Board. Washington: Conference Board, 2006.

Chan, Andy, and Tommy Derry, eds. *A Roadmap for Transforming the College-to-Career Experience*. Winston-Salem, NC: Wake Forest University, 2013. http://rethinking success.wfu.edu/files/2013/05/A-Roadmap-for-Transforming-The-College-to-Career -Experience.pdf.

Charles, Camille Z., Mary Fischer, Margarita Mooney, and Douglas Massey. *Taming the River: Negotiating the Academic, Financial, and Social Currents in Selective Colleges and Universities*. Princeton, NJ: Princeton University Press, 2009.

Chronicle of Higher Education. "MOOC Madness." October 1, 2012. http://chronicle .com/section/Online-Learning/623/.

Coleman, James S. *The Adolescent Society: The Social Life of the Teenager and its Impact on Education*. New York: Free Press of Glencoe, 1961.

Damaske, Sarah. "Brown Suits Need Not Apply: The Intersection of Race, Gender and Class in Institutional Network Building." *Sociological Forum* 24 (2009): 402–24.

Damon, William. *The Path to Purpose: Helping Our Children Find Their Calling in Life*. New York: Simon and Schuster, 2008.

Davidson, Adam. "The Dwindling Power of a College Degree." *New York Times*, November 23, 2011. http://www.nytimes.com/2011/11/27/magazine/changing-rules-for -success.html.

Delbanco, Andrew. *College: What it Was, Is, and Should Be*. Princeton, NJ: Princeton University Press, 2012.

Dewey, John. *The School and Society*. Chicago: University of Chicago Press, 1915.

DiPrete, Thomas A., and Claudia Buchmann. *The Rise of Women: The Growing Gender Gap in Education and What it Means for American Schools*. New York: Russell Sage Foundation, 2013.

Durkheim, Émile. "On Education and Society." In *Power and Ideology in Education*, edited by Jerome Karabel and A. H. Halsey, 92–104. Oxford: Oxford University Press, 1977.

———. *Moral Education: A Study in the Theory and Application of the Sociology of Education*. New York: Free Press, [1925] 1961.

———. *The Rules of Sociological Method*. New York: Free Press, [1895] 1950.

Edelman, Lauren. "Legal Ambiguity and Symbolic Structures: Organizational Mediation of Civil Rights Law." *American Journal of Sociology* 97 (1992): 1531–76.

———. "Legal Environments and Organizational Governance: The Expansion of Due Process in the Workplace." *American Journal of Sociology* 95 (1990): 1401–40.

Edwards, Julia. "Stephen Trachtenberg Is Not Sorry." *National Journal*, October 1, 2012. http://www.nationaljournal.com/features/restoration-calls/stephen-trachtenberg-is-not-sorry-20120927?page=1.

Eide, Eric, and Geetha Waehrer. "The Role of the Option Value of College Attendance in College Major Choice." *Economics of Education Review* 17 (1998): 73–82.

Fain, Paul. "New Yardstick of Quality." *Inside Higher Ed.* July 10, 2013. http://www.insidehighered.com/news/2013/07/10/voluntary-performance-measures-gates-backed-group.

Field, Kelly. "Student Aid Can Be Awarded for 'Competencies,' Not Just Credit Hours, U.S. Says." *Chronicle of Higher Education*. March 19, 2013. http://chronicle.com/article/Student-Aid-Can-Be-Awarded-for/137991/.

Fischer, Claude S., Michael Hout, Martín Sánchez Jankowski, Samuel R. Lucas, Ann Swidler, and Kim Voss. *Inequality by Design: Cracking the Bell Curve Myth*. Princeton, NJ: Princeton University Press, 1996.

Fischer, Karin. "A College Degree Sorts Job Applicants, but Employers Wish It Meant More." *Chronicle of Higher Education*, March 12, 2013. http://chronicle.com/article/The-Employment-Mismatch/137625/#id=overview.

Flanagan, Constance, and Peter Levine. "Civic Engagement and the Transition to Adulthood." *The Future of Children* 20 (2010): 159–79.

Ford, Karly Sarita, and Richard Arum, "Same-College Partnering: Educational Homogamy 1975–2005." Working paper. New York: New York University, 2013.

Franke, Ray, Sylvia Ruiz, Jessica Sharkness, Linda DeAngelo, and John Pryor. *Findings from the 2009 Administration of the College Senior Survey (CSS): National Aggregates*. Report of the Cooperative Institutional Research Program at the UCLA Higher Education Research Institute. Los Angeles: UCLA Higher Education Research Institute, 2010.

Friedman, Thomas. "How to Get a Job." *New York Times*, May 28, 2013. http://www.nytimes.com/2013/05/29/opinion/friedman-how-to-get-a-job.html?src=ISMR_AP_LO_MST_FB.

Fuhrman, Susan H., and Richard F. Elmore. *Redesigning Accountability Systems for Education*. New York: Teachers College Press, 2004.

Furstenberg, Frank. "On a New Schedule: Transitions to Adulthood and Family Change." *The Future of Children* 20 (2010): 67–87.

Furstenberg, Frank F., Rubén G. Rumbaut, and Richard A. Settersten. "On the Frontier of Adulthood: Emerging Themes and New Directions." In *On the Frontier of Adult-*

hood: *Theory, Research, and Public Policy,* edited by Richard Settersten, Frank Furstenberg, and Rubén Rumbaut, 3–28. Chicago: University of Chicago Press, 2008.

Gadja, Amy. *The Trials of Academe: The New Era of Campus Litigation.* Cambridge, MA: Harvard University Press, 2009.

Gerber, Theodore P., and Sin Yi Cheung. "Horizontal Stratification in Postsecondary Education: Forms, Explanations, and Implications." *Annual Review of Sociology* 34 (2008): 299–318.

Ginsberg, Benjamin. *The Fall of the Faculty: The Rise of the All-Administrative University and Why It Matters.* Oxford: Oxford University Press, 2009.

Gitlin, Todd. Foreword to *The Lonely Crowd,* by David Riesman, xi–xx. New Haven: Yale University Press, 2001.

Goldin, Claudia Dale, and Lawrence F. Katz. *The Race between Education and Technology.* Cambridge, MA: Harvard University Press, 2009.

Gose, Ben. "Liberal-Arts Colleges Ask: Where Have the Men Gone?" *Chronicle of Higher Education,* June 6, 1997. https://chronicle.com/article/Liberal-Arts-Colleges-Ask -/75455/.

Granovetter, Mark. *Getting a Job: A Study of Contacts and Careers.* Chicago: University of Chicago Press, [1974] 1995.

Grigsby, Mary. *College Life through the Eyes of Students.* Albany: State University Press of New York, 2009.

Grubb, W. Norton, and Marvin Lazerson. "Vocationalism in Higher Education: The Triumph of the Education Gospel." *Journal of Higher Education* 76 (2005):1–25.

Grusky, David B., Beth Red Bird, Natassia Rodriguez, and Christopher Wimer. *How Much Protection Does a College Degree Afford? The Impact of the Recession on Recent College Graduates.* Report of Pew Charitable Trusts, Economic Mobility Project. Washington: Pew Charitable Trusts, 2013.

Hauser, Robert M., and John Robert Warren. "Socioeconomic Indexes for Occupations: A Review, Update and Critique." *Sociological Methodology* 27 (1997): 177–298.

Hersch, Richard. "Going Naked." *AAC&U Peer Review* 9 (2007): 4–8.

Hoffer, Thomas, Andrew M. Greeley, and James S. Coleman. "Achievement Growth in Public and Catholic Schools." *Sociology of Education* 58 (1985): 74–97.

Hopkins, Louis B. "Personnel Procedure in Education: Observations and Conclusions Resulting from Visits to Fourteen Institutions of Higher Learning," in *Educational Record* 7. Washington: American Council on Education, 1926.

Hout, Michael. "More Universalism and Less Structural Mobility: The American Occupational Structure in the 1980s." *American Journal of Sociology* 93 (1988): 1358–1400.

Hunter, James Davison. *The Death of Character: Moral Education in an Age without Good or Evil.* New York: Basic Books, 2008.

Hurtado, Sylvia, and Deborah Faye Carter. "Effects of College Transition and Perceptions of the Campus Racial Climate on Latino College Students' Sense of Belonging." *Sociology of Education* 70 (1997): 324–45.

Imber, Jonathan, ed. *Therapeutic Culture: Triumph and Defeat.* Piscataway, NJ: Transaction Press, 2004.

Jacob, Brian, Brian McCall, and Kevin M. Stange. "College as a Country Club: Do Colleges Cater to Students' Preferences for Consumption?" NBER working paper no. 18745. Cambridge, MA: National Bureau of Economic Research, 2013.

Jay, Meg. *The Defining Decade: Why Your Twenties Matter—and How to Make the Most of Them Now*. New York: Hachette, 2012.

Johnson, Valen E. *Grade Inflation: A Crisis in College Education*. New York: Springer Verlag, 2003.

Jones, Dennis. *Outcomes-Based Funding: The Wave of Implementation*. Report of the National Center for Higher Education Management Systems and Complete College America. Boulder, CO: National Center for Higher Education Management Systems, 2013. http://www.completecollege.org/pdfs/Outcomes-Based-Funding-Report-Final .pdf.

Kalleberg, Arne L. "Work Values and Job Rewards: A Theory of Job Satisfaction." *American Sociological Review* 42 (1977): 124–43.

Kamenetz, Anya. *DIY U: Edupunks, Edupreneurs, and the Coming Transformation of Higher Education*. White River Junction, VT: Chelsea Green Publishing, 2010.

Katz, Stanley N., James Grossman, and Tracy Steffes. *The History Major and Undergraduate Liberal Education*. Report of the National History Center Working Group to the Teagle Foundation. New York: Teagle Foundation, 2008.

Kimmel, Michael. *Guyland: The Perilous World Where Boys Become Men*. New York: Harper, 2008.

Kirp, David L. *Shakespeare, Einstein, and the Bottom Line: The Marketing of Higher Education*. Cambridge, MA: Harvard University Press, 2003.

Klein, Stephen, Ou Lydia Liu, James Sconing. *Test Validity Study Report*. Washington: Fund for the Improvement of Postsecondary Education, 2009. http://cae.org /images/uploads/pdf/13_Test_Validity_Study_Report.pdf.

Klein, Stephen, Richard Shavelson, and Roger Benjamin. "Setting the Record Straight." *Inside Higher Ed*, February 8, 2007. http://www.insidehighered.com/views/2007/02 /08/benjamin.

Klinenberg, Eric. *Going Solo: The Extraordinary Rise and Suprising Appeal of Living Alone*. New York: Penguin, 2012.

Kuh, George D. "The Other Curriculum: Out-of-Class Experiences Associated with Student Learning and Personal Development." *The Journal of Higher Education* 66 (1995): 123–55.

Kuh, George D., Jillian Kinzie, Jennifer A. Buckley, Brian K. Bridges, and John C. Hayek. *What Matters to Student Success: A Review of the Literature*. Washington: National Postsecondary Education Cooperative, 2006.

Kuh, George D., Jillian Kinzie, John H. Schuh, and Elizabeth J. Whitt. *Student Success in College: Creating Conditions that Matter*. San Francisco: Jossey-Bass, 2005.

Labaree, David F. "Public Goods, Private Goods: The American Struggle over Educational Goals." *American Educational Research Journal* 34 (1997): 39–81.

Lagemann, Ellen. *Private Power for the Public Good: A History of the Carnegie Foundation for the Advancement of Teaching*. Middletown, CT: Wesleyan University Press.

Lareau, Annette. *Unequal Childhoods: Class, Race, and Family Life*. Berkeley, CA: University of California Press, 2003.

Learned, William, and Ben Wood. *The Student and His Knowledge: A Report to the Carnegie Foundation on the Results of the High School and College Examinations of 1928, 1930, and 1932*. A Report of the Carnegie Foundation. New York: Carnegie Foundation for the Advancement of Teaching, 1938.

Lemann, Nicholas. *The Big Test: The Secret History of the American Meritocracy*. New York: Farrar, Straus, and Giroux, 1999.

Levine, Arthur, and Diane Dean. *Generation on a Tightrope: A Portrait of Today's College Student*. San Francisco: Wiley, 2012.

Lewin, Tamar. "Official Calls for Urgency on College Costs." *New York Times*, November 11, 2011. http://www.nytimes.com/2011/11/30/education/duncan-calls-for-urgency-in-lowering-college-costs.html?smid=pl-share.

———. "Value of College Degree is Growing, Study Says." *New York Times*, September 21, 2010. http://www.nytimes.com/2010/09/21/education/21college.html.

Lin, Nan. "Social Networks and Status Attainment." *Annual Review of Sociology* 25 (1999): 467–87.

Liu, Yujia, and David B. Grusky. "The Payoff to Skill in the Third Industrial Revolution." *American Journal of Sociology* 118 (2013): 1330–74.

Loss, Christopher P. *Between Citizens and the State: The Politics of American Higher Education in the 20th Century*. Princeton, NJ: Princeton University Press, 2012.

Lumina Foundation. *The Degree Qualifications Profile*. Indianapolis, IN: Lumina Foundation, 2011.

———. "Tuning USA." Lumina Foundation. http://tuningusa.org/About/What_is_Tuning.aspx.

MacArdle, Megan. "Is College a Lousy Investment?" *Newsweek*, September 9, 2012. http://www.thedailybeast.com/newsweek/2012/09/09/megan-mcardle-on-the-coming-burst-of-the-college-bubble.html.

Malczewski, Joan. "Weak State, Stronger Schools: Northern Philanthropy and Organizational Change in the Jim Crow South." *Journal of Southern History* 75 (2009): 963–1000.

Manzoni, Anna. "An Intersectional Approach to Measuring Youth Pathways to Independence." Paper presented at the spring 2013 meeting of RC28, Trento, Italy, May 16–18, 2013.

Matasar, Richard. "A Commercialist Manifesto: Entrepreneurs, Academics and Purity of Heart and Soul." *Florida Law Review* 48 (1996): 781–811.

McCabe, Donald L., Linda Klebe Treviño, and Kenneth D. Butterfield. "Cheating in Academic Institutions: A Decade of Research." *Ethics & Behavior* 11 (2001): 219–32.

McPherson, Miller, Lynn Smith-Lovin, and James M. Cook. "Birds of a Feather: Homophily in Social Networks." *Annual Review of Sociology* 27 (2001): 415–44.

Mills, C. Wright. *The Sociological Imagination*. New York: Oxford University Press, 1959.

Milner, Murray. *Freaks, Geeks, and Cool Kids: American Teenagers, Schools, and the Culture of Consumption*. New York: Routledge, 2004.

Nathan, Rebekah. *My Freshman Year: What a Professor Learned by Becoming a Student*. Ithaca, NY: Cornell University Press, 2005.

National Governors Association. *Degrees for What Jobs? Raising Expectations for Universities and Colleges in a Global Economy*. Report of the NGA Center for Best Practices. Washington: National Governors Association, 2011. http://www.nga.org/files/live/sites/NGA/files/pdf/1103DEGREESJOBS.PDF.

National Research Council. *Education for Life and Work: Developing Transferable Knowledge and Skills in the 21st Century*. Washington: National Academies Press, 2012.

National Survey of Student Engagement (NSSE). *Assessment for Improvement: Tracking Student Engagement over Time—Annual Results from 2009*. Bloomington: Indiana University Center for Postsecondary Research, 2009.

National Survey of Student Engagement (NSSE). *Promoting Engagement for All Students: The Imperative to Look Within*. Bloomington, IN: Indiana University Center for Postsecondary Research, 2008.

Newman, Katherine. *The Accordion Family: Boomerang Kids, Anxious Parents, and the Private Toll of Global Competition.* Boston: Beacon, 2012.

Organisation for Economic Co-operation and Development (OECD). *Education at a Glance 2012: OECD Indicators.* OECD Publishing, 2012.

———. *OECD Skills Outlook 2013: First Results from the Survey of Adult Skills.* OECD Publishing, 2013.

———. *Synergies for Better Learning: An International Perspective on Evaluation and Assessment.* OECD Publishing, 2013.

———. *Time for the U.S. to Reskill? What the Survey of Adult Skills Says.* OECD Publishing, 2013.

Orr, Dominic, Christoph Gwosc, and Nicolai Netz. *Social and Economic Conditions of Student Life in Europe: Synopsis of Indicators, Final Report, Eurostudent IV 2008–2011.* Report of Eurostudent. Hannover, Germany: Eurostudent, 2011.

Pascarella, Ernest T., Charles Blaich, Georgianna L. Martin, and Jana M. Hanson. "How Robust Are the Findings of Academically Adrift?" *Change: The Magazine of Higher Learning,* May/June 2011: 20–24.

Pascarella, Ernest T. and Patrick Terenzini. *How College Affects Students: A Third Decade of Research.* San Francisco: Jossey-Bass, 2005.

Pike, Gary R., and George D. Kuh. "Relationships among Structural Diversity, Informal Peer Interactions and Perceptions of the Campus Environment." *Review of Higher Education* 29 (2006): 425–50.

Pryor, John H., Syvia Hurtado, Victor B. Saenz, Jose Luis Santos, and William S. Korn. *The American Freshman: Forty Year Trends, 1966–2006.* Report of the Cooperative Institutional Research Program at the UCLA Higher Education Research Institute. Los Angeles: UCLA Higher Education Research Institute, 2007.

Riesman, David. *The Lonely Crowd: A Study of the Changing American Character.* New Haven: Yale University Press, [1950] 2001.

———. *On Higher Education: The Academic Enterprise in an Era of Rising Student Consumerism.* New Brunswick, NJ: Transaction Publishers, 1980.

Robbins, Alexandra. *Pledged: The Secret Life of Sororities.* New York: Hyperion, 2004.

Roksa, Josipa. "Estimating Value of Higher Education: The State of Knowledge and Future Directions." Working paper. Charlottesville, VA: University of Virginia, 2013.

Roksa, Josipa, Teniell L. Trolian, Ernest T. Pascarella, Cindy A. Kilgo, Charles Blaich, and Kathleen S. Wise. "Racial Gaps in Critical Thinking: The Role of Institutional Context." Paper presented at the 2014 AERA meeting, Philadelphia, Pennsylvania, April 3–7, 2014.

Rosenbaum, James E. *Beyond College for All: Career Paths for the Forgotten Half.* New York: Russell Sage Foundation, 2001.

Rosenfeld, Michael J. *The Age of Independence: Interracial Unions, Same-Sex Unions, and the Changing American Family.* Cambridge, MA: Harvard University Press, 2007.

Rotherham, Andrew J. "Actually, College Is Very Much Worth It." *Time Magazine,* May 19, 2011. http://www.time.com/time/nation/article/0,8599,2072432,00.html.

Schneider, Barbara, and David Stevenson. *The Ambitious Generation: America's Teenagers Motivated but Directionless.* New Haven: Yale University Press, 1999.

Schoeni, Robert, and Karen Ross. "Material Assistance from Families during the Transition to Adulthood." In *On the Frontier to Adulthood: Theory, Research, and Public Policy,* edited by Richard Settersten, Frank Furstenberg, and Rubén Rumbaut, 396–416. Chicago: University of Chicago Press, 2005.

Seltzer, Judith A., and Suzanne M. Bianchi. "Demographic Change and Parent-Child Relationships in Adulthood." *Annual Review of Sociology* 39 (2013): 275–90.

Settersten, Richard A., and Barbara E. Ray. *Not Quite Adults: Why 20-Somethings Are Choosing a Slower Path to Adulthood, and Why It's Good for Everyone.* New York: Bantam Books, 2010.

———. "What's Going On with Young People Today? The Long and Twisting Path to Adulthood." *The Future of Children* 20 (2010): 19–41.

Silva, Jennifer M. *Coming Up Short: Working Class Adulthood in an Age of Uncertainty.* New York: Oxford University Press, 2013.

Slaughter, Sheila, and Gary Rhoades. *Academic Capitalism and the New Economy.* Baltimore: John Hopkins University Press, 2004.

Small, Mario L., and Christopher Winship. "Black Students' Graduation from Elite Colleges: Institutional Characteristics and Between-Institution Differences." *Social Science Research* 36 (2007): 1257–75.

Smith, Christian, with Melinda Lundquist Denton. *Soul Searching: The Religious and Spiritual Lives of American Teenagers.* New York: Oxford University Press, 2005.

Southern Association of Colleges and Schools Commission on Colleges (SACSCOC). *Credit Hours Policy Statement.* Decatur, GA: SACSCOC, 2012. http://www.sacscoc .org/subchg/policy/CreditHours.pdf.

Sperber, Murray. *Beer and Circus: How Big-Time College Sports is Crippling Undergraduate Education.* New York: Henry Holt, 2001.

Stainburn, Samantha. "Promises, Promises." *New York Times,* October 26, 2009. http://www.nytimes.com/2009/11/01/education/edlife/01forprofit-t.html.

Stevens, Mitchell. *Creating a Class.* Cambridge, MA: Harvard University Press, 2007.

Stevens, Mitchell, Elizabeth Armstrong, and Richard Arum. "Sieve, Incubator, Temple, Hub: Empirical and Theoretical Advances in the Sociology of Higher Education." *Annual Review of Sociology* 34 (2008): 127–51.

Stuber, Jenny M. *Inside the College Gates: How Class and Culture Matter in Higher Education.* Lanham, MD: Lexington Books, 2011.

Svenson, Ola. "Are We All Less Risky and More Skillful Than Our Fellow Drivers?" *Acta Psychologica* 47 (1981): 143–48.

Swartz, Teresa Toguchi, Douglas Hartmann, and Jeylan T. Mortimer. "Transitions to Adulthood in the Land of Lake Wobegon." In *Coming of Age in America: The Transition to Adulthood in the Twenty-First Century,* edited by Mary C. Waters, Patrick J. Carr, Maria J. Kefalas, and Jennifer Holdaway, 59–105. Berkeley: University of California Press, 2011.

Taylor, Shelley E., and Jonathon D. Brown. "Illusion and Well-Being: A Social Psychological Perspective on Mental Health." *Psychological Bulletin* 103 (1988): 193–210.

Thompson, Derek. "The Value of College Is: (a) Growing (b) Flat (c) Falling (d) All of the Above." *Atlantic Monthly,* September 27, 2011. http://www.theatlantic.com /business/archive/2011/09/the-value-of-college-is-a-growing-b-flat-c-falling-d-all-of -the-above/245746/.

Thomson, Susan. "Male Students' College Achievement Gap Brings Concern." *Washington Post,* August 31, 2003.

Tierney, William G. "An Anthropological Analysis of Student Participation in College."
    Journal of Higher Education 63 (1992): 603–18.
Tinto, Vincent. *Leaving College: Rethinking the Causes and Cures of Student Attrition.*
    Chicago: University of Chicago Press, 1994.
US Census Bureau. *Statistical Abstracts 2012.* Washington: US Census Bureau, 2012.
US Department of Education. *A Test of Leadership: Charting the Future of U.S. Higher
    Education.* Report of the Secretary of Education's Commission on the Future of
    Higher Education. Washington: US Department of Education, 2006.
US Department of Education, College Affordability and Transparency Center.
    "College Scorecard." Washington: US Department of Education, 2013. http://www
    .whitehouse.gov/issues/education/higher-education/college-score-card.
US Department of Education, National Center for Education Statistics (NCES). *Bacca-
    laureate and Beyond Longitudinal Study (B&B).* Washington: US Department of
    Education, National Center for Education Statistics, n.d.
————. *Digest of Educational Statistics, 2006.* By Thomas D Synder, Sally A. Dillow, and
    Charlene M. Hoffman. NCES 2007-017. Washington: US Department of Education,
    National Center for Educational Statistics, 2007.
US Department of Health and Human Services, Office of the Assistant Secretary for
    Planning and Evaluation. *Pathways to Adulthood and Marriage: Teenagers' Attitudes,
    Expectations, and Relationship Patterns.* By Robert G.Wood, Sarah Avellar, and Brian
    Goesling. PP08-66. Washington: US Department of Health and Human Services,
    2008.
Vaisey, Stephen. "Education and its Discontents: Overqualification in America,
    1972–2002." *Social Forces* 85 (2006): 835–64.
Voluntary Institutional Metrics Project. *A Better Higher Education Data and Information
    Framework for Informing Policy.* Washington: HCM Strategists, 2013. http://www
    .hcmstrategists.com/pdf/gates_metrics_report.pdf.
Waters, Mary C., Patrick J. Carr, and Maria J. Kefalas. Introduction to *Coming of Age in
    America: The Transition to Adulthood,* edited by Mary C. Waters, Patrick J. Carr, Maria
    J. Kefalas, and Jennifer Holdaway, 1–27. Berkeley: University of California Press,
    2011.
Waters, Mary C., Patrick J. Carr, Maria J. Kefalas, and Jennifer Holdaway, eds. *Coming of
    Age in America: The Transition to Adulthood.* Berkeley: University of California Press,
    2011.
Wightman, Patrick, Megan Patrick, Robert Schoeni, and John Schulenberg. "Historical
    Trends in Parental Financial Support of Young Adults." PSC report no. 13-801. Ann
    Arbor: University of Michigan Population Studies Center, 2013.
Williams, Alex. "Saying No to College." *New York Times,* November 30, 2012. http://www
    .nytimes.com/2012/12/02/fashion/saying-no-to-college.html?smid=pl-share.
White House. "Fact Sheet on the President's Plan to Make College More Affordable: A
    Better Bargain for the Middle Class." Washington: White House, 2013. http://www
    .whitehouse.gov/the-press-office/2013/08/22/fact-sheet-president-s-plan-make
    -college-more-affordable-better-bargain-.
White, Lawrence. "Judicial Threats to Academe's 'Four Freedoms.'" *Chronicle of Higher
    Education,* December 1, 2006. http://chronicle.com/article/Judicial-Threats-to
    -Academes/20260/.
Wright, David L., William F. Fox, Matthew N. Murray, Celeste K. Carruthers, and Grant
    Thrall. *College Participation, Persistence, Graduation, and Labor Market Outcomes: An*

Input-Adjusted Framework for Assessing the Effectiveness of Tennessee's Higher Education Institutions. Report of HCM Strategists' Context for Success Project. Washington: HCM Strategists, 2012. http://www.hcmstrategists.com/contextforsuccess/papers .html.

Xie, Yu, and Jennie Brand. "Who Benefits Most from College? Evidence from Negative Selection in Heterogeneous Economic Returns to Higher Education." *American Sociological Review* 75 (2010): 273–302.

Zielinski, Dave. "Effective Assessments." *HR Magazine* 56 (2011). http://www.shrm.org /publications/hrmagazine/editorialcontent/2011/0111/pages/0111zielinski.aspx.

Index

Page numbers followed by the letter *f* refer to figures.

AAC&U. *See* Association of American Colleges and Universities
AASCU. *See* American Association of State Colleges and Universities
academically adrift, 2, 6; higher education and, 12
Academically Adrift (Arum and Roksa), 112, 127
academic capitalism, 7
academic dishonesty, 135
academic engagement, of students, 33–37, 120
academic pursuits, marginalization of, 6–7
accordion families, 87
accountability: colleges and, 122; at institutional level versus state/federal, 127; state and federal schemes for, 124
ACPA. *See* American College Personnel Association
adaptive testing, 128
administrators: adoption of personnel perspective by, 8–10; growing role of, versus faculty, 6–7
adrift: academically, 2, 12; post-college examples of being, 1–4

adulthood, transitions to, 15–16; individual trajectories and, 17; social backgrounds and, 17
AHELO. *See* Assessment of Higher Education Learning Outcomes
American Association of State Colleges and Universities (AASCU), 21
American College Personnel Association (ACPA), 9
American parenting, 85
APLU. *See* Association of Public and Land-Grant Universities
Armstrong, Elizabeth, 14, 28–29, 70–71
Arnett, Jeffrey, 83
Aronson, Elliot, 47
Assessment of Higher Education Learning Outcomes (AHELO), 20, 139
assessments: competency-based, 129; computer-based, 128–29; course, 10; growing use of, politics and, 131–32; longitudinal, of students, 131; normative values and, 122–25; performance-based, computers and, 128–29; potential to improve higher education and, 132; of student learning, higher education and, 8; technical issues and, 125–27

Association of Public and Land-Grant Universities (APLU), 20
Association of American Colleges and Universities (AAC&U), 122–23

Babcock, Philip, 35
Baccalaureate and Beyond (B&B) Longitudinal Study, 47
basic skills. *See* generic competencies
Becker, Howard, 10
Beginning Postsecondary Students (BPS) Longitudinal Study, 137–38
Bellah, Robert, 85
blended learning, 128
Brint, Steven, 11–12
Brown, Jonathon, 106
business majors, earnings of, 63–65

CAAP. *See* Collegiate Assessment of Academic Proficiency
capitalism, academic, 7
career fairs, 69–70
career placement. *See* employment; job searches
Carnegie Foundation for the Advancement of Teaching, 130–31
character formation, 14
cheating, 135
Children of the Great Depression (Elder), 17
Chronicle of Higher Education, The, 128
civic engagement, 98–105, 120; factors affecting low levels of, 103–5; individual characteristics and, 103; role of colleges, 101–2, 102f; school context and, 102–3; views of graduates on US state of affairs and, 104–5
CLA (Collegiate Learning Assessment), 5, 20, 126, 137–39, 140–41; measurement of cross-institutional variation of learning, 40–46; measurement of general collegiate skill, 37–40
CLA performance, 118, 133–34, 221n10; computers and, 129; education level required for jobs, 63; experiencing unemployment and, 61–63, 62f; incomes of graduates and, 63; job satisfaction and, 76; living arrangements and, 89; negative early-career outcomes and, 60; post-college success and, 80; self-reported job skill requirements and, 77

Coleman, James, 26
college career resources, 67, 72, 219n28, 219n30; job quality and, 73–74
college experiences, examples of, 26–29
college freshmen, living at home and, 16
college graduates. *See* graduates
college loan debts, living arrangements and, 87–88
college relevance, perceptions of, 77–79
colleges. *See* higher education
College Scorecard, 124
college selectivity, 219n10; post-college living arrangements and, 89; job searches and, 70
Collegiate Assessment of Academic Proficiency (CAAP), 21, 139
Collegiate Learning Assessment. *See* CLA
Coming of Age in America (Swartz et al.), 109–10
competencies. *See* creative competencies; generic competencies
competency-based assessments, federal government and, 129
computer-based assessments, 128–29
corporatization, of higher education, 6–7
Council for Aid to Education (CAE), 20, 137, 139
course evaluations. *See* assessments
creative competencies, decreasing return of, 18–19. *See also* generic competencies
credentials, state accountability schemes and, 124
Culture of American Families Survey, 85
current events, engagement with, 84–85
Current Population Surveys (CPS), data from, 18

Damon, William, 111
Dean, Diane, 99, 108
Degrees for What Jobs? (National Governors Association), 124
Delbanco, Andrew, 120
Determinants of College Learning (DCL) dataset, 137
Dewey, John, 135
digital learning, 120–21, 128
direction, lack of, college graduates and, 110–12
"do-it-yourself" education, 120–21
"drifting dreamers," 110

Durkheim, Émile, 12, 26
duty, development of, 14

educational matching theory, 76
educational transformations, 12
educators, student authority and, 8
Eide, Eric, 50
Eight-Year Study (Progressive Education Association), 130–31
Elder, Glen, 17
emerging adults/adulthood, 6, 83–84, 112–14; being adrift and, 133; benefits of, 107; transitions to, 15–16; unforgiving economic environment and, 14–18
emerging adult societies, 16–17
employers: former, job searches and, 71–72; requests for transcripts and, 74–75
employers, colleges and, for job searches, 67
employment: methods of finding, 66–68, 68f; positive, graduates two years after graduation and, 65–66
engagement. See civic engagement; political engagement
ethnic backgrounds. See racial/ethnic backgrounds, graduates living at home and
EUROSTUDENT survey, 35
evaluations, course. See assessments

faculty, declining role of, versus administrators, 6–7
Fall of the Faculty, The (Ginsberg), 7
Family Educational Rights and Privacy Act (FERPA, 1974), 10
federal accountability schemes, for colleges, 124
federal government, competency-based assessments and, 129
FERPA. See Family Educational Rights and Privacy Act
financial assistance from parents, after graduation, 90–92
financial independence, 84
"flipped classrooms," 128
formal means, of job searches, 68–69
freshman, college, living at home and, 16
Fund for the Improvement of Postsecondary Education (FIPSE), 139
Furstenburg, Frank, 17, 92

Generation on a Tightrope (Levine and Dean), 108
generic competencies, 51–52, 134; CLA measurement of, 37–40; higher education and, 19–20; labor market success and, 18–19; measurements of, 20–21. See also creative competencies
Ginsberg, Benjamin, 7–8
Gitlin, Todd, 13
Going Solo (Klinenberg), 89
Goss v. Lopez, 9–10
graduates: African-American, finding partners two years after college, 95; Asian, finding partners two years after college, 95; features of efforts to define competencies, skills, and knowledge for, 123; having partners, and proportion of women on campus, 95; independent living and, 85–92; lack of direction and, 110–12; lifetime earnings of, 216; optimism and, 105–12; optimism of, and labor market conditions, 109–10; percentage entering graduate school, 47–51, 47f, 48f, 50f; positive employment two years after graduation and, 65–66; preparation for life after college and, 51–52; unskilled occupations and, 64–65; vagueness of, 110–12; views of, on US state of affairs and civic engagement, 104–5
graduate school: college majors and rate of attendance, 49–51, 50f; graduate programs and decision to attend, 48–49; option value of, 50; proportion of undergraduates attending, 47, 48f; undergraduate experiences/CLA performance and decision to attend, 48, 49f
Granovetter, Mark, 66, 68
grit, development of, 14
Grusky, David, 18–19
Guyland (Kimmel), 89

Hamilton, Laura, 14, 28–29, 70–71
Hauser, Robert, 58
higher education: accountability and, 122; admission criteria and personnel perspective of, 13–14; adoption of personnel perspective and, 8–11, 13–14; assessment of student learning and, 8; being defined by preferences of undergraduates, 119–20;

higher education (*cont.*)
  as business, 7–8; challenges of making
    comparisons across institutions of, 127;
    changes in student-faculty ratios and,
    7–8; corporatization of, 6–7; cross-
    institutional variation of learning in,
    40–46; declining role of faculty versus
    administrators in, 6–7; digital learning
    and, 120–21; educational transforma-
    tions and, 12; FERPA and, 10; focus
    on personal development and social
    engagement and, 11–12; generic compe-
    tencies and, 19–20; increasing costs of,
    120–22; as investment, 53–54, 215n1;
    labor market outcomes and, 54–55; lack
    of validation instruments and, 126–27;
    normative values for judging, 122–25;
    personal development and, 25–26, 51;
    potential to improve, assessments and,
    132; reasons for importance of, 54; re-
    sponsibilities of, 132; student reflections
    on experiences, 46–47; technical issues
    for judging, 125–27; in twenty-first
    century, 6–14; using graduate wages for
    evaluating, 124–25
Higher Education Research Institute
    (UCLA), 35, 46, 130
"hooking up," 93, 113
Hout, Michael, 61

income: selectivity of college attended and,
    63–64; senior CLA scores and, 63–64
independence: difficulty obtaining, gradu-
    ates and, 85–92; financial, 84; psycho-
    logical, 83–84
inner-directed dispositions, 13
Integrated Postsecondary Education System
    (IPEDS), 125–26
internships: job quality and, 73–74; job
    searches and, 71–72

Jacob, Brian, 11
job loss, 62–63
job quality, job search methods and, 73–75
job rewards: defined, 75; job satisfaction
    and, 75
job satisfaction: CLA performance and,
    76; educational matching and, 76; job
    rewards and, 75; self-reported job skill
    requirements and, 76–77

job searches, 66–68, 219n33; college selec-
    tivity and, 70; formal means of, 68–69;
    former employers and, 71–72; intern-
    ships and, 71–72; methods for, 66–67;
    methods for, and job quality, 73–75; on-
    campus resources for, 69–71; persistence
    and, 68–69; personal ties and, 72–73;
    volunteer opportunities, 71–72

Kalleberg, Arne, 75
Kamenetz, Anya, 120
Kimmel, Michael, 89
Kirp, David, 6–7
Klinenberg, Eric, 89
Kuh, George, 51

Labaree, David, 100, 124
labor market conditions: living arrange-
    ments and, 87, 88f; optimism of gradu-
    ates and, 109–10
labor market outcomes, 54–55, 57f, 141–43;
    factors associated with negative early-
    career, 60–66; social backgrounds and,
    61; two years after graduation, 55–59,
    55f, 59f; unskilled occupations, 64–65.
    See also unemployment
labor market success: creative competen-
    cies and, 18–19; generic skills and, 18;
    improving, 79–81
Lagemann, Ellen, 130
LEAP (Liberal Education and America's
    Promise) Initiative, 123
learning, student: cross-institutional varia-
    tion of, 40–46; technology and, 128–
    29
learning outcomes, measuring and improv-
    ing, 128–33
Lemann, Nicholas, 130
Levine, Arthur, 99, 108
Liberal Education and America's Promise
    (LEAP) Initiative, 123
Liu, Yujia, 18–19
living arrangements, 84, 88; college fresh-
    man and, 16; of college graduates two
    years after graduation, 85, 86f; college
    loan debts and, 87–88; with friends, 89;
    independently, 89; labor market condi-
    tions and, 87; with parents, 85–87, 86f;
    with partners, 89; racial, ethnic, and
    social backgrounds and, 88–89

loan debts, college, and graduates living at home, 87–88
Lonely Crowd, The (Riesman), 12, 51
longitudinal assessments, of students, 131
Loss, Christopher, 8–9, 13
Luminat Degree Qualifications Profile, 123

Making the Grade (Becker et al.), 10
Malczewski, Joan, 130
MAPP. *See* Measurement of Academic Progress and Proficiency
Marks, Mindy, 35
Matasar, Rick, 7
Measurement of Academic Progress and Proficiency (MAPP), 21, 139
Mills, C. Wright, 4–5
Mills, Judson, 47
"MOOC Madness," 128
Moralistic Therapeutic Deism, 11

National Governors Association, 124
National Student Clearinghouse, 129
National Survey of Student Engagement (NSSE), 34, 129–30
Newman, Katherine, 15
news consumption, 84–85, 99–100, 101f
normative values, assessment of higher education and, 122–25

on-campus resources, for job searches, 69–71
online learning. *See* digital learning
optimism, college graduates and, 105–12
option value, of graduate program, 50
Organisation for Economic Cooperation and Development (OECD), 20
"other-directed" dispositions, 12–13, 51

parental support, after graduation, 90–92
parenting, American, 85
partners, romantic, 96f; African-American graduates finding, two years after college, 95; Asian graduates finding, two years after college, 95; college as source for, 93–95, 94f; education levels of, 96; finding romantic, 93–98; men finding, two years after college, 95; proportion of women on campus and probability of graduates having, 95; role of colleges in finding, 96–98, 97f
part-time jobs, 71–72

Paying for the Party (Armstrong and Hamilton), 28–29
performance-based assessments, computerized, 128–29
perseverance, development of, 14
persistence, job searches and, 68–69
personal contacts, job searches and, 66–67, 72–73
personal development, emphasis on, 51
personal exploration, focus on, 14
personnel perspective, 13; admission criteria and, 13–14; adoption of, 8–11
political engagement, 99; individual characteristics and, 103; role of colleges, 101–2, 102f; school context and, 102–3
positive employment outcomes, graduates two years after graduation and, 65–66
post-college success: choice of field of study and, 80–81; CLA performance and, 80; perceptions of college relevance and, 77–79
Proficiency Profile, 21
Programme for the International Assessment of Adult Competencies (OECD), 20
Progressive Education Association, 130–31
psychological independence, 83–84

racial/ethnic backgrounds, graduates living at home and, 88–89
recruiting events, on-campus, 69–70
responsibilities: of faculty, 132; of higher education, 134; of individuals, 132; of schools, 132; young adults and, 98–99
Rhoades, Gary, 7
Riesman, David, 11, 12–13, 26, 51
Rockefeller Foundation, 130–31
romantic partners. *See* partners, romantic
Rosenfeld, Michael, 16

Schneider, Barbara, 110
Schneider, Mark, 125
self-directed learning, 120–21
self-exploration, 11
Silva, Jennifer, 11
skills, basic. *See* generic competencies
Slaughter, Sheila, 7
Smith, Christian, 11
sociability, institutional focus on, examples of, 29–32

social backgrounds, living at home and,
    88–89
social development, focus on, 14
social engagement, emphasis on, 51
social integration, 33
social networks, 216n5; role of, in job
    searches, 66–67
social obligation, development of, 14
Social Science Research Council (SSRC),
    137, 138
social sensibilities, 46, 51; focus on, 26
social skills, development of, 12–13
social well-being, 11
Sociological Imagination, The (Mills), 4–5
Spellings Commission, 122
standardized tests, 130–31. *See also*
    assessments
state accountability schemes, for colleges,
    124
STEM (science, technology, engineering,
    and mathematics) fields, development
    of concept inventories of core concepts
    in, 123, 124
Stevens, Mitchell, 13
Stevenson, David, 110
student learning: higher-education assess-
    ment and, 8; marginalization of, 6–7
students, consumer preferences of, 10–11
student service model, 9
study times, 115–16
success stories, 115–19
Swartz, Teresa Toguchi, 109–10

Taylor, Shelley, 106
technology: data collection/analysis for indi-
    vidual learning outcomes and, 129–30;
    increased administrative capacity for us-
    ing data and, 131; learning and, 128–29

Test of Leadership, A (Spellings Commission),
    122
therapeutic ethic, 11
time use, students and, 33–37, 212n29
tolerance of difference, 32–33
Trachtenberg, Stephen, 7
transcripts, employers and, 74–75
transformations, educational, 12
transitions, to adulthood, 15–16; individual
    trajectories and, 17; social backgrounds
    and, 17
Tuning USA Project (Lumina Foundation),
    123

unemployment, probability of, by CLA per-
    formance and field of study, 60–62, 61f.
    See also labor market outcomes
universities. *See* higher education
unskilled occupations, graduates and,
    64–65

vagueness, of college graduates, 110–12
Vaisey, Steven, 76
values: colleges and, 99; normative, for judg-
    ing higher education, 122–25; work, 75
Voluntary Institutional Metrics Project, 126
Voluntary System of Accountability (VSA),
    139
volunteering, 99
volunteer opportunities, job searches and,
    71–72

Waehrer, Geetha, 50
wages, graduate, for evaluating colleges,
    124–25
Warren, John Robert, 58
Waters, Mary, 15
work values, defined, 75